Culture and Customs
of Mali

Map of Mali. (Cartography by Bookcomp, Inc.)

Culture and Customs of Mali

DOROTHEA E. SCHULZ

Culture and Customs of Africa
Toyin Falola, Series Editor

GREENWOOD

AN IMPRINT OF ABC-CLIO, LLC
Santa Barbara, California • Denver, Colorado • Oxford, England

Library of Congress Cataloging-in-Publication Data

Schulz, Dorothea Elisabeth.
    Culture and customs of Mali / Dorothea E. Schulz.
        p. cm. — (Culture and customs of Africa)
    Includes bibliographical references and index.
    ISBN 978-0-313-35912-5 (hardcopy : alk. paper) — ISBN 978-0-313-35913-2 (ebook)
1. Mali—Civilization.   2. Mali—Social life and customs.   I. Title.
    DT551.4.S45   2012
    966.23—dc23   2011036674

ISBN: 978-0-313-35912-5
EISBN: 978-0-313-35913-2

16   15   14   13   12   1   2   3   4   5

This book is also available on the World Wide Web as an eBook.
Visit www.abc-clio.com for details.

Greenwood
An Imprint of ABC-CLIO, LLC

ABC-CLIO, LLC
130 Cremona Drive, P.O. Box 1911
Santa Barbara, California 93116-1911

This book is printed on acid-free paper ∞

Manufactured in the United States of America

For Ulrich

Contents

Series Foreword

Africa is a vast continent, the second largest, after Asia. It is four times the size of the United States, excluding Alaska. It is the cradle of human civilization. A diverse continent, Africa has more than fifty countries with a population of over 700 million people who speak over 1,000 languages. Ecological and cultural differences vary from one region to another. As an old continent, Africa is one of the richest in culture and customs, and its contributions to world civilization are impressive indeed.

Africans regard culture as essential to their lives and future development. Culture embodies their philosophy, worldview, behavior patterns, arts, and institutions. The books in this series intend to capture the comprehensiveness of African culture and customs, dwelling on such important aspects as religion, worldview, literature, media, art, housing, architecture, cuisine, traditional dress, gender, marriage, family, lifestyles, social customs, music, and dance.

The uses and definitions of "culture" vary, reflecting its prestigious association with civilization and social status, its restriction to attitude and behavior, its globalization, and the debates surrounding issues of tradition, modernity, and postmodernity. The participating authors have chosen a comprehensive meaning of culture while not ignoring the alternative uses of the term.

Each volume in the series focuses on a single country, and the format is uniform. The first chapter presents a historical overview, in addition to information on geography, economy, and politics. Each volume then proceeds to examine the various aspects of culture and customs. The series highlights the mechanisms for the transmission of tradition and culture across generations:

the significance of orality, traditions, kinship rites, and family property distribution; the rise of print culture; and the impact of educational institutions.
The series also explores the intersections between local, regional, national,
and global bases for identity and social relations. While the volumes are organized nationally, they pay attention to ethnicity and language groups and the
links between Africa and the wider world.

The books in the series capture the elements of continuity and change in
culture and customs. Custom is represented not as static or as a museum ar-
tifact but as a dynamic phenomenon. Furthermore, the authors recognize
the current challenges to traditional wisdom, which include gender relations,
the negotiation of local identities in relation to the state, the significance
of struggles for power at national and local levels and their impact on cultural traditions and community-based forms of authority, and the tensions
between agrarian and industrial/manufacturing/oil-based economic modes of
production.

Africa is a continent of great changes, instigated mainly by Africans but
also through influences from other continents. The rise of youth culture, the
penetration of the global media, and the challenges to generational stability
are some of the components of modern changes explored in the series. The
ways in which traditional (non-Western and nonimitative) African cultural
forms continue to survive and thrive—that is, how they have taken advantage of the market system to enhance their influence and reproductions—also
receive attention.

Through the books in this series, readers can see their own cultures in a different perspective, understand the habits of Africans, and educate themselves
about the customs and cultures of other countries and people. The hope is
that the readers will come to respect the cultures of others and see them not
as inferior or superior to theirs but merely as different. Africa has always been
important to Europe and the United States, essentially as a source of labor,
raw materials, and markets. Blacks are in Europe and the Americas as part
of the African diaspora, a migration that took place primarily because of the
slave trade. Recent African migrants increasingly swell their number and vis-
ibility. It is important to understand the history of the diaspora and the newer
migrants as well as the roots of the culture and customs of the places from
where they come. It is equally important to understand others in order to be
able to interact successfully in a world that keeps shrinking. The accessible
nature of the books in this series will contribute to this understanding and
enhance the quality of human interaction in a new millennium.

Toyin Falola
Frances Higginbothom Nalle Centennial Professor in History,
The University of Texas at Austin

Acknowledgments

Tʜᴇʀᴇ ɪs ᴀ Tuareg proverb that says "A hand that holds a poking stick will not get burnt," meaning "whoever relies on efficient support has nothing to fear." This book is a good illustration of this proverb because it is, in the fullest sense of the word, a work of collaboration and dialogue. It brings together insights gathered in innumerable encounters and conversations during the more than 20 years I spent working on and in Mali. If in these pages I managed to capture some of the complexities and richness of Malian cultural and social life, I owe this principally to the hospitality, generosity, and patience of those I lived and worked with in Mali. For this, I thank friends and family in Mali, as well as those countless others who, over all these years, have acquainted me with Malian culture, politics, and history.

I am grateful to Toyin Falola, editor of the "Culture and Customs" series and also a long-standing colleague and friend. I thank him for entrusting this book project to me and thank Kaitlin Ciarmello from ABC-CLIO Publishers for her superb advice in composing this book.

In Cologne, Carolin Maevis did a first-rate job in assisting me with preparing the final version of the manuscript. Souleymane Diallo's excellent input and feedback on several chapters was important for balancing any "Mande-centric" bias I might have brought otherwise to the portrayal of Mali's diverse regional cultures and histories.

My daughter Dussuba Johanna might not be aware of the place she has in this book, but her humor, quick-wittedness, and zest of living continue to be a source of inspiration and delight. Last but not least, I thank Ulrich Thon, without whose thoughtful support and steady encouragement it would have been hard to bring this work to completion.

Chronology

c. 800–1200 Empire of Wagadu (Ghana), located in the region of present-day northwestern Mali and adjacent areas of Mauritania, with the capital Kumbi Saleh.

1100–1400 Empire of Mali, emerging from a small kingdom located at Kangaba, near the upper Niger River, and expanding into a vast empire under the legendary ruler Sundjata Keita. At the zenith of its might in the 14th century, the Mali Empire spanned large areas of contemporary Mali, Senegal, Gambia, and southern Mauritania. Under its tutelage, Gao, Djenné, and Timbuktu became thriving centers of commerce and Muslim erudition, attracting scholars from throughout Africa and from Asia.

c. 1335–1591 Gradual expansion of the Songhai Empire of Gao. Toward the end of the 15th century, under the Sonni dynasty, the Songhai Empire became the dominant political formation in this area of West Africa, covering an area stretching from Kebbi in the east to Djenné in the west and to the Mossi area in the south.

1591 An invasion by armed forces from the area of today's Morocco put an end to the Songhai Empire, taking over control of its gold and salt trade networks across the Sahara.

1600–c. 1865 Several smaller kingdoms, including the kingdoms of Jaara (c. 1500–1900), Segu (1600–1862), and Kaarta (1633–1854), fought for dominance over the area. The kingdom of Macina, whose origins went back to the early 1400s, expanded into a theocratic state under the leadership of the Muslim scholar Cheikou Amadou in 1810. Starting in 1852, the Tukulor Muslim military leader El Hadj Umar Tall launched his military campaign from his home base, the Futa Djallon (in present-day western Senegal). After defeating the kingdom of Kaarta in 1854 and Macina and Segu in 1862, the Tukulor Empire became an important power player in the wars against French colonial occupation.

1865   In response to the fragmentation of the Tukulor Empire after El Hadj Umar Tall's death and under his son Ahmadou, the warrior chief Samori Touré, moving in from the Guinea highlands, established military and administrative control over vast areas of southern Mali, until his final military defeat by French colonial troops in the 1890s.

1876–92   French colonial troops, moving in from the area of present-day Senegal, gradually established control over areas formerly occupied by the Tukulor Empire. In 1892, after Ahmadou's final defeat, France declared the area of contemporary Mali a distinct colony, to be named French Sudan (Soudan Français).

1902–4   The area of present-day Mali was incorporated into the French administrative unit Senegambie and Niger.

1904–20   The area of present-day Mali became part of the French colonial administrative unit Upper Senegal and Niger.

1920   The areas of present-day Niger and Mali were administratively separated, with the latter being renamed French Sudan.

1937   The French Sudan was reconstituted as a separate administrative entity of the West African French colonial territories.

1946   The creation of two political parties, the PSP (Parti Soudanais Progressiste) and the US-RDA (Union Soudanaise–Rassemblement Démocratique Africain), marked the formal beginning of the struggle for independence from Mali.

1956   Similar to other colonies of the AOF, the French Sudan was granted limited self-government. The US-RDA won the National Assembly elections to represent the French Sudan.

1958   The degree of autonomy of the French Sudan was expanded as it became a member of the Communauté Française and was renamed Sudanese Republic (République Soudanaise). After Mamadou Konaté's death, Modibo Keita established himself as uncontested party leader.

1959   Under the leadership of Modibo Keita, head of US-RDA, and Léopold Senghor, the leader of the independence movement in

Senegal, Mali and Senegal joined to constitute the Malian Federation (Fédération du Mali) in January 1959.

1960   The Malian Federation was granted independence from France on June 20, 1960. Due to leadership struggles and disagreements over the political orientation of the Malian Federation, this political entity was dissolved two months later. On September 22, 1960, Mali declared its independence as a separate nation-state. Modibo Keita, the prime minister of the Malian Federation, became the first president and head of the single-party US-RDA, which adopted an "African socialist" agenda of economic development.

1961   The creation of the Malian National Army.

1963–64   An uprising of Tuareg groups in the north against the central government was bloodily repressed.

1967   In response to the deepening economic crisis and a rising opposition within the ruling party, President Keita initiated certain political and economic reforms that, however, failed to remedy the shortcomings of a highly centralized national economy and political regime.

1968   A military coup under the leadership of Lieutenant Moussa Traoré put an end to the US-RDA party rule and initiated a decade-long military regime under the military body CMLN (Comité Militaire de la Libération Nationale), headed by Moussa Traoré. Under his leadership, the country gradually moved from its former alignment with socialist countries, such as the USSR, China, and Cuba, to a closer alliance with Western countries.

1970–74   A pervasive drought in the northern regions of Mali rendered the situation of the politically and economically marginalized northern populations life-threatening. With rising numbers of famine deaths, broad segments of the northern population migrated to the neighboring countries. Another drought-related famine in 1984–85 seriously affected rural areas throughout the country and compelled even more people in the north to migrate. Food and financial aid provided mainly by France and the European Union ended up, to a major extent, in the private bank accounts of party members and state officials.

1979   A new constitution, approved already in 1974 by a referendum, came into force. It stipulated the one-party rule of the newly created party UDPM (Union Démocratique du Peuple Malien) under the presidency of Moussa Traoré.

1980–85   Bloody repression of repeated student protests that were initially directed against the oppressive political environment under UDPM rule and later opposed the austerity measures implemented under the dictate of Western donor organizations.

1989   A democracy movement initiated by university professors, lawyers, and other professional groups publicly called for the granting of multiparty democracy and freedom of expression.

1990   Tuareg groups in the north joined in a well-organized military rebellion against the central government.

1991   On March 26, 1991, following months of violent confrontations between the state security forces and students with other supporters of the democracy movement in Bamako, a coup by a group of military officers under Lieutenant-Colonel Amadou Toumani Touré put an end to the UDPM single-party rule. Under the transitory military regime of the CTSP (Comité de Transition pour le Salut du Peuple), a new constitution was put into place, granting multiparty democracy and civil rights.

1992   The legislative elections established the party ADEMA-PASJ (Alliance pour la Démocratie au Mali–Parti Africain pour la Solidarité et la Justice) as the winner. Its secretary-general Alpha Oumar Konaré, a prominent representative of the democracy movement, was elected the first president of democratic Mali.

1992–96   After a peace treaty (National Pact) signed between the CTSP and the Tuareg oppositional groups, the situation of civil war continued in the north of Mali until 1996. Following the peace treaty, measures of greater political and economic integration of the northern regions were implemented, along with an administrative reform that granted these regions greater budgetary autonomy.

1997   Alpha Oumar Konaré was reelected president, under heavy contestation by oppositional parties and an electoral participation of no more than 27 percent of the total population.

2002   Presidential elections established Amadou Toumani Touré (who ran as an independent candidate), the leader of the military coup against former president Traoré as the new president. Two months later followed the parliamentary elections.

2007   President Toumani Touré was reelected president for a second term, followed by new parliamentary elections.

2010   Celebrations of the 50 years of independence from French colonial rule.

2011   Mariam Kaïdama Cissé was appointed the first female prime minister.

2012   Next presidential elections occur in April.

1

Introduction

Maa mana kè maa si o si ye, i ka kè a nyuman ye.
Whoever you are, strive to honor the social group you come from.

—Bamana proverb

Soa andi horoma afofti.
Get to know yourself.

—Fulani proverb

THE REPUBLIC OF Mali is a landlocked country bordered on the north by Algeria, on the east by Niger and Burkina Faso, on the south by Ivory Coast and Guinea, and on the west by Senegal and Mauritania. It covers an area of 482,077 square miles (1,248,574 sq km) and has a population of more than 12 million. Mali has an annual growth rate of 2.7 percent and an infant mortality rate higher than both world and African standards. The country is shaped into a northern and a southern triangle, with the northern triangle encompassing the Sahara desert and the arid zone of the Sahel. Throughout Mali, population densities are low, particularly in the more remote northeastern and eastern parts where densities are about three people per square mile. This trend has been reinforced since the droughts of the 1970s and 1980s, which forced many people with a nomadic lifestyle in these northern regions to migrate to more southern zones and urban areas of the country. Bamako, the capital and largest city, is located on the shore of the Niger River in Mali's southwest; it has a population of approximately one million.

The territory of present-day Mali includes a great diversity of peoples and cultures that, prior to French colonial rule, were organized into different political forms, ranging from centralized polities to more decentralized structures.

French colonial occupation of the region started in the mid-19th century, as the French military entering the area from the western Atlantic coast gradually subjugated the area that was to be integrated into the French West African colonial territory after 1880 (named French Sudan in 1920). Senegal and Mali together formed the French Sudan and together they reached independence under the name Mali Federation. After the secession of Senegal from the federation on August 22, 1960, the Sudanese Republic changed its name to the Republic of Mali on September 22, 1960. The country's first government, under President Modibo Keita and his party US-RDA (Union Soudanaise–Rassemblement Démocratique Africain), ended on November 18, 1968, when President Keita's single-party rule was overthrown by a military coup under the leadership of Colonel Moussa Traoré. The new military regime, CMLN (Comité Militaire de la Libération Nationale), ruled the country until 1979, when it was replaced by a civilian government still under firm control of President Traoré and his single-party UDPM (Union Démocratique du Peuple Malien). In 1990, following mounting opposition to his regime, Traoré lost the support he had enjoyed among Western powers, especially France and the United States, and was overthrown in March 1991 by a military coup led by Lieutnant-Colonel Amadou Toumani Touré. Touré's military regime ensured Mali's peaceful transition to democracy. In 1992, following Mali's first democratic elections, Alpha Konaré and his party ADEMA (Alliance pour la Démocratie au Mali) formed the country's new government. The current president, Amadou Toumani Touré, was elected in 2002 and reconfirmed in office in 2007. Although both Presidents Konaré and Touré experienced periods of vehement contestation on the part of oppositional parties, the political situation has remained relatively stable since the introduction of multiparty democracy in 1991.

LAND, CLIMATE, AND VEGETATION PATTERNS

More than half of the country's total area lies in the Saharan and Sahelian zones of the northern triangle. The Niger River flows through the interior of the country for more than 1,000 miles and serves as the country's major trading and transport artery. It rises in the Fouta Djallon in the south and flows to the northeast across the Manding Plateau. Reaching Koulikoro, north of Bamako, it spreads out in a valley. The town of Mopti marks the site of the confluence of the Niger and the Bani Rivers. Beyond Mopti, it spreads out into an interior delta, branching out into numerous streams and lakes as it flows northward and, at Karbara, eastward. The river effects a great turn southward, the Niger Bend, and continues past Gao and Ansongo. Because some areas of the river flood during specific seasons of the year, they provide highly fertile agricultural soil and pasture for livestock along the riverbanks. The flow of the Niger reaches its seasonal peak on the upper Niger between July and October, in the delta between early October and November, and at the bend between December and January. The second most important element of the country's drainage system is the Senegal River, whose tributaries flow in a northwesterly direction across western Mali for more than 400 miles (640 km).

Mali's climate is hot and dry, with the sun near its zenith during most of the year. The country has three distinct vegetation and climate zones: the Sahara desert in the north, where rainfall is virtually absent and where daytime temperatures range from 117°F to nearly 140°F (47°C to 60°C) and the nighttime temperature drops to 39°F (4°C); the arid Sahelian zone, with average temperatures between 73°F and 94°F (23°C and 36°C); and the Sudanic zone of the south, whose temperatures range between 75°F and 86°F (24°C to 30°C) and which, similar to the Sahel, has alternating dry and rainy seasons. The dry season, characterized by low humidity and high temperatures, begins in November and lasts until early June. Also characteristic of the dry season are the harmattan and alize winds blowing from the east and northeast respectively. The monsoon wind, in contrast, blows from the southwest during the rainy season. Rainfall in the Sahelian zone ranges from 8 to 20 inches (200–510 mm) per year, whereas the Sudanic zone receives between 20 and 55 inches (1,400 mm) of rain in a year.

Two vegetation zones correspond to the country's two southern climate zones. The Sahelian zone has mostly steppe vegetation with drought-resistant trees, such as the baobab, acacia, mimosa, palmyra, and doum palm. The Sahel lacks densely covered tree areas, an absence that has been reinforced by late 20th-century processes of overgrazing, soil erosion, and deforestation and by sustained periods of drought. The Sudanic zone encompasses areas of savannah and of forest corridors, with the kapioka tree, the nere (*Parkia biglobosa*), the cailcedra (*Khaya senegalensis*), and the karité (*Butyrospermum parkii*) as the most important trees.

Beyond the Niger valley, the soils are often poor. The desert region is composed primarily of sand, rock, and gravel. Because the iron-bearing soils of the southern regions have been exposed to strong evaporation for a long time, they are frequently covered by a tough red crust that bars agricultural exploitation.

Because of significant regional discrepancies in climate and vegetation, forms of livelihood differ widely, along with the conditions for subsistence cultivation and cattle herding. Most settlements (villages and towns) are located in Mali's southern triangle, whereas in the northern triangle, at least historically, a significant part of the population combined cattle herding with a nomadic or seminomadic lifestyle.

PEOPLES

Mali is a multiethnic nation that comprises more than 12 ethnic groups, each of them speaking its own language. Still, ethnicity, as a marker of social and cultural identity, is extremely fluid in Mali. For centuries, the characteristically high mobility of the Malian people has created a web of social relations and commercial networks that crisscrosses the country, transcends national boundaries, and blurs clear-cut divides between Mali's different peoples and cultures. These networks are based on kinship, alliance, and common regional origin. In a given locale, certain clans may be considered to belong to a particular ethnic group even though they might have adopted the language and certain cultural traditions of another, often the locally dominant, ethnic group. Families are organized hierarchically—in terms of not only sex but also age and generation—and they are generally patrilineal, patrilocal, and polygynous. In spite of the fluidity of ethnic identities, several broad categories can be distinguished. Most of Mali's nomads and seminomads live in the northern triangle and come from three groups of people, who, partly because of their different modes of livelihood, are today considered distinct ethnic groups: the Fulani, the Moors, and other Berber groups (including the Tuareg) who refer to themselves as Imazighen (or Kel Tamasheq) and speak Tamasheq. The last live in the northern Sahelian and Sahara regions. Prior to the arrival of French troops and throughout the colonial period, the livelihoods of the Kel Tamasheq were shaped by the networks of exchange and caravan trade they maintained with the neighboring Songhai people, who lead a sedentary life. The Kel Tamasheq exchanged their animals for corn and millet cultivated by the Songhai agriculturalists. Also in these areas, particularly to the northwest, along the Mauretanian border, live the Moors, who are Berber groups of Arab-Spanish origin and who speak varieties of Hassaniya, a language that draws heavily on spoken Arabic. The Fulani are cattle-herders who lead a nomadic or seminomadic lifestyle. All three groups have marked social classes: nobles at the top, followed by groups that specialize in a particular trade and whose members only marry among each other, and finally the ex-serfs, whose ancestors were once captured among Mali's southern populations and who therefore are not of Berber origin. Whereas some of these groups maintain a nomadic lifestyle, most of them have seen themselves obliged to live in permanent settlements over the past decades, following the economic hardship brought about by postindependent governmental policy and also by the droughts of the 1970s and 1980s. These northern peoples, particularly those who identify themselves as Imazighen, share a resentment of a colonial and postcolonial history that brought about their own political and economic marginalization within the emergent Malian state, a state whose legitimacy and claim to shared nationhood they have challenged repeatedly. In the early 1990s, a significant number of these Berbers were forced to leave the country because of military and ethnic conflict. Most spent several years in refugee camps in Mauritania, Burkina Faso, and Algeria, but they have been largely repatriated since 1997. In some areas of Mali's northern triangle, Berber groups coexist with other ethnic groups, such as the sedentary Songhai in the Niger delta between Ansongo and Djenné and the Fulani pastoralists in the Macina region southwest of Timbuktu and in the Sahelian region bordering Mauritania. Farther to the south, a number of ethnic groups, all of them sedentary agriculturalists, exist who also share common histories of settlement, migration, and intermarriage, although they often trace their origins back to different family histories and identities. The numerically strongest group among them is composed of lineages who identify themselves as Bamana (in the literature often referred to as Bambara), live in the areas bordering the upper Niger River, and claim the cultural and political heritage of the 18th-century empire of Segu. Their language, Bamanakan, serves as the lingua franca in Mali's southern triangle. In some areas along the Niger River, the Bamana have formed long-standing ties with other ethnic groups, among them the Somono, Bozo, Tukulor, and Khasonke. The Maninka (Malinke) in the southwest part of the country consider themselves bearers of the traditions of the medieval Mali Empire. Closely related to them and to the Bamana (in terms of shared histories, political traditions, and language) are the Jula (Dioula), who live in and across the southern border regions. All three groups have a similar tiered system of social stratification, with freeborn and aristocratic families at the top of the social hierarchy, dependent groups of professional specialists, and families of ex-serfs at the bottom of the social hierarchy. Another ethnic group that claims a long-standing aristocratic political heritage and is organized along similar patterns of social stratification is the Soninke, who, as descendants of the founders and subjects of the Ghana Empire, live in the western Sahelian zone. The Senufo in Mali's southeast claim the political heritage of the 19th-century kingdom of Kenedugu. Other ethnic groups, in contrast—such as the Bobo, Minianka, and Dogon—do not look back on the same centralized political traditions. They live in Mali's east and southeast, with the Dogon occupying the plateau region east of the city of Mopti.

Islam spread to the area of contemporary Mali in several historical movements. Peoples in the north of Mali have been exposed to Islamic influence by Almoravid warriors moving into the region from across the Sahara since the 11th century. Under the kingdom of Mali in the 13th and 14th centuries, Jula traders created islands of Muslim faith and practice in the savannah towns of southern Mali and northern Ivory Coast. In the 15th and 16th centuries, the northern cities of Timbuktu, Djenné, and Gao turned into centers of Islamic erudition and into nodal points not only for trade in salt, slaves, and gold but also for scholarly intellectual exchange across the Sahara. From there, Islamic culture expanded southward as the Songhai Empire extended its control to Segu in the 16th century. But only in the colonial period did broad segments of the rural population, especially in Mali's southern triangle, convert to Islam. Today Islam is the religion of approximately 85 percent of the total population, rural and urban. Because local practices and institutions of Islam are infused with traditional understandings of esoteric knowledge and power, there exists considerable debate among Muslims about proper religious observance. The few Christians, primarily Catholic, are mostly Dogon and Bobo and compose little more than 1 percent of the total Malian population. Traditional religious practices that are still mostly unaffected by Islam are to be found among the Bobo, the Senufo, the Minianka, and the Dogon.

The majority (about 3/4) of Mali's population live in rural areas; settlement patterns vary with people's modes of livelihood. Those who live on agriculture and cattle herding typically live in thatched dwellings grouped together in villages of about 120 to 550 inhabitants that are surrounded by fields and grazing lands. Interspersed with these villages lie small, temporary settlements (hamlets) where people live and work during the cultivation and harvest seasons (June to October). In the northern triangle, settlement patterns used to reflect the nomadic lifestyle of the majority of the population, with temporary hamlets forming at water points and along transhumance routes. Nowadays, with people's growing move toward a sedentary lifestyle, these temporary agglomerations have been turned into more permanent forms of settlement and villages.

Some of the country's towns—such as Segu, Mopti, Gao, Timbuktu, and Nioro du Sahel—have existed for centuries. Other urban centers of contemporary Mali, among them the capital Bamako, Kayes, and Kita, became important only with French colonial occupation. The historical cities usually emerged as trade entrepôts on the Niger River and along other long-distance trade routes that connected trans-Sahara commerce to the savannah areas in Mali's south and beyond. Built in the typical Sudanese style of architecture, these cities became poles of attraction for a thriving culture of Muslim erudition and commerce, with some of them being closely affiliated with certain religious clans and Sufi orders.

Since the late 19th century, urbanization and the migration of youth in search of labor have weakened the family's authoritarian structure.

Nevertheless, especially in rural areas, authority and control within the family remains in the hands of the eldest male of the senior generation. In the regions to the north of Mali, authority within many families of the Tuareg, Moors, and others has been substantially undermined by ecological degradation and concomitant migration, as well as by the political crises that made refugees of numerous groups beginning in the 1970s.

LANGUAGES

French, the former colonial language, prevails as the country's language of administration and politics. Since independence, Bamanakan (the language spoken by the Bamana) has been promoted as the country's lingua franca, a trend facilitated by the fact that historically, this language—as well as its close affiliates, Maninkakan and Julakan—served as the language of communication in long-distance trade and travel. However, it is important to keep in mind that the majority of the country's northern population either do not know or refuse to speak Bamanakan because they associate it with the political and cultural hegemony of Mali's southern ethnic groups and with their own histories of political and economic marginalization since the colonial period. Ironically, then, and similar to many other African postindependent nations, the diversity of and internal competition among national languages has contributed to the persistence of French as the main language of administration, communication, and mass media. This does not preclude, however, that the majority of the population continue to use their mother tongues, numbering more than 15, in daily social and economic life. Most of these tongues are recognized officially as national languages.

There are also clear indications of a governmental effort to support a recent trend toward administrative decentralization by promoting Mali's diverse linguistic and cultural heritage. For instance, starting with the first democratically elected government of President Alpha Oumar Konaré, significant steps were undertaken to effect school education at the elementary level in the country's different national languages. In the same period, Malians have also witnessed the expansion of programs featuring national languages and diverse oral and musical traditions on national radio and television, as well as on the many local radio stations that have emerged since the early 1990s.

EDUCATION

Throughout Mali's colonial and postcolonial history, efforts have been made, particularly on the part of Muslim religious leaders and intellectuals, to establish an educational infrastructure parallel to the state schooling system, yet so far these attempts have been to no avail. Primary and secondary school education continues to takes place under close scrutiny of the state administration. Elementary and higher education is free of charge. Starting in the mid-1990s, the former secondary education system was substantially revised, and a university was created. Yet these amendments did not substantially improve the conditions for teaching and research. State institutions of higher learning are seriously understaffed and suffer from dysfunctional research facilities. The situation is further compounded by the fact that since the political changes of the 1990s, secondary education has been disrupted by prolonged periods of student unrest and strikes. Although at face value these strikes were animated by an effort on the part of students to struggle for an improvement of the state bursary system, the strikes also reflect a widespread dismay among Mali's urban, schooled youth about the lack of economic and professional opportunities. In response to the instability, low quality, and failing infrastructure of the state school system, there has been a trend toward the privatization of the secondary school education, particularly of technical colleges and trade centers, since the late 1990s. Yet the mushrooming of private institutions of higher education brings with it its own problems and does not resolve fundamental problems, such as the cementing of economic privilege and a general lowering of educational standards.

RESOURCES, OCCUPATIONS, AND ECONOMY

The main bases of rural economies are subsistence agriculture and/or raising livestock. Since colonial times, many rural households have supplemented their income through cash-crop production and by sending younger members of the family for seasonal labor to other West African countries. In recent decades, partly in response to the droughts of the 1970s and 1980s, patterns of labor migration have grown more diverse as more and more younger people, especially men, leave for Europe and the United States in search of additional income.

The inland Niger delta is an important area of commercial agriculture. Dating back to colonial times, the floodwater of the Niger River has sometimes been retained for swamp rice cultivation and has been made available for irrigation, particularly in the southwestern section of the inland Niger delta. Important subsistence crops are millet, rice, corn, peanuts, wheat, and, to a lesser extent, manioc, yams, and sweet potatoes. Apart from cotton, the most important cash crop, sugarcane and peanuts are also grown for the market. Wherever water reserves allow them to do so, people grow fruits and vegetables in market gardens. Livestock (cattle, sheep, goats, and chickens) is important both commercially and to supplement daily staple foods. Fishing is another important sector of subsistence and cash-crop economies.

Only about one-fifth of the labor force is employed in industry (such as food processing); small-scale commerce is an important domain of income-generating activities, even though the revenue it generates is often limited.

Commercial exploitation of mineral deposits, among them iron, bauxite, and manganese, has been limited. The exploitation of gold reserves, most of which are located near the borders with Senegal and Guinea, has provided a source of income since the colonial period. Nowadays, with increasing liberalization of the economy, Mali's gold reserves have become a point of attraction for multinational corporations (mostly from South Africa, Canada, and China). In the border zone to Senegal, minor quantities of diamonds are mined.

In the absence of extensive industry (which employs less than one-fifth of the labor force), many people struggle to make a living from small-scale commerce. Others engage in manufacturing enterprises that specialize in food processing or in the making of consumer goods, such as blankets, cotton thread, and printed fabric. These activities are destined mainly for the domestic market. But there are also Malian handicrafts that are increasingly produced for an international tourist market, such as clothing, pottery, shoes, baskets, and wood carvings, and these are renowned for their aesthetic complexity and high quality throughout West Africa.

History

Early History

Rock paintings and inscriptions as well as Paleolithic and Neolithic remains give evidence of the existence and livelihoods of indigenous people throughout the area of present-day Mali. Most evidence of Paleolithic industry has been found in the Sahara and Sahelian zones. The oldest human skeletal evidence, found in 1927 at Asselar (Sahara), dates back to the Neolithic age (5000 BCE).

The characteristically high mobility and openness of Malian peoples and cultures has a long heritage. For more than a millennium, it has been rooted in long-distance travel and intellectual and commercial connections that enabled and accompanied a trade in gold and in slaves, ivory, civet, and gum arabic along trans-Saharan caravan routes that connected the Niger River valley and its southern extensions to locations in the Sahara and North Africa. Already in the centuries before the Common Era, there was a succession of flourishing urban entrepôts along the Niger and across the Sahelian and Sahara zones that owed their wealth and success to the trade in Saharan salt and in gold deposits coming in from the gold-mining areas in the west and southwest (the present-day border zones to Senegal and Guinea).

Starting in the middle of the third century BCE, the inland delta of the Niger River witnessed the emergence of the thriving trade center and city culture of Jenne-Jeno. The complexity, richness, and sophistication of this early civilization has been documented in fascinating detail through terracotta statues and other archeological finds at Jenne-Jeno and neighboring sites. Around the 13th century CE, the city was eclipsed by another trade entrepôt in the vicinity, Djenné, which owed its prosperity to Soninke traders whose commercial activities were instrumental to the spread of Islam along the then-existing routes connecting the southern savannah regions to trans-Sahara trade.

Early and Medieval Political Formations

Long-distance trade in gold and salt, from early on combined with a cosmopolitan culture of Muslim erudition and religious practice, was pivotal to the emergence of several highly centralized polities. Between the fourth and the 11th centuries, the Soninke polity of Ghana established its economic and political hegemony over the area between the Niger and Senegal Rivers, hailing from its center near present-day Nema, about 100 kilometers north of the Malian border with Mauritania. Ghana and its successors, Mali and the Songhai polity of Gao, are commonly referred to as kingdoms in the scholarly and popular literature. Yet it is important to keep in mind that their administrative structure and economic and social organization differed significantly from that of European medieval kingdoms and empires.

The Almoravid invasion of 1076 put an end to the already failing political and economic power of Ghana. Two centuries later, another hegemonic formation emerged in the southwest, on the upper Niger: the legendary Maninka (Malinke) empire of Mali, which lasted until the 15th century and was rendered famous by the travel accounts of Ibn Battuta, who visited the area in 1352–53. It is in this period that the legendary ruler Mansa Musa (ruling from 1307 to 1332), on his famed pilgrimage to Mecca in 1324, is said to have caused one of the first economic depressions in history by lavishly spending enormous amounts of gold on his way from Egypt to Arabia, thereby effecting a plunge in local gold prices that was to last for at least 12 years. During the period of Mali hegemony, the caravan routes gradually shifted east through Djenné and Timbuktu (founded in the 11th century as a seasonal camp by Berber nomads). Mali's decline in the 15th century left a political vacuum filled by the emergence of a new political and economic power farther east, the Songhai polity, with the city Gao and its famed mosque (built in 1324–25) at its center. Under Songhai hegemony, Djenné and Timbuktu thrived as centers of commercial activity and Islamic erudition. Songhai hegemony effectively ended in 1591, when a Moroccan army crossed the Sahara, attacked and destroyed Gao, and triggered a period of political chaos and decline in long-distance trade. Moroccan usurpation also put an abrupt end to the thriving culture of Muslim teaching and learning in Timbuktu, as renowned scholars were executed and most of the local holdings in manuscripts were destroyed. Only decades after the hegemony of the Songhai had come to an end, new trade routes in gold and slaves emerged, yet they pointed increasingly toward the coast, where the new trading posts established by Europeans offered new opportunities for trade in slaves, gold, and salt.

After the collapse of the Songhai Empire, no single polity established military control over the region. The reach of the Moroccan invaders remained limited to the region of Timbuktu and Gao. Several small successor political formations arose. In 1737, groups of Tuaregs seized control of the Niger Bend. One century later, in 1833, troops of the Fulani kingdom of Macina (stretching west of the Niger Bend and covering part of what are now the areas of Mopti and Segu) defeated whatever had remained of Moroccans' military power. Farther down to the south, another center of political and economic power had emerged already in the early 18th century. Founded by the Bamana warrior family of Kulubali in 1712, the polity of Segu extended its reach south and southwest, basing its power on military expeditions and the forceful extraction of tributary payments in currency and slaves. It lasted until its demise under the onslaught of El Hadj Umar Tall's jihad, which led to the establishment of Tukulor rule after 1861. Already in 1753, a split in the Kulubali dynasty in Segu had led to the establishment of a second Bamana polity, Kaarta, in what is now western Mali. This polity was equally defeated by El Hadj Umar Tall (in 1854). El Hadj Umar Tall was killed in a skirmish with the Fulani in 1864; the vast territories he had brought so swiftly under his military control were divided among his sons and commanders. His eldest son, Amadou Tall, became head of the Segu Tukulor polity, yet his position remained instable as the predominantly Bamana population mounted constant revolts against his rule.

Already in the late 17th century, the Senufo political formation of the Kenedugu controlled the area of what is today the border region with Burkina Faso. The 19th-century capital Sikasso of the Kenedugu showed remarkable resilience to the military attack of Samori Touré in 1887 yet only a decade later surrendered to French military occupation (in 1898).

French Colonial Rule

French colonial troops moving in from the western coastal area started to subjugate populations in present-day Mali in the 1880s. Once subjected to French colonial control, this area became part of French Sudan and was administered with other French colonial territories as the Federation of French West Africa.

The French had established military presence at Médine (in western Mali) already by 1855. They considered the Segu Tukulor polity a principal obstacle to their occupation of the Niger River valley. Wary of the competition on the part of the British colonial empire over this region of West Africa, they sought to extend their territory eastward through both diplomatic overtures and military undertakings. Primarily as the result of the diplomatic efforts of Captain Gallieni, who signed protectorate treaties with representatives of the local political establishment in Bafoulabé and Kita, by 1880 French military control extended from Médine 200 miles (320 km) east to Kita.

Reactions to French occupation differed considerably from one region to another. In some areas of the French Sudan, locally powerful families and clans mounted sustained military opposition to colonial encroachment. In other locations, certain segments of the local population, in contrast, facilitated the arrival of the French troops, mainly because they sought French support in their own local power struggles for political and economic control. In still other areas, such as the south and southeast of the Sudan, French military clashed with the troops of military and political leaders, most notably Samori Touré, whose empire-building endeavor since the 1860s coincided with the arrival of the French occupational forces.

In 1883, Gustave Borgnis-Desbordes initiated a number of military campaigns against the Tukulor polity of Segu and against the forces of Samori Touré. The same year, Borgnis-Desbordes captured Bamako, then a small, unimportant locale on the Niger. From 1890 to 1893, Colonel Louis Archinard engaged in a series of military operations that ultimately allowed him to conquer Segu in 1893. Samori Touré's troops were subsequently driven into the northern area of present-day Ivory Coast. Between 1894 and 1899, French troops gradually conquered first Timbuktu and then the entire area of the southern Sahara. But the French colonial administration never managed to pacify or bring under full control all nomadic groups in the north.

In 1893, Albert Grodet was appointed the first civilian governor of colonial French West Africa (AOF), but resistance to French control continued until Samori Touré's defeat and capture in 1998, the same year that saw the conquest of the Kenedugu polity of Sikasso by French forces. In 1904, the Kayes-Bamako portion of the railroad that linked Dakar in present-day Senegal with the Niger River was completed. As Bamako became the colony's administrative center, it doubled in size from 1902 to 1912 and continued to grow rapidly thereafter.

Similar to other areas of the French colonial territories, the Sudan was divided into administrative units (cercles), each of them composed of cantons headed by (appointed) chiefs. These chiefs were essential to the functioning of the colonial administration because it was their responsibility to collect taxes, recruit men for forced labor, and select the children to be sent to the colonial schools. Because of their intermediary position between the colonial administrators and the colonized population, the chiefs often encountered considerable contestation on the part of local political factions.

How colonial administrators put into practice the French colonial policy of indirect rule depended on the ways locally powerful clans had reacted to French occupation. In some locales, the French left the established political authorities in power. In other cases, traditional chiefs were replaced by members of competing clans or of branches of the same chiefly lineage; or they were effectively neutralized by an elaborate *divide et impera* strategy on the part of the administration, which sought to bypass traditional authorities by governing through appointed chiefs.

French colonial policy, although nominally guided by republican ideals, applied different standards of the rights of man when dealing with its colonial subjects. Violence and physical coercion remained integral features of French colonial conquest and administration. Domestic slavery and slave trade (which had fed into the transatlantic slave trade since the 17th century) were widespread when the French military troops started to occupy the area of the French Sudan. Although France had nominally abolished slavery under the Second Republic in 1848, slaves of different status remained a pervasive social and economic feature in the French West African territories well into the early decades of the 20th century. For local populations, colonial labor conscription blurred the lines between established forms of slavery and colonial forms of forceful labor recruitment.

The French colonial powers viewed the area of the French Sudan as markedly less important economically and politically than the adjacent areas of present-day Senegal and Ivory Coast, yet this did not preclude the forceful extraction of labor such as for the colonial rice irrigation scheme of the Office du Niger, cotton production, and the construction of the railway Dakar-Niger. Forced labor, as well as military conscription and taxation, triggered several local revolts whose spread and repercussions remained limited, however, and never led to a marked disruption of production and trade. During the two world wars, the French drafted heavily in the French Sudan. Many of the so-called Senegalese riflemen (*tirailleurs sénégalais*) were actually recruited among the Bamanakan- and Maninkakan-speaking populations of the southern French Sudan. After their return from both wars, these veterans generally enjoyed considerable standing within the colonial administration; they also garnered respect from the local population, which often considered them bearers of new ideas and technological innovation.

Colonialism, Law, and Culture

An important process by which colonial administration sought to implement control over local populations was the establishment of a system of legal regulation. The French Parliament was invested with full legislative powers and with functions allowing for a direct administration of colonies, thus covering the domain of criminal law, public matters, and political and administrative regulation. The governor-general of the AOF, seated in St. Louis (present-day Senegal), promulgated legislation in the form of ordinances and of administrative orders.

A 1903 decree by the governor of colonial French West Africa that the French Civil Code should be applicable throughout the French West African territory marked the establishment of a dual legal system, with two distinct bodies of law and spheres of their application. French positive law (Code Napoléon) regulated the affairs of French citizens and *assimilés,* that is, French expatriates, non-African foreigners, and those Africans who had acquired French citizenship. The rest of the colonized population, the so-called French subjects, were adjudicated under Indigenous Justice, that is, according to various indigenous or customary laws among which Islamic law held a privileged position. Both customary law (including Islamic law) and modern law were applied by French administrator-judges (the former in the *Tribunaux Indigènes*), who relied on the advice of experts (assessors) in local legal norms and practices. Some administrators invested great efforts in compiling and systematizing local customary conventions. In regions with a Muslim majority, one of the two assessors or advisers to the judge was either an expert in Islamic jurisprudence or some other Muslim notable. Because French magistrates usurped the power of decision making in disputes over divorce, land use rights, succession, and so forth, they severely reduced the political powers of village elders, Muslim notables, and other dignitaries considered experts in conventional legal regulations. However, it is also likely that a number of these notables and other experts in traditional legal conventions, by contributing to the standardization of different customary laws, were able to enhance their personal powers and to buttress the structural position of the group they represented. Also, in spite of the seemingly overarching powers of colonial administrators, their possibilities to enforce their rulings were actually weak and by and large limited to the administrative centers and the immediate surrounding areas.

Another important venue for the maintenance of colonial order was a colonial schooling system. Here, a new class of African literati was trained to be employed as clerks, technicians, interpreters, and teachers in the lower ranks of colonial administrative apparatus. Colonial schooling was therefore decisive for the emergence of a new political elite whose power position was grounded in their Western school education, in contrast to Muslim scribes and their background in Arabic literacy and religious and ritual knowledge.

As another side effect of colonial school education, a novel African culture of intellectual exchange and of consumerism emerged in the new urban centers of the French colonial territories. Pamphlets and printed press publications allowed members of this new African elite to establish real-time and imaginary ties to the colonial metropolis and to intellectuals living in other places of French West Africa; these ties proved to be pivotal to incipient nationalist tendencies.

Independence Movements

Endeavors by indigenous elites to move the colonized peoples of colonial French West Africa to independence started already in the late 1930s. At that time, intellectuals trained at the French institution of higher learning, the École William Ponty in Dakar, organized themselves in voluntary associations whose stated purposes were mainly cultural and sportive while also providing a platform to discuss politics. In these circles moved forerunners and leading activists of the French West African independence movement, among them Mamby Sidibe, Mamadou Konaté, and Modibo Keita. French colonial administration sought to contain the influence of these groupings by creating an umbrella cultural association. In 1937, the first trade unions were created in the French Sudan, among them a teachers' union founded by Konaté. In contrast to the cultural associations that served as a platform for the new elite of African literati, the trade unions constituted embryonic forms of mobilization of the urban masses.

A moment of radical rupture came toward the end of the Second World War, when General de Gaulle convened the Brazzaville Conference (1944) and committed France to far-reaching reforms yet avoided the issue of independence. The Loi Lamine Gueye of 1946 granted some limited citizenship rights to natives of the African colonies. The same year witnessed the creation of political parties that were to lead the different territories of French West Africa to independence.

In the area of the French Sudan, two parties competed for a following. Most notably, and in contrast to party formations in many other African colonial territories, ethnic affiliation played a negligible role in mobilizing followership for either of the two parties. The party PSP (Parti Soudanais Progressiste) adopted a more moderate stance toward the colonial powers, aiming at greater autonomy though in collaboration with France. It counted among its ranks many conservative forces, among them notables and religious leaders who owed their political influence to the support of the colonial administrators.

Led by Fily Dabo Sissoko, a schoolteacher and canton chief, the PSP was originally the more successful political party, but it lost political terrain to its competitor, the US-RDA (Union Soudanaise–Rassemblement Démocratique Africain) party, in the 1956 legislative elections. The latter adopted an explicit anticolonial rhetoric and a socialist orientation and had its stronghold in urban areas and among the lower social classes of the population. During these times of independence struggle, the US-RDA also counted among its ranks many younger Muslim activists and merchants with close ties to the Arab-speaking world.

The *Loi Cadre* (framework law) of 1956 granted universal suffrage, a move that played to the advantage of the US-RDA with its strong base among the socially and politically underprivileged segments of French Sudanese society. The *Loi Cadre* also invested the Territorial Assemblies with greater autonomy, giving them extensive powers over internal affairs and thus limiting the executive powers of the governor-general. The French Empire was renamed the French Union. The Constitution of the French Fifth Republic of 1958 initiated further changes in the colonial administrative structures. Designated a member of the French Union, the Republique Soudanaise was granted full internal autonomy. Soon afterward, the French Sudan and Senegal merged to form a new political body, the Malian Federation (Fédération du Mali), which declared full independence on June 20, 1960.

After the failure and subsequent dissolution of the Malian Federation (on August 20, 1960), the former French Sudan proclaimed itself the independent Republic of Mali on September 22, 1960, and withdrew from the French Community. Its new constitution was a slightly revised version of the initial constitutional text (drafted for the Malian Federation in January 1959).

Socialism and Single-Party Rule under President Keita (1960–68)

President Modibo Keita, whose US-RDA party had dominated the last years of preindependence politics, moved quickly to declare a single-party state. A charismatic leader and articulate proponent of an African path to socialism, he put a special emphasis on gaining cultural and political independence from France. Sided by leading ideologues of the ruling party, among them Seydou Badian Kouyaté, President Keita proclaimed a socialist policy based on extensive nationalization and oriented toward a fundamental restructuring of rural subsistence economies. Fundamental to the implementation of these policies were party structures created to mobilize workers, women, and youth at the regional and local levels.

The US-RDA also established close diplomatic relations and economic ties to communist and socialist countries and pushed cultural exchange programs with the USSR, China, and Cuba. The new government sought financial independence from the Franc Zone by issuing a nonconvertible currency, the Franc Malien, in 1962. Yet this policy was reverted subsequently when a continuously deteriorating economy prompted the ruling party's decision in 1967 to rejoin the Franc Zone.

Modibo Keita's ambitious project of establishing an economically prosperous and politically and culturally independent African nation was thwarted by a number of impediments, among them an extremely hierarchical administrative and political apparatus (a legacy of French colonial rule) and the considerable resistance on the part of broad segments of the population to the state-orchestrated restructuring of rural economies. During this period, the government was also repeatedly challenged by separatist movements in the north led by certain groups of Tuaregs. President Keita bloodily repressed these tendencies; his government's persistent economic, political, and cultural marginalization of northern peoples was continued under his successor, President Traoré.

In 1967, faced with growing financial difficulties, an ailing national economy, and growing popular discontent, US-RDA's governmental policy became more radicalized and oppressive. A popular militia—created in 1967 and composed of party youth who were to uncover corruption, identify dissenters with the party line, and pursue breaches of the party directives—only added to a general atmosphere of popular unrest.

In November 1968, in a situation of mounting political and economic instability, a group of officers led by Lieutenants Moussa Traoré and Yoro Diakite seized the opportunity of Keita's absence from the capital to mount a coup d'état. Keita and key members of his government were arrested, and a new government under the CMLN was declared. Traoré became president of the CMLN; Diakite became chief of state yet was soon replaced by Traoré. Accused of treason and sentenced to life imprisonment with hard labor, Diakite died under doubtful circumstances in a prisoners' working camp in 1973. Traoré, now head of state, also eliminated other political competitors and critics, such as Malik Diallo, another member of the CMLN.

The CMLN was composed of 14 former graduates from the military school, all of them from very modest educational backgrounds and totally inexperienced in administrative and economic matters. After the coup d'état, the CMLN declared as the main purpose of the regime change a reversion of the flawed economic policies of Keita's government. Notably, the new regime did not distance itself from the socialist agenda of the preceding government. Yet over the years, particularly since the late 1970s, clear efforts were made to establish closer contact with leading powers of the Western capitalist world.

Significant parts of the population, especially in Mali's rural areas, initially welcomed the regime change and the measures taken by the CMLN, such as the dissolution of US-RDA party structures and parapolitical bodies, the termination of compulsory political rallies and indoctrination sessions, the dismantling of collectivized agriculture, and the encouragement of private trade. However, over the years, the CMLN's lack of experience and competence became more and more evident. Power struggles within the CMLN, compounded by the government's evident lack of political direction and consistent policy, translated into an emergent culture of ad hoc political decision making, clientelism, mismanagement, and personal appropriation of state funds. Occasional dissent within the military and by civilian elements—most notably unions, students, and teachers—only led to bloody repression and to a stronger centralization of political power in the hands of Traoré and a few confidants. The situation did not change after the return to civilian rule but was instead compounded by a series of droughts in the 1970s and 1980s. In 1974, a new constitution was approved by popular referendum, but the country returned to civilian rule only in 1979.

Leading members of the newly created ruling party UDPM (Union Démocratique du Peuple Malien) were the same as those who had been in charge during military rule. Moussa Traoré was elected president of the new civil government. Although the new constitution established party structures and thus at least formally granted civilians the opportunity to participate in national and local elections, for instance in 1985, these changes did not alter the fundamental framework of state politics, partly because the UDPM—the only legal party—occupied all the seats in the National Assembly. UDPM party structures were established at the levels of the administrative subdivisions (cercle and arrondissement).

Traoré's military and later civilian rule witnessed two armed border conflicts with neighboring Upper Volta (which was renamed Burkina Faso in 1984) over a border area, in 1974–75 and again in December 1985. Foreign policy under President Traoré followed pragmatic considerations. Close relations to the socialist and communist bloc were maintained, and relations with the Western world, especially with France and the United States, were significantly extended. This development manifested itself in the heavy influx of foreign investment and donor money. Parallel to the extension of diplomatic and economic relations with the West ran the intensification of ties to the Arab-speaking world, particularly since the late 1970s. The creation of a national Muslim organization (Association Malienne pour Unité et le Progrès de l'Islam [AMUPI]) in the mid-1980s allowed Traoré to channel and control the funds coming in from private and public donors in the Arab-speaking Muslim world who sought to expand an Islamic infrastructure of proselytizing through the construction of schools and mosques. Even if these funds dried up in subsequent years, Traoré continued to grant special privileges to Muslim interest groups, in spite of the secular constitution of Mali's second republic, partly because of the persistent influence and mobilizing potential of certain Muslim religious leaders and intellectuals.

As a corollary of intensified ties to the Western world, starting in the mid-1980s, Mali submitted to the structural adjustment policy measures of the World Bank and the International Monetary Fund (IMF). The government consented to a program aiming at the reduction of public expenses, the reduction of social welfare provisions, the shrinking of the bureaucratic apparatus, and the privatization of many of the state-owned enterprises. These measures, as well as other elements of the IMF-imposed austerity program, increased dissatisfaction particularly among an urban population faced with a situation of continued misappropriation of state funds by leading party and state officials.

The Era of Multiparty Democracy: Presidents Konaré and Touré (1991–present)

The call for democratic reform that swept the African continent following the events in Eastern and Central Europe in the late 1980s had momentous repercussions in Mali. An urban-based democracy movement, organized by an alliance of civil servants, high school teachers, and lawyers, pushed for the granting of civil rights and the introduction of multiparty democracy. President Traoré's attempt to stifle these claims initiated a series of demonstrations, riots, and bloody clashes of urban youth with police forces and the military in major urban centers. On March 26, 1991, a group of 17 military officers under the leadership of Lieutenant-Colonel Amadou Toumani Touré arrested Moussa Traoré and suspended the constitution. The new military leaders swiftly organized a return to civilian rule and held a national conference in August 1991 that was attended by major associations and unions. Major results of the national conference were a charter for political parties, an electoral code, and a draft constitution (approved by popular referendum in January 1992). The period between January and April witnessed municipal, legislative, and presidential elections. Alpha Konaré, a well-known leader of the democracy movement, won the presidency with his party ADEMA, but it is important to note that voter participation was mainly restricted to the urban areas and did not exceed 30 percent of Mali's total population. Konaré was inaugurated as the president of the Third Republic on June 8, 1992.

The introduction of multiparty democracy in 1991 heralded a new era of civil rights and of a thriving culture of civil society initiatives illustrated by a mushrooming of grassroots organizations and of private media institutions, most notably local radio stations. Nevertheless, many hopes that urban Malians had put in democratic reform and in President Konaré's election were not borne out. The efforts of the new government were hampered by a hierarchically organized and widely inefficient state bureaucratic apparatus. A weak economy plagued by the effects of recent neoliberal reform, decreasing foreign aid, the devaluation of the CFA franc by 50 percent in January 1994, a persistent political culture of clientelism and misappropriation of state funds, and a continued degradation of the natural environment added to the challenges the new government faced. The first period of President Konaré's presidency was also disrupted by repeated clashes between security forces on one side and students and other groups of urban youth on the other who, dismayed by the realization that they did not reap the benefits of the political changes they had brought about, destroyed public buildings and physically assaulted members of the new government. Political life was also punctured by the interventions of oppositional parties.

Finally, the government faced persistent political unrest in Mali's north, where, starting in June 1990, armed attacks against state actors and institutions had increased; they were engineered by groups who framed their discontent with their economic and political marginalization as an ethnic confrontation between Tuaregs and a central state run by a southern Bamana-Maninka elite; their call for greater autonomy led to clashes with the military. The situation became more complicated in the course of 1994 and 1995 when armed groups of Tuaregs clashed with other segments of the northern population, who launched an operation of self-defense that, in all likelihood, received logistical support from the government in Bamako. In an attempt to resolve this civil war, the government and an alliance of opposing factions signed a pact in 1996 to end the fighting and restore stability in the north. The pact granted autonomy to the north as well as providing an increase in government resource allocation. It created favorable conditions for the gradual repatriation of the majority of a civil population that had fled the country during armed conflict. Since then, the situation has calmed down, even though in some pockets of the north multiple parastatal structures of power have emerged and vie each other for the allocation of the resources of the central state.

The next round of elections in 1997 was hampered by administrative difficulties; allegations by the oppositional parties of electoral fraud resulted in a court-ordered annulment of the legislative elections held in April 1997. Several influential oppositional parties boycotted the subsequent presidential elections in May 1997, from which President Konaré and his ADEMA party emerged with overwhelming strength. During the subsequent two-round legislative elections (July and August 1997), ADEMA won more than 80 percent of the National Assembly seats. Konaré's second and last term as president was overshadowed by charges of human rights abuses and of a thriving culture of political clientelism that illustrated the de facto single-party rule of the ADEMA.

All political parties participated in the next general elections (June and July 2002). After conducting a general census, the government put together a new list with the correct number of potential voters to prepare for the elections. Touré, who had led the military coup against Traoré and secured Mali's peaceful transition to multiparty democracy, emerged as the second democratically elected president. As an independent candidate, he integrated the dominant AMUPI party as well as representatives of oppositional parties into his government. Reelected in the presidential elections of 2007, he is currently serving his second term as president of Mali's Third Republic.

Political and Administrative Reform Since 1992

Since the mid-1990s, under pressure of Western donor organizations, the Malian state has embarked on an ambitious project of administrative decentralization and juridical reorganization. The reform led to greater administrative powers and financial autonomy at the—newly created—local level (the so-called commune) and to the creation of elected municipal councils, headed by elected mayors. The country now consists of eight regions, in addition to the capital district of Bamako. Each region is made up of a number of districts (or *cercles*) that break down into several *communes*, which, in turn, are divided into villages or quarters.

The law reform project, financed by a consortium of Western donors since 1999, was set up to improve the effectiveness and credibility of the judiciary and to create structures of extrajudicial arbitration to deal with property and land use issues. Another objective was to mend inconsistencies within the Malian legal code that are in part due to codes inherited at independence from France, yet they also derive from the fact that until then, the state had refrained from codifying crucial domains of family law.

The new constitution of 1992 stipulates a multiparty democracy that allows for the free formation of political parties as long as these are not based on claims to religious, ethnic, gender, or regional exclusivity. The constitution also stipulates a five-year-term presidency (with a limit of two terms) that grants the president authority as the chief of state and commander in chief of the armed forces. The president presides over the Council of Ministers, a governmental body that comprises the prime minister (who is appointed by the president as head of government) and other ministers. This council adopts law proposals that are then presented to the National Assembly for approval. Numerical representation in the National Assembly is arranged according to the size of the population of each administrative district. Deputies are nominated for a five-year-term through direct election and by party or independent list. At present, there are 16 political parties represented in the assembly that are aggregated into five parliamentary groups.

The constitution provides for the independence of the judiciary but also invests the Ministry of Justice with the power to appoint members of the judiciary staff and to oversee their work. In addition to the Supreme Court, there also exist a high court of justice and a constitutional court, each of which are granted the powers to try high-standing state and party officials.

2

Religion and Worldview

Titt ti hak iyfal Yalla ad hakk arr tiyyat.
If God closes one of your eyes, He will open your other one.

—Tuareg proverb

Don borey fonda, cimi fonda no.
The voice of the ancestors is the true voice.

—Songhai proverb

MALI IS RICH in religious history and civilization; to date, a variety of world-views and religious beliefs and practices coexist and often intermingle. Whereas in many other countries religious difference has turned into a source of conflict in recent years, Malian people continue to show great tolerance; many of them refrain explicitly from turning disagreements over religious matters into violent confrontations.

Islam made its presence felt in the area of present-day Mali in the 11th century, although at that time its reach remained by and large limited to urban centers of the north. In subsequent centuries, particularly in the 15th and 16th centuries, rich merchants and the rulers of the Songhai Empire transformed the northern cities of Timbuktu, Djenné, and Gao into centers of Islamic erudition. From there, Islamic culture expanded southward as the Songhai Empire of Gao extended its control to Segu. After massive conversion, which started in the early 19th century and continued throughout the colonial period, Islam constitutes Mali's predominant religion today. Approximately 85 percent of the total Malian population, urban and rural, consider themselves Muslims. Yet many of them combine Islam with traditional religious beliefs and practices. This holds true more often in some regions of the south than in the north. The few Christians, primarily Catholic, are mostly Dogon and Bobo and comprise less than 2 percent of the total Malian population. Traditional religious practices that are still mostly unaffected by Islam are to be found mostly among the Dogon, the Senufo, and the Minianka.

When speaking of Malian religions, it is important to keep in mind that what in the Western world is classified as *religion* and *worldview* does not constitute a neatly separable field of action and knowledge to many people in Mali. Rather, as in so many other African societies, religious beliefs and practices interlace tightly with the domain of politics and with the field of knowledge relating to people's physical and emotional well-being, which in Western industrial society is commonly referred to as the domain of "health" and "medicine." Herein resides the continued, far-reaching significance of religious practices and beliefs for the ways many Malians organize and make sense of their daily lives, relate to each other, and seek to mold their future and that of their beloved ones.

As in other societies, religious practices, and the rituals, myths, and texts that accompany them, have deep emotional reverberations and significances. They are essential to how people make sense of the universe, of the origins of humankind, and of their own existence. These emotional and existential attachments are in force independently of a person's educational background. That is, a civil engineer's educational background in the sciences does not preclude a deep devotion to his faith, nor the regular observance of what he considers a religious obligation.

A person's worldview, understood as a framework of ideas and beliefs through which an individual interprets the world and interacts with it, is always in flux. An important dimension of worldviews or religious belief systems is that they offer knowledge about phenomena and dynamics whose workings are not immediately evident to one's perceptive capacities; these phenomena are commonly referred to as supernatural or transcendent.

Many Malians, while being socialized into set systems of beliefs and ritual practice, help to write forth particular religious traditions. Simultaneously, however, they also transform them, by introducing changes, innovations in response to their own experiences and attempts to deal with the challenges, desires and hopes their lives confront them with. Therefore, rather than assume that "religion" and "worldview" are static systems, we should understand them as ever-changing sets of beliefs and practices in which ritualized forms of action play a central role.

Worldviews make themselves manifest (among other things) in various oral and written texts, such as poems, songs, epics, and creation myths, as well as in other instantiations of cultural creativity, such as music, dance, and decorative arts. Analysis of these varied forms of cultural production therefore provides access to people's views of the world, to their ideas about their own origins and those of humankind.

Worldviews and religious beliefs are often fragmentary in character. That is, they do not constitute homogenous and neatly bounded knowledge systems. Rather, different elements are involved in a process of constant mixing, merging, and mutual transformation. In Mali, this process is particularly evident in the ways elements of Muslim belief and practice have been incorporated into local religions, and vice versa. Since Islam has become rooted in the various regional and local cultures of Mali, some of its practices and elements have been subject to revision and transformation.

A pervasive feature of Malian religions—one that establishes their resonance with other African religious traditions—is the deep conviction that there exists a world of invisible, occult powers beyond this palpable and visible universe. This other world is supernatural in the sense that scientific knowledge or commonsensical modes of explanation are insufficient to account for its workings. In the eyes of numerous Malians, however, this does not preclude the existence of such invisible forces. While some local Malian religions conceive of these transcendental powers as ancestor spirits or as spirits affiliated with natural elements, other religious traditions, first and foremost among them Islam, view them as evil-doing or good-natured spirits—that is, as demons (*jine*) and angels whose workings are circumscribed by the overarching powers of one supreme God. Common to these different ways of conceiving these supernatural forces is the conviction that these occult powers exist and that they occasion, and can be held responsible for, natural events and human success, misfortune, and failure. For instance, the worldly powers of chiefs, rulers, and politicians are generally thought to be grounded in esoteric forms of power and knowledge. Accomplishment, ambition, intelligence, or one's capacity to exert physical coercion are never sufficient to explain a person's political and economic success. Rather, many people believe that only those who can control invisible forces (or who successfully rely on specialists in esoteric knowledge and power in order to do so) can hold and maintain worldly power. Many people thus tend to explain a person's election to political office, or sudden wealth, as the result of his or her successful mobilization of occult powers. There is also the common belief that many illnesses, as well as other instances of personal misfortune, have been occasioned by others (often, frighteningly, those who live close by, such as family, neighbors, and friends) who, out of envy or spite, decided to use evil forces against the afflicted person.

In line with the belief in an occult world of power underneath the visible and mundane world, Malian societies have developed various rituals, ceremonies, and religious institutions that allow them to communicate with spirits and other supernatural beings. These ritual activities are often described—in the scholarly literature and in local parlance—as a form of sorcery. This term is slightly distorting because it fails to capture the complexity of beliefs that underlie these practices. In fact, in Mali, several domains of esoteric knowledge and power exist; they can be seen as the result of people's historically amassed insights into how to deal with the invisible powers that shape their daily fate.

Each of these areas of occult expertise can be described as a medico-religious knowledge system; each system comprises an ensemble of beliefs and practices oriented toward ensuring and restoring emotional, physical, and psychological well-being. Each medico-religious system depends on religious experts whom people may consult to seek remedies to their misfortunes and afflictions. Different kinds of ritual and religious experts can be distinguished according to the kind of esoteric knowledge on which they rely. Yet some experts also purposefully combine strategies and devices drawn from different occult knowledge systems. Consultation generally evolves through a sequence of procedures and steps: a diagnosis of the origins of the malaise; the identification of the perpetrator, ancestor spirit, or other mystical power that caused the affliction; and the preparation of the cure itself, which usually involves the invocation of God's healing and protective powers or the supplication of other occult forces. Techniques for diagnosing the affliction and its origins range from divination practices drawing on the Qur'an and Arabic literacy to the deciphering of signs written in dust, sand, and soil to the throwing of gravel or cowry shells. Very often, the cure implies a sacrifice or offering, either to God or to the invisible forces whose assistance the expert seeks.

The habit of consulting with experts in esoteric knowledge to tackle the difficulties and dilemmas of daily life has been a long-standing feature of Malian social life. To these experts, then, providing esoteric services for clients has constituted an important source of additional income. However, there are also indications that these esoteric works are currently spreading in urban areas, thereby turning into a fee-for-service occupation. This process has been closely related to the spread of money as a general currency and to shrinking income opportunities in urban Mali.

This move toward greater commercial exploitation of esoteric knowledge, and the rituals it involves, demonstrates that it would be misleading to view the continued significance of religious beliefs and practices as a sign of Malians' rootedness in traditional beliefs or even their resistance to modernization. Rather, the diverse ways in which many Malians engage with what they consider manifestations of divine power or of occult forces show how they purposefully devise and revise religious practices and beliefs to address the challenges of modern life and social change and to tackle personal dilemmas, sorrows, and fears.

ISLAM

Islam's Historical Expansion in the Area of Present-Day Mali

Muslim thought and practice has been present for centuries, particularly in the northern areas of contemporary Mali. The great extent to which Muslim moral reasoning, religious practice, and literate traditions have shaped other religious traditions of Mali demonstrates that far from deriving from allegedly unchanging or static local traditions and customs, contemporary Malian culture is the result of a centuries-long engagement of local actors with various external and internal dynamics of revision and change. As a religion and civilization, Islam inspired translocal mobility, social flexibility, and various forms of cultural malleability and adaptation.

More than 85 percent of the Malian population is nominally Muslim, yet many people, particularly in the more remote rural areas of the southern triangle, combine Muslim religious practice with diverse beliefs and rituals taken from local religions that preceded Islam. Muslims scholars, among them those of a reformist mindset, condemn these people's combination of Islam with other religious beliefs as unlawful and non-Islamic. In contrast, those who engage in these hybridized religious practices feel that nothing is wrong in their combination of different faiths and refer to their ways of adhering to Islam as "walking on two paws."

Islam spread in the area of contemporary Mali largely through peaceful means. Its presence in the northern confines of present-day Mali dates back to the 10th century of the Common Era, when Muslim traders of Berber origin, living in the southern Saharan commercial centers of Awdaghust and Tadmekka, traded with the capitals of the Sudanic polities Ghana and Gao. These capitals thus functioned as southern termini of trans-Saharan Muslim commerce; they were considered part of Bilad-al-Sudan ("the Land of the Black People"), a zone where Islamic faith and civilization had not yet been brought to the infidels. Starting in the 11th century, however, the situation changed as Muslim warriors of Berber origin, the Almoravids, extended their military jihad across the Sahara. They, as well as Muslim traders, established a permanent presence in the commercial centers of the polities of Ghana and Gao. Although the rulers of these polities gradually converted to Islam from the 11th century, Islam remained for centuries a minority religion closely tied to the professional identity and elite status of urban families of traders and scholars. A notable illustration of this uneven distribution of Islam is the situation in the 13th- and 14th-century polity of Mali: the rulers of Mali, as well as their families, had formally converted to Islam (a conversion that did not prevent them from turning to experts of traditional religions for support in times of crisis). Yet the majority of the (rural) population continued to be attached to conventional fertility rites and the worship of ancestors and other incarnations of supernatural power.

By the 15th century, Muslim traders had spread their commercial ties, intellectual influence, and faith to the fringes of the forest south of present-day Mali. Central to the urban-based Muslim diaspora was not only a shared submission (the literal meaning of Islam) to God's injunctions, but also a common language (Julakan, very close to Bamanakan), a legal system based on what Muslims considered the divinely ordained law—the shari'a—and a shared professional identity. Being a trader, in other words, meant converting to Islam.

Islam remained the religion of a minority of urban literati until the late 18th century, when a number of Muslim scholars and political leaders engaged in movements of reform and state building that radically transformed the societies throughout colonial French West Africa. Most of these jihad movements were initiated by Fulani and Tukulor scholars and reformists with strong ties to Sufi-related forms and understandings of proper Muslim practice. These leaders' reformist and educational zeal and the state-building endeavors that accompanied them were fundamental to the spread of Islam from urban to rural areas and therefore to the transformation of Islam from an urban minority religious to a mass religion of mostly nonliterate rural populations.

The first reform movement with repercussions for the practice of Islam across wide areas of West Africa was initiated by Uthman dan Fodio, the founder of Sokoto Caliphate in late-18th-century Hausaland (northern Nigeria). Uthman was a strong defender of Qadiriyya Sufi practice; his reformist movement and state-building endeavor strongly influenced the reasoning of scholars and religious leaders in the area of present-day Mali.

The second reformist movement of wider regional importance was led by Seku Amadu Bari, who founded the theocratic state of Macina, in the middle delta of the Niger River after his victory over the Segu polity in 1818.

The reformist endeavor with the most far-reaching consequences for the spread and practice of Islam in Mali's southern triangle was that of the scholar El Hadj Umar Tall, who transformed his project of returning to the proper teachings of Islam into a military jihad. Born in the Futa Toro (northern Senegal and southeastern Mauritania) into a Tukulor family, El Hadj Umar Tall studied in the Futa Jalon (present-day Guinea) and became a practitioner of the Tijaniyya Sufi path. By then, the Tijaniyya Sufi order was firmly established in Algeria and Morocco yet was relatively new to Sahelian West Africa. After his return from a two-year stay in Medina and Mecca (1818–20), El Hadj Umar spent six years in Hausaland and then returned to the Futa Jalon, where he spent most of the 1840s building a significant Tijaniyya community. Starting in the late 1840s, El Hadj Umar Tall became more and more convinced that waging military jihad, not writing and teaching, was the right way of bringing Islam to the mass of infidels living in the surrounding areas, thereby making them part of the Muslim world, the dar al-Islam. In 1852, he launched a jihad that was to bring vast areas within and beyond the confines of present-day Mali under his military and religious leadership.

Although El Hadj Umar Tall's religiously inspired conquest of vast areas of southern Mali was a historical stepping-stone for the spread of Islam, the religion continued to be associated with urban-based trade and erudition. Broad segments of the rural populations in the south converted to Islam only in the course of the colonial period. Younger men were often the first ones in a family to adopt the Muslim faith. Not only did these men associate Muslim faith and practice with a modern, educated, and civilized African identity that constituted an alternative to the modernism represented by the European colonial culture. To them, Muslim identity also opened up new intellectual and business ties to the Arab-speaking Muslim world.

Because historically Islam had been thoroughly rooted only in urban areas of the north, it was initially only here that Muslim women of elite background accessed religious education and passed on their knowledge to other women. Because of a lack of written documentation, little is known about female Muslim leaders and teachers in these times. Nevertheless, oral accounts of more recent historical periods document that there were a few women, usually connected to prestigious families of Muslim scholars and traders, who garnered much respect because of their pious conduct and religious erudition.

Central elements of Islam, as they have been practiced and taught in the surroundings of present-day Mali since the early 20th century, testify to the successful incorporation of Islam into established local religious ideas and notions of the transcendental world. Most notably, people found it easy to find a correspondence for their belief in occult forces in the angels and demons, for which Islam makes ample room. Since their arrival in this part of the Muslim world, mystical traditions of Islam, as they are represented by Sufi orders, have enjoyed great popularity throughout West Africa. One reason for this popularity is that there are strong resonances between local religious traditions and the mystical traditions passed on by the leaders of Sufi orders. Local religions often assign very special functions to religious experts in dealing with the spirit world. Similarly, Sufi-related religious practices and spiritual exercise revolve around the belief in the spiritual guidance provided by the leader of a Sufi order. Disciples of Sufi practice emphasize the importance of human intercession in their communication with God. These disciples consider the leaders of Sufi orders to be holy men (singular, *wali*) whose spiritual leadership and closeness to God allow them to communicate with God on behalf of ordinary believers. In the eyes of many believers, the intercession of these holy men and of other specialists in Muslim esoteric knowledge is necessary for a variety of practices, such as asking for God's special benedictions and fabricating amulets, talismans, and other protective works.

Contemporary Dynamics of Islam and Muslim Religious Practice

At present, especially in towns whose pasts are connected to prestigious traditions of Sufi practice and leadership, religious specialists derive exquisite prestige from the special divine blessing (*baraka*) their families are said to hold and that, according to a widely held belief, gives them privileged access to esoteric knowledge. Their special expertise is also related to their Qur'anic school education, such as Arabic literacy and the knowledge of particularly powerful suras and names of God. This knowledge qualifies them to diagnose the sources of affliction, to fabricate works, to speak over them (that is, recite passages from certain suras), and, occasionally, to inscribe sacred verses on their surface.[1]

For some of the leading families associated with Sufi orders, all these practices constitute a source of considerable wealth, as people offer them generous gifts in return for the esoteric undertakings they effect on the behalf of followers. Muslim religious specialists who live in other areas of Mali, in contrast, do not have the same cachet of genealogical privilege and high-prestige spiritual powers. Nevertheless, some of them turn their expertise in dealing with occult powers into a full-time profession as they seek to make a living in a situation of shrinking income resources in urban areas. Some of them combine Muslim techniques of engaging with occult forces with procedures taken from other medico-religious belief systems, thereby illustrating how Islam's encounter with local religions leads to the transformation of each of these religious systems.

Islam has been transformed in this area of West Africa not only through its blending with local forms of engaging with supernatural powers. For a long time, Muslim religious practices have been continuously reassessed and revised in response to different reformist endeavors undertaken by Muslim scholars and activists. As a result, present-day Muslim thought and practice are characterized by a considerable degree of variation. A prominent example of the diversity of Muslim beliefs and practices is spirit possession; whereas some Muslims consider it part and parcel of Muslim religious practice, other Muslims challenge this view and contend that engaging with spirits is un-Islamic and blasphemous.

These disagreements among different Muslim leaders and practitioners over what constitutes true Islam can be traced back to the times of French colonial administration when, starting in the late 1930s, a number of male intellectuals returned to the French Sudan after spending years of study at religious institutions in Saudi Arabia and Egypt. After their return, they denounced as un-Islamic certain ways Islam was practiced in the region (such as the custom of soliciting Muslim specialists' esoteric expertise) and criticized Muslims who supported these religious conventions. The reformist-minded intellectuals also revised the traditional Qur'anic educational system to make it accessible to broader segments of the population and to teach them Arabic literacy. Their activities contributed to the unsettling of the credentials and legitimacy of traditional religious authority. The repercussions of these changes are still palpable today. For instance, broader access to Islamic education prompted youth and women to reformulate their self-understandings as responsible and knowledgeable Muslims.

Until the 1970s, most women, especially those from a non-elite background, could gain only limited knowledge in religious and ritual matters. Since then, new grassroots organizations have emerged, such as Muslim women's educational circles in which women are trained in Arabic and in ritual knowledge. In contrast to earlier times, most of these women are from the urban lower and lower middle classes. Their groups resemble the informal structures of mobilization that have been mushrooming throughout the Muslim world since, roughly, the mid-1970s. Inspired by a transnational *da'wa* movement, these groups aim to reform the moral and the social and highlight the importance of religious instruction and Arabic literacy. The activities of Muslim women in Mali also demonstrate how their project of moral reform perpetuates a long-standing Muslim tradition of internal critique and reform. The learning activities of these women, as well as the fact that their female leaders disseminate their teachings on audiotapes and local radio, indicate a broadening of access to religious knowledge, a process that in earlier historical periods already exacerbated struggles over religious authority and leadership.

CHRISTIANITY

In spite of sustained efforts on the part of Christian missionaries since colonial times, to date, Christians in Mali are a small minority in numerical terms; yet they have been generally appreciated and treated with respect by their Muslim compatriots. Confronted with the upsurge of a symbolism and an infrastructure of Islamic awakening in Mali's public arenas since the 1980s, some groups of Christians express heightened concern about what they fear as a governmental move toward greater support of Muslim interest groups. However, it seems that so far their concerns have been largely unfounded. Until his recent death, Luc Sangaré, the late archbishop of Bamako, was a highly influential opinion leader who garnered great respect among many urban Muslims. Also, both governments of democratic Mali have regularly invited Christian interest groups to participate in public debate in their function as representatives of Malian civil society, along with speakers of Muslim groups. Christian evangelists and missionaries are seeking out converts among those who adhere to local religious traditions, but it is hard to compete with the much more popular and accessible religion of Islam.

OTHER MALIAN RELIGIOUS TRADITIONS

Because the populations of the north have been exposed to the influence of Islam for a longer period of time, Malian religious traditions that differ from and often preceded Islam are today practiced mostly in Mali's southern triangle. In the scholarly and popular literature, these religions and worldviews are often referred to as indigenous or as African. Yet this denomination is misleading insofar as it suggests that Islam is not indigenous and an intricate element of Malian culture but foreign to it. Given the centuries-long presence of Islam in this area of West Africa, this depiction is clearly inadequate. For lack of a better term, the following discussion refers to these other religions as local, mainly because their practice and impact was most often restricted to specific localities.

People who adhere to local religious traditions are the minority in Mali. Nevertheless, they have affected Malian history and culture in important and long-lasting ways. These religions embody central ideas about the values that help maintain and perpetuate humankind and community and about the codes of conduct that ensure the congruence of individual behavior with communal norms. Similar to other societies, in Africa and elsewhere, that are primarily organized according to the needs of rural subsistence production, Malian societies attribute central importance to communal aspects of life; their rituals therefore embody, and help to perpetuate, rules that encourage moral conservatism and stipulate the respect for parents and elders and for traditional norms.

All Malian religions make room for the transmission of these rules and norms. The norms are passed on in the course of a person's initiation into the codes and secrets of a particular association or society, or else they are conveyed along with rituals that accompany a person's transition from one stage of his or her life cycle to another. In many local societies, these transitions are marked by male and female circumcision rituals, which bear deep religious significance. In other words, circumcision constitutes an important step in becoming a member of the adult world. It is preceded by the initiate's gradual preparation for this life cycle event, usually during an extended period of seclusion. During this period, girls and boys are taught central norms, moral values, and rules of conduct considered necessary for the maintenance and reproduction of social order and communal life.

Central to many local religious traditions are beliefs in, and rites related to, the powerful hold of ancestors and other spirits over communal well-being and individual success. Humans must constantly strive to appease ancestors by catering to their needs and demands. Occurrence of social strife and physical affliction indicates that the always precarious coexistence with spirits has tipped off-balance. In this worldview, crop and cattle productivity are directly associated with the "spirits of the land." In a given locale or community, certain families, referred to in local languages as "guardians of the earth," were—and still are—believed to hold particular knowledge and esoteric power that allows them to communicate with the world of invisible forces and spirits. It is the task of these families of ritual specialists to mediate between the world of transcendental powers and that of everyday life and to convey to human beings what wishes or unfulfilled promises kept ancestors and other spirits from granting physical well-being, fertility, and worldly success.

Closely related to the beliefs in the influence of ancestor spirits and other invisible forces on humans' daily actions and well-being are rites that in many agricultural societies of southern Mali, at least historically, aimed at ensuring the fertility of soils, plentiful harvests, and the perpetuation of human community. A notable example of these rites is the *ciwara* dance, rendered internationally famous by its emblem, the carved wooden representation of the mythical antelope spiritual being (*ciwara*) that taught humans the art of farming. The *ciwara* mask performance has been practiced by Bamana agriculturalists as part of a sequence of annual rituals whose function is to secure and celebrate fertility, productivity, and social and moral order.

In recent decades, Islam and Christianity have been making inroads into even remote rural societies, yet pockets of settlements persist in which people give primacy to traditional worldviews and religious practices and seek to fend off the influence of Muslim or Christian converts. Some of these adherents to local religious traditions view the book religions as a threat not only to their established religious conventions and local values, but also to the special status and powers associated with families specializing in the communication with the world of invisible forces.

Secret Societies

Secret societies play an eminent role in numerous local religious traditions, even though their workings, reach, and relevance have been affected by the incorporation of Islam and Christianity into local communities throughout even the most remote rural areas of Mali. The primary purpose of these organizations is to preserve and pass on the values, the rules of conduct, and the esoteric knowledge considered necessary to ensure the harmonious functioning and longevity of a given community. All this knowledge is restricted, that is, it is treated as a secret to be revealed only to those initiated into the society. Membership in a secret society is therefore conditional upon a lengthy initiation process, in the course of which the candidate gradually acquires the knowledge that the society is held to control and protect. Much of this secret knowledge pertains to the regulation of the relations between different status and age groups of society, as well as to the ways in which humans may manipulate their natural environment and seek to call on the assistance of invisible forces and the spirits of the wilderness. Very often, initiation into a secret society culminates in the ritual act of circumcising the initiate. Most secret societies in Mali are for men only, yet there also exist a few societies drawing primarily on female initiates. Mask performances and specific instruments to be used during rituals play an important role in most secret societies and their ceremonies.

Associations of hunters (singular *donson* in Bamanakan) are one particular instance of a secret society; they are found in several local religious traditions in Mali and throughout West Africa. An important characteristic of these men-only associations is that they cut across social distinctions that are otherwise so relevant to social organization in these societies, such as different status, birth, political rank, and ethnic background. Hunters are generally considered to be closer to the wilderness, that is, the zone beyond the realm of civilization and humanity. They are therefore said to know about the inner forces of nature and to control its mystical powers through various secrets. Some hunters are also consulted in their function as experts of plant-related medicinal knowledge. Hunters' esoteric knowledge and powers are legendary; they have found entry into various forms of poetry and oral recitation, most notably the "hunters' songs" and "hunters' epics." The special instrument associated with hunters' mystical powers and the way in which they pass on their knowledge is the *donson ngoni,* a six-stringed guitar.

Spirit Possession

Spirit mediums and possession rituals constitute an important element in several Malian medico-religious systems. Although there are Muslims who decry these practices and attendant beliefs as un-Islamic, they are also an essential characteristic of how certain Malian Muslims deal with different kinds of affliction and misfortune. Spirit mediums have a special ability—or God-granted gifts—to receive messages from spirits; they are thus considered mediators between humankind and the world of invisible forces and ancestor spirits. People consult with spirit mediums for personal, financial, social-relational, or health reasons. Spirits take temporary possession of the body of their medium, thereby putting them into a trance state during which a medium loses his or her normal personality and verbal and nonverbal communication patterns. By sharing the mind and body of the medium, a spirit conveys to its medium its expectations, wishes, and information that will allow the medium to diagnose the origins of a person's affliction and establish what cure will be necessary. Most spirit mediums need to undergo a period of apprenticeship during which they lean how to host, that is, how to deal with the spirit who takes possession of their body. In many cases, particular drum rhythms and forms of drumming are essential to summoning specific spirits into their mediums' body.

In addition to these features that many local religious traditions share, each of them also bears certain specific traits. In what follows, notable characteristics of certain local religions will be presented. Yet much of what the following sketch presents as a consistent local religious tradition no longer exists in pristine and internally consistent form. Whereas individual elements of beliefs, worldviews, and rituals are still valid, others have been largely abandoned under the influence of Islam and Christianity, modern school education, and the intensification of migratory exchange connecting remote rural locals to urban areas in Mali and abroad.

Tuareg Religion

The religious practices of the Kel Tamasheq (Tuareg) exemplify how pre-Islamic religious beliefs, cosmology, and ritual have been absorbed into Islam and are considered by believers an essential element of their Muslim belief and religious practice. In fact, it is difficult to distinguish between Islamic and non-Islamic elements of the Kel Tamasheq worldview, for instance, when it comes to analyzing local explanatory frameworks that account for the causes of malaise and misfortune. Because at first Tuareg were reluctant to embrace Muslim faith and religious practice, they were renowned among the different Berber groups of North Africa for their lax attitudes toward observing Muslim ritual obligations. Also, they only loosely applied Islamic codes of ethical conduct, such as those requiring chastity for women before marriage. Today, there exists some variation among different Tuareg groups with regard to the extent to which they subscribe to Islamic norms and social and religious regulations. Because boys are preferentially exposed to traditional Qur'anic school education, men are often more likely to know the prescribed prayers; girls and women, in contrast, tend to use Tamasheq terms. In Tuareg groups more influenced by recent Muslim reformist-trend scholars, female chastity and women's withdrawal from public life have gained in importance. Still, the division of labor and other social tasks among these groups render impossible a strict practice of female seclusion.

Important Tuareg rituals are closely related to life cycle ceremonies, such as name giving, (male) circumcision, weddings, and funerary rites. Another important ceremony is the initial men's face-veil wrapping, which takes place around the age of 18 years, helps to reestablish and celebrate reserve and modesty as elements of masculinity, and marks the transition from boyhood to manhood and adult status. A separate set of ritual acts marks the transition of female Tuareg from girlhood to puberty status and later womanhood.

The blending of Islamic and other sources of esoteric knowledge is also vividly illustrated in the coexistence of different kinds of experts of religio-medical knowledge. Muslim religious experts, popularly called *ineslemen,* are often considered to maintain particularly close relations to God that manifest themselves in their special spiritual powers. Muslim experts are called upon to officiate in rites of passage and Islamic rituals, and people also consult them to cure certain (god-made) afflictions. Blacksmiths are also considered important in maintaining good relations with the world of invisible powers; people call on them, too, to help them deal with physical affliction and social misfortune and to perform specific ritual duties during life cycle ceremonies. Yet another kind of ritual expert plays a central role in Tuareg spirit-possession rituals.

Bamana Religion

Bamana religion revolves around the belief in the existence of one supreme creator god, Mansa Dembali, who delegates the governance of the world to lesser spiritual beings. According to Bamana mythology, the Sky, associated with masculinity, functions as the husband of the Earth, associated with femininity, by fertilizing her regularly through its sacred semen (rain) and by letting its light shine on her. As agriculturalists, the Bamana invest particular attention and energy into maintaining good relations with the Earth, through set sequences of annual rites asking the Earth for permission to sow and for forgiveness for breaking the soil to plant. In these rituals, women, as bearers of human fertility, take over very particular functions. Other domains of subsistence production are similarly structured by rituals aiming at reconciling the spirits of the natural world with humans' extraction of natural resources.

According to Bamana belief, after the creation process was over, the supreme God retired into a remote area of the sky. Human beings therefore need to direct their daily requests, demands, and sacrificial offerings to the lesser spiritual beings, some of whom are venerated through fixed sets of rituals linked to particular worship communities, among them the Nya, Ntomo, Nama, and Komo secret societies.

Although most Bamana today consider themselves Muslims and have replaced belief in Mansa Dembali with a worship of the Muslim supreme god, many continue to practice non-Islamic rituals, in particular those serving to honor ancestors, who are considered to continue to watch over, and interfere with, human affairs. To ensure that a deceased family member becomes an ancestor in the proper sense (that is, one who will protect, rather than disrupt, family affairs), people feel they need to accurately perform the funerary rites of the 1st, 3rd, 7th, and 40th days after the death has occurred.

Illustrative of the long-standing ritual traditions of the Bamana are performances such as the *ciwara* dance and the *ntomo* dance, linked to male initiation ceremonies. All these ritual ceremonies, whether related to initiation, ancestors, or the agricultural circle, have resulted in an enormous pantheon of ritual objects.

Although Bamana male and female initiation societies (*jow*) have lost social significance, they still constitute an essential, defining element of Bamana religious practice and social organization. The *jow* are composed of several age-related educational stages, or societies. As male and female initiates move through the six societies, they learn about the dual material and spiritual nature of the world and acquire carefully channeled insider knowledge, that is, secret knowledge. Initiates are also taught vital lessons about the norms and rules of social life that are meant to serve the maintenance of social and moral order and guarantee the well-being of the individual and the community.

Dogon Religion

Dogon worldview and religious practices are among the best known religious traditions of sub-Saharan Africa. The Dogon owe this renown significantly to the writings and scholarship of the French anthropologist Marcel Griaule and his team of researchers, among them most notably the anthropologist Germaine Dieterlen. Griaule's team came across the Dogon for the first time in 1931 during a research expedition across the Sudan, from West to East Africa. The research team continued its research on the Dogon during subsequent research trips spanning the period between the 1930s and the 1960s. Much of the work of Griaule and his fellow researchers focused on Dogon cosmology, religious beliefs, and ritual practices. Among the most important works resulting from this decades-long research endeavor are Marcel Griaule's *Masques Dogons* (1938) and *Dien d'Eau* (1948, the English translation of which appeared in 1965 under the title *Conversations with Ogotemmeli*). Griaule documented in detail what he and Dieterlen considered to be an elaborate Dogon cosmology and philosophical system of explaining the material and spiritual origins of the universe. Griaule also reported a sophisticated Dogon account of the star system of Sirius.

Subsequent generations of scholars have called into question these accounts, arguing that Griaule and Dieterlen based their insights on accounts provided by few selected (and in some cases rather marginal) people and attributed to the Dogon worldview greater internal consistency, and distinctiveness from an Islamic worldview, than what was actually the case. Whether these critiques apply or not, it is the case that at present, the Dogon cosmology no longer exists in any pristine form, distinct from Muslim— or Christian—ways of accounting for the origins of social and moral order. After all, today about 10 percent of the Dogon population are Christians. Also, since the mid-19th century, the neighboring Fulani have played an important role in the conversion to Islam by certain segments of the Dogon population. It is important to note, however, that although numerous Dogon embrace certain tenets of Islam or Christianity, they have rejected others; in many cases, the new elements are blended with those of conventional Dogon worldview and religious practice.

The Dogon are believed to have originated in the Manding Mountains near the borders of Equatorial Guinea and Mali; they migrated to their current homeland, the Bandiagara plateau and foothills, only in the 18th century, where they subjected and ultimately wiped out the local Tellem population. Elements of Dogon traditional religion reflect the extent to which Tellem culture and worldview was absorbed into, and lived forth in, Dogon mythological accounts (for example, of the mythical Nommo ancestors).

Dogon religious beliefs, as they are reported in the works of Griaule and his fellow researchers, are complex, and knowledge of them is unevenly distributed among different members of Dogon society. Dogon religion centers on the belief in Amma, the supreme Creator God, and in the existence of other categories of lesser spiritual beings whom the Dogon should worship through distinct cults. Among these lesser deities are, first, spirits of the water who emerged as Amma's offspring; the Lebe, the incarnation of the earth and its fertilizing properties; and the Yurugu, mythical ancestors from whom the members of the four Dogon groups are thought to have descended. Apart from these lesser deities, Dogon religion also makes room for the existence of various good-natured and evil spirits who inhabit the bush, trees, and other elements of the natural world.

Interaction with these spirits is importantly effected through mask performances. That is, the spirits are believed to take temporary material form in
the masks carved by Dogon ritual specialists and brought to spiritual life in
elaborate dance ceremonies. Because they are meant as concrete expression of
ancestor and other spirits, these carvings are carefully hidden away, viewed
and handled only by those initiated into the rites.

Young men are initiated into secret societies whose ideological cores these
mask performances constitute; women, in contrast, remain strictly excluded.
As is the case of secret societies of other ethnic groups, Dogon secret society
is characterized by a special language of the initiates, a strict etiquette, obligations, and specific prohibitions.

As Amma, the Creator God, is believed to have withdrawn from the realm
of worldly matters, much of Dogon religious practice centers on rituals relating to the maintenance of good relations between the living and the world
of spirits, among them particularly the spirits of the deceased, the ancestor
spirits. Family elders play an important role as ritual experts in this ancestor
cult, a role that corresponds to their dominant position in Dogon social and
political life.

Funerary ceremonies are essential to the communication with ancestors
because it is through these ceremonies that a deceased (male) family member
is transformed into an ancestor in the proper sense of the term. Dogon funerary ceremonies comprise two kinds of rites: those following death and relating directly to the deceased person and his journey to the spirit world; and
the *dama* rites that mark the end of the mourning period. Sacrificial offerings
to ancestor spirits play a role in all these rituals. Depending on the status and
importance of the deceased person, funerary ceremonies may also include
mask performances that are meant to facilitate the passage of a deceased male
family elder to the ranks of ancestor spirits.

Communication with the spirit world is also effected through three principal cults, the Awa, Lebe, and Binu, all of which require the expertise of ritual
specialists. Awa cult ceremonies involve mask performances of cult initiates
who dance with spectacularly painted masks. In close analogy to the funerary
rites described previously, the Awa cult ceremonies are intended to facilitate
the transition of the soul of a deceased family elder to the world of ancestor
spirits. Beyond this immediate purpose, the Awa cult aims at restoring order
to the spiritual forces disturbed by the death of one of the Dogon's mythological ancestors, the Nommo.

The cult of Lebe, the lesser deity associated with human and natural fertility, is directed toward the agricultural cycle. Its importance is manifested in
the existence of a Lebe shrine in almost every Dogon village. The chief ritual
expert of the Lebe cult is called Hogon, the person considered to be the oldest

direct descendant of the founder of the Dogon. Apart from officiating agricultural ceremonies, the Hogon's task is to make regular offerings to Lebe to ensure the purity of the soil, a precondition for fertility and plentiful harvest.

The cult of Binu relates mostly to the communication with ancestors; it also has complex associations with the Dogon creation myth (as it has been reported by Marcel Griaule and his colleagues), particularly with the importance it accords to the lesser deity named Nommo. Nommo, the first living being created by Amma, soon multiplied to become four sets of twins. One of the Nommo twins rebelled against Amma and the order he had established and thereby brought disorder into the cosmos. To restore order and purify the universe, Amma cut up the body of another of the Nommo. These scattered body parts of one Nommo became the sites of Binu shrines throughout the Dogon region. These shrines, whose facades are often painted with graphic signs and mystic symbols, are considered to host the Binu, spirits of other mythical ancestors of the Dogon who make themselves known to their descendants by taking the form of an animal that in a family's mythical past became a Dogon clan's protector; today, this animal is honored as the clan's totemic animal. Ritual experts in charge of communicating with the Binu ancestor spirits make regular offerings (of blood and millet porridge) to them to ensure their benevolent protection.

The core of the Dogon ancestor ritual complex is the Sigi ceremony. It takes place once every 60 years, which used to correspond roughly to a Dogon person's lifespan. The purpose of the ceremony is to honor the dead ancestors so as to ensure their benevolence and protection. A central element of the Sigi ceremony is a series of mask dances performed during a period of seven days. During this time, new masks are carved and dedicated to the ancestors, to serve as their temporary, material incarnations.

Senufo Religion

The Senufo in southwestern Mali comprise several subgroups, among them the Minianka, who are often considered a separate ethnic group in spite of the many commonalities that both groups share.

Similar to other agricultural societies of southern Mali, Senufo traditional religious beliefs posit the existence of a (male) creator god who after completing the creation of the universe retreated from worldly affairs. Senufo also believe in lesser deities and a variety of spirits, among them ancestor spirits and those associated with the wilderness. The latter are believed to take the form of various animals, such as lizards, tortoises, crocodiles, and pythons. What distinguishes the Senufo from neighboring peoples is their predominantly matrilineal social organization, a feature that mirrors the strong emphasis on gender duality and complementarity evinced in Senufo creation myths and in the relatively flexible nature of female and male membership in secret societies. According to Senufo mythical accounts of the origins of humankind, the first celestial beings, Maleeo and Kolotyolo (Ancient Mother and Creator God), were male and female, and the first humans, Yiriigifolo or Nyehene, were created as a couple, too.

Although Senufo religious practice and attendant rituals have changed substantially under the influence of Islam and Christianity, the Poro secret society (for men) and the Sandogo secret society (for women) continue to play an important role in various ceremonies and rituals, such as those aiming to ensure agricultural productivity and those establishing communication between the living and the world of ancestors. The Poro society also plays an eminent role in funerary rituals. Both secret societies are open to membership by representatives of the opposite sex; in the case of the Poro society, only prepubertarian or women beyond menopause may join. In many of their rituals, mask dance performances play a central role. Also important to Senufo religion is the divination system, closely associated with the Sandogo society.

As we have seen, religious practices and beliefs remain fundamental to many Malians' everyday experiences and to the ways in which they conduct social and political life. Whether in town or in remote areas of the countryside, people accord a central and enduring relevance to religion, as a blueprint for moral order and action, as a source of knowledge and civilization, and as a way of understanding what constitutes the—visible or hidden—foundations of the social and material world they live in.

Note

1. Strictly speaking, the esoteric knowledge that Muslim religious specialists are held to control encompasses three distinct areas of expertise that receive very diverse appreciation. The most respectable among these forms of expertise is related to prophetic revelation, such as visions and dreams. The second kind of expertise encompasses knowledge about the power of formula, words, numbers, and letters and their manipulation. The third and least respectable expertise (and the one whose legitimacy has historically generated the most heated debates among Muslim scholars) is related to practices of predication, such as astrology and geomancy. See Louis Brenner, "Sufism in Africa," in *African Spirituality: Forms, Meanings, and Expressions,* ed. J. Olupona (New York: Crossroad Publishing Company, 2000), 324–49.

3

Literature and Media

Fòko nyuman ni tinyè tè kèlèn ye.
A good way of saying something is not the same as (saying) the truth.
—Bamana proverb

Haala wéla kasso halakha hulè wala.
Speech is not good, but nothing can be resolved without speaking.
—Fulani proverb

FOR CENTURIES, MALIAN literary traditions have evolved at the crossroads of Muslim, Arabophone erudition and of regional- and local-language-based intellectual production. To date, Mali enjoys an international reputation for its rich oral and musical traditions. In recent decades, Mali has also gained a significant presence in the canon of written world literature. Also, with the implementation of the UNESCO World Heritage project in Timbuktu and Djenné, Mali has made the headlines of leading newspapers around the world because of its rich historical archive of written manuscripts.

The links between contemporary literary production in Mali and its colonial past are manifold. Written literature is deeply rooted in Western school education and in the language and literary conventions mediated through French schooling. Written literature is also informed by the views of a modern African subject, European civilization, and progress and enlightenment that were promoted through colonial and later postcolonial schooling. From the 1950s onward, these views were also disseminated by mass media, especially through the French colonial newspaper *Le Soudanais* and radio station Radio Soudan. Yet Mali's written literary traditions did not start with colonial rule but, rather, can be traced back to a centuries-long literary production of Muslim scribes and erudite Arabophones.

These historical layers of institutional innovation and cultural creativity mark out the terrain of intellectual and literary productivity that links up with earlier aesthetic conventions and preferences. Most significantly, there are a number of contemporary Malian writers who draw on the various oral traditions of Mali and integrate into their writings the human experience and insights condensed in parables, proverbs, songs, and genres of social critique that have traditionally targeted various ills of society, such as the excesses of patriarchal and gerontocratic forms of power. By recuperating the narrative techniques and stylistics of various oral genres, these Malian writers walk in the footsteps of Mali's rich heritage in orature, as scholars of African literature often refer to the nonwritten literary texts of Africa. Amadou Hampâté Bâ, for instance, a world-famous Malian historian and novelist, spent much of his life writing these oral traditions down for the world to remember. Another internationally acclaimed Malian writer who successfully integrated literary conventions of orature into his work is Yambo Ouologuem. His *Le devoir de violence* won the Prix Renaudot in 1968, yet its legacy was stained by accusations of plagiarism.

Apart from these instances of Malian literature winning international acclaim, Malian writers still struggle to mark their place in postcolonial and world literature. At a national level, Malian authors face various economic, political, and logistical impediments to make their literary production relevant and accessible to the majority of the national population. Very often, these struggles at the national level affect their chances of gaining recognition in an international arena of literary production and reception. In spite of these difficulties in reaching and appealing to a national readership, Malian writers such as Ahmadou Hampâté Bâ, Massa Makan Diabaté, Aicha Fofana, Aoua Keita, Moussa Konaté, and Fily Dabo Sissoko have become authors of international renown. The fact that the annual Literary Festival, initiated since the early 1990s at St. Marlo, has branched out to Bamako, Dublin, and Sarajevo also shows that Malian written literature has found its place in world literature.

ORAL LITERATURE: THE EMOTIONAL AND AESTHETIC RESONANCES OF THE SPOKEN WORD

Developments in Malian written literature since the late colonial period ran parallel to, and often fed on, the continued high valuation attributed to oral texts. Even today, to many Malians, orature remains a key source of pride in their own cultural and political traditions, and they consider oral texts to be more expressive of their aesthetic preferences than any kind of written literature. To the majority of Malians, oral texts, especially those related to their home communities, embody historical experience and events and capture timeless human wisdom. Oral performances therefore bear great emotional significance and generate long-lasting commitments.

The high valuation of the spoken word, and the multifarious functions oral genres accomplish in society, is a characteristic feature of many African societies. Earlier generations of scholars focused on the prevalence of the spoken word in African societies and often argued that many Africans' (and other nonliterate societies') conventional preference for oral texts and for oral forms of passing down history indicated a particular mindset, one centered on repetition and reproduction of form rather than on transformation and innovation. Scholars who argued along these lines very often, either implicitly or explicitly, depicted this mindset of oral cultures as intellectually inferior to societies that relied on literacy to pass down past experiences and events. However, the heuristic insights generated with such a schematic opposition between written and oral texts and forms of communication are very limited. It seems more useful not to posit a hierarchy (and clear-cut divide) between written and oral literary production, but to understand them as contrasting and also complementary and overlapping domains of cultural creativity.

This view offers a more adequate portrayal of the landscape of literary production in Mali. It recognizes the fact that there are so many ways in which Malian writers, as well as many other African authors, draw on oral traditions. It also grants an understanding of the ways in which written and oral literature interlock, inform, and inspire each other and therefore contribute to the continued liveliness of African literary productions, be they orally transmitted or conveyed in written form.

Oral Tradition

Oral tradition refers to a range of textual and literary productions that are passed down not by employing written scripts but in oral form. A society's oral traditions comprise accounts of historical events and persons, as well as other texts that store cultural values and social norms, such as proverbs and fables. Oral traditions therefore have a strong pedagogical function and play a key role in ensuring the continuation of the social and moral universe. Oral traditions reflect on existing political structures and forms of social organization and on the attendant ideologies. They also provide a blueprint for the making of future social and political order. In this sense, whenever a particular oral tradition concerns issues of political organization, it can be said to have a strong legitimating function for the political status quo or for the political order that those in control of the oral tradition seek to secure for the future. The situation-dependent and variable functions of oral traditions indicate that their transmission does not imply a simple process of mere reproduction of existing texts; rather, it very often involves an adaptation and thus a transformation of these texts and of their inherent teachings, in accordance with the requirements of the current situation. Very often, this process of adaptation also involves an attempt to project those political relations that are said to have existed in the past into the future, as a blueprint for a future political order that one seeks to establish.

Societies differ in the ways they organize and institutionalize the transmission of oral traditions. In some societies, the transmission process is very little formalized, and oral texts can be told by anyone—that is, by nonspecialists. In other societies, the patterns of oral transmission are highly routinized and organized; sometimes these societies rely on specialists of the spoken (and sung) word to memorize and pass down their oral texts. Most societies that belong to the contemporary Malian nation-state have historically relied on a very elaborate and formalized system of passing down their various oral traditions. Prior to the arrival of French colonial troops in the second half of the 19th century, and still throughout the colonial period, Mali's literary traditions were transmitted mainly by word of mouth. Some oral genres, such as proverbs, fables, riddles, and certain songs (for instance, those linked to particular dance performances, see chapter 8), were memorized and told by anyone in society. Other oral genres, such as family genealogies, certain forms of praise, and heroic epics, could be performed and transmitted only by a distinct group of people. These specialists of the spoken word were in charge of reciting or singing histories and stories known by heart on very specific social and ritual occasions. Some of these occasions had a restricted audience; others involved a wider public, as in the case of family celebrations, funerals, and other community celebrations. Still today, the specialists of the spoken word play an eminent role in the social life of families and local communities. In the Mande-speaking areas of southern Mali, these specialists are called *jeliw* (Bamanakan, singular *jeli*) or *jaliw* (Maninkakan, singular *jali*). Some of them, especially women, have enjoyed a remarkable success and international reputation as singers over the last decades thanks to mass media.

The oral traditions that the specialists of oral performances pass down are often associated with Mali's different regional histories and centralized polities. The most famous of these, the Sundjata epic, is tied to the history of the Manding, the area covering approximately the triangle between Bamako, Kita, and Kurusa. Other epics, such as the one of Sonni Ali Ber and that of

Dinga, relate to the Songhai Empire and the Soninke kingdom respectively. Although the facticity of these historical narratives has not always been confirmed and their reliability as sources of historical knowledge remains open to debate, epics such as that of Sundjata Keita serve as a key symbolic and expressive blueprint for the ordering and justification of social and political relations between different groups and families today. Other important oral genres that are similarly connected to the histories of centralized polities and that are equally performed by these specialists are praise songs and genealogies. These two genres may also relate to the political histories of individual families, usually those who occupy positions of political and economic power in a particular setting.

There are also certain oral traditions that are transmitted by groups considered to be of inferior social origin. A notable example of this kind of texts is oral traditions that relate to the Soninke kingdom of Jaara (whose center was located in the town of Niono) and that have been passed down by female slaves. Finally, oral genres exist that are associated with distinct social groups and practices, such as the hunters' music, which is tied to the ritual activities and knowledge of hunters (see chapter 4). Whether oral traditions are in the hands of specialists, as in the case of the *jeliw,* or of nonspecialists, their memorization and recitation usually require years-long training, musical and rhetorical expertise, and extraordinary cognitive capacities.

THE HISTORICAL RELEVANCE OF ARABIC AND OTHER SCRIPTS FOR MALIAN LITERARY CREATIVITY

African societies are commonly associated with oral forms of transmission and literary production. Yet this image is very partial and misleading in the case of certain ethnic groups and regional literary traditions that form part of contemporary Mali. Especially in the northern triangle of Mali, Islam, in its association with Arabic literacy and literature production, played a key role in promoting and spreading literacy centuries before the arrival of French colonial troops.

Recent historical research into inscriptions in Arabic and Tifinagh (the script in which Tamasheq, the language of the Tuareg, has been written for perhaps two thousand years) that have been found as funerary epigraphs in the area around Gao in northeastern Mali evidences the existence of a rich corpus of medieval scriptural sources. Both scripts were in use in this region already between the 11th and the 15th centuries. These scriptural sources, as well as the UNESCO project, which was recently initiated to preserve handwritten scriptures of the Timbuktu libraries of the 18th and 19th centuries, refute the still common view of an Africa without history and of a dark continent that did not have writing scripts before the arrival of Western travelers, missionaries, and colonial troops in the 18th and 19th centuries.

We owe much of our historical knowledge about the political, social, and economic organization—of urban life more particularly—of several Malian ethnic groups to the writings by Arabic travelers and historians such as El Bekri (11th century), Ibn Khaldoun, Al Omari, and Ibn Battuta (14th century), and Leo Africanus (early 16th century). Also, starting in the 15th century (and intensifying between the 16th and 20th centuries), there were several Muslim scribes of African origin who lived along the Niger Bend, such as Mahmud Kati and Abdherramane es Sadi, to whom we equally owe important historical information about urban civilization in this region. In the case of several centralized polities in southern Mali, too, important written documentation about social and political life stems from the writings of literate Muslims.

Prior to and during most of the 19th century, Muslim scribes and scholars used Arabic script not only for purposes of religious scholarship and debate and to compose exegetic and pedagogical texts. They also composed literature in local languages, most notably Fulfulde and Tamasheq. Their primary objective in doing so was to help spread the Muslim faith. The literature in local languages and written in Arabic script was referred to as *ajamiyya* (non-Arabic) literature. Poetry was one of its most important and widespread forms; its composition was based on poetic conventions that were adaptations from Arabic prosody. Pieces of narrative poetry recounted the deeds of important leaders of religio-political movements and their special exploits in spreading the Muslim faith. There also existed *ajamiyya* praise poetry on behalf of religious leaders, as well as of others who had served the cause of Islam. All these forms of poetry served to commemorate the history of those who had helped spread Islam in the area and to explain their objectives to subsequent generations of Muslim scholars and political authorities. Other praise poetry was composed to laud the Prophet Muhammad. Similar to these diverse genres of poetry, *ajamiyya* pedagogical texts were geared toward facilitating an understanding of Islam. In a social setting in which the majority of people did not understand Arabic, the *ajamiyya* literature thus played a critical role in promoting knowledge about Islam and in convincing people about its civilizing force.

The instrumental role of the *ajamiyya* literature notwithstanding, Muslim scribes who used Arabic script to circulate their ideas in languages that were more widely spoken in the local contexts in which they lived never overcame a major impediment. That is, the Arabic alphabet and script is not well suited to Fulfulde sounds and to those of other local languages. This difficulty was recognized by later generations of intellectuals interested in composing literature in local languages. Approximately a century after the time when important pieces of the *ajamiyya* literature were produced, Souleymane Kanté, a Guineatn intellectual with family ties to southern Mali who worked in colonial Ivory Coast, sought to remedy this situation. Reportedly enraged by the argument of a Lebanese journalist that Africans' cultural and intellectual inferiority manifested itself in the fact that their languages could not be transcribed, Kanté set out to prove the contrary. After experimenting with writing Maninkakan in Arabic script for two years, in 1949, he decided to invent a script capable of accommodating the tonality of Mande languages, something the Arabic script failed to do. The result of his efforts was the writing system N'ko ("I speak" in Bamanakan and Maninkakan), which since its creation has enjoyed wide popularity among Maninkakan-speaking intellectuals across the Guinean, Malian, and Ivorian national borders. The literature Kanté produced in the N'ko script comprises compilations of oral local histories and of medicinal knowledge but also translations of French publications. Because of the close association of the script with the Maninka and Bamana cultural traditions, it is very unlikely that it will become the primary writing system for broad segments of the Malian population. Nevertheless, Kanté's initiative presents an interesting example of an effort on the part of intellectuals to deal with dilemmas of literary production created by colonial rule. These dilemmas equally applied to other African colonial and postcolonial contexts, as the examples of Chinua Achebe and Ngugi wa Thiong'o illustrate.[1] The situation in which Kanté as well as other African authors worked was one in which colonial language policy posed highly adverse conditions for writing in local languages. Under the French colonial policy of *assimilation,* writers and artists were held to engage in artistic production within the framework of the Francophonie. Literature was to be produced exclusively in French and thereby to follow to established literary and aesthetic preferences of the French *civilisation.* Throughout the French colonial territories, the legacy of this strong pressure on conformity and integration into the Francophonie was not only evident in those authors who, at least to a certain extent, agreed to conform to these aesthetic conventions and judgments; it also manifested itself in the attempts of those authors who, through more experimentally oriented writings, sought to expand or even to work against the grain of established aesthetic preferences, such as by using new words and idiomatic expressions that were translated from an African language lexicon. The most well-known representative of this kind of effort to Africanize the French language in the Mande-speaking realm is Ahmadou Kourouma, a native of the part of the colonial territory that today constitutes Ivory Coast, whose widely acclaimed novel *Les Soleils des Independences* (*The Suns of Independence*) made extensive use of Maninka/Jula idiomatic expressions and therefore partakes in the Manding cultural realm.

A far-reaching consequence of French assimilationist cultural policy was that there never emerged a significant body of written literature in one of Mali's national languages. This severely restricted—and continues to limit—the readership for Malian literature. Another serious implication of French colonial language policy was that French was the exclusive language of mass media, that is, of the newspaper *Le Soudanais* and, after its creation in 1958, of the Radio Soudan. The legacy of this language policy continued in post-colonial times. French remained the most important language of communication. Even the privileged position of Bamanakan, which was gradually elevated to the primary national language after independence, can be seen as a direct outcome of French colonial language policy, which discouraged or directly repressed any artistic expression in local languages. Bamanakan owed its privileged position as official national lingua franca to the effort of post-colonial governments to replace French as primary language of communication. At the same time, this replacement created new dilemmas of language choice and limited readership for Malian writers because it perpetuated the relations of inequality between different national languages and bolstered the dominance of southern cultures and oral traditions. In short, Malian authors of written literature still struggle with the effects of colonial and postcolonial language policy because no matter which language they choose, they will find only a (regionally and linguistically) limited audience.

COLONIAL LITERARY PRODUCTION

Since the 1920s, a body of literature emerged in the area of today's Mali that was written mostly by French explorers and members of the colonial military of that time. Strictly speaking, Malian literature written in French only dates from the 1950s onward, the decade that witnessed the publication of novels and poetry collections by authors such as Amadou Hampâté Bâ, Ibrahima Mamadou Ouane, Seydou Badian, and Fily Dabo Sissoko.[2]

Fily Dabo Sissoko, one of the leaders of the political independence struggle of the 1940s and 1950s, has been recently elevated to the status of a father of Francophone Malian literature by leading Malian intellectuals, a claim that is undoubtedly related to the new political environment granted by the government of Alpha Konaré after 1992, an environment that facilitated the public rehabilitation of Sissoko as a politician and of his work. Sissoko occupies a prominent position in the history of Malian literature not only because he was among the few authors who wrote both poetry and novels in colonial times. He also embodies the ambitions and creative potential of the first generation of a Malian intellectual elite, as well as the institutional and political limitations this elite had to face under French colonial administration and in the first years after independence. Born in Horokoto, an insignificant hamlet near Bafoulabé (southwestern Mali) in 1900, Sissoko moved through the different echelons of the colonial school system. This training was geared toward preparing him, like so many of his contemporaries educated in the French colonial school system, for future employment in the colonial administration. After working for some years as a schoolteacher and supervisor, Sissoko took his father's place as the canton chief of Niamba in 1933. Sissoko became involved in the emergent independence movement of the 1940s. After 1945, as a cofounder of one of the two parties leading the independence movement, the Parti Soudanais Progressiste (PSP), he became Deputy of the Sudan. Starting in the mid-1950s, however, as the competing party, US-RDA, gained in influence and popular support under the leadership of Modibo Keita, Sissoko's political career took a downfall. Under US-RDA rule in postindependent Mali, Sissoko no longer occupied a political office. In 1962, has was accused of a conspiracy against the government of Modibo Keita and sentenced to death. After an amnesty by the president, he was imprisoned in Kidal, in Mali's far north. There he died under doubtful circumstances, together with several other highly influential intellectuals. Sissoko is the author of four collections of poems, of numerous political essays and ethnographic writings, and of a collection of Maninka proverbs. In 1955, his novel *La passion de Djimé* and his collection of poems *Harmakhis* appeared. This year is often taken as a turning date, marking the transition from an earlier, ethnographically oriented Malian literature to one marked by artistic creativity. A characteristic feature of Sissoko's literary work is his explicit attachment to the cultural and religious traditions of his ancestors, an attachment that put him in clear contrast to other Sudanese writers of his time, especially to Amadou Hampâté Bâ, whose literary productions cannot be considered independently from his self-understanding as an observant Muslim.

Amadou Hampâté Bâ was the other towering literary figure of colonial Mali. A historian by training, he also collected and translated various oral traditions and ethnographic texts. Hampâté Bâ was born in Bandiagara and wrote poetry in French and in his native Fulfulde, and he also published memoirs (*Amkoullel*) and a novel (*L'étrange destin de Wangrin*) providing formidable accounts of an African experience of colonialism. Given that Hampâté Bâ received only limited formal French education (in addition to his training at Qur'anic schools), his literary work in French is all the more remarkable. Equally noteworthy is his career that led him from working as a junior colonial administrator to becoming a researcher at the well-known IFAN (L'Institut Français [now Fondamentale] d'Afrique Noire) in Dakar, Senegal, to serving as a diplomat, first in the UNESCO executive council and then as Mali's ambassador to Côte d'Ivoire (where he died in 1991). Over the years of his work in the French colonial administration and later at the IFAN in Dakar, he became an important contributor to the colonial project of re-cording—and of simultaneously defining and creating—African tradition. Moreover, in a situation of heightened controversy among Muslims over cor-rect religious practice, he also became a defendant of religious conventions in line with Sufi-related understandings of Islam.

Aoua Keita's notable autobiography, one of the few Malian autobiographies by a woman writer, is a rich source of information on the situation of women in the colonial period and their possibilities for political action. Keita was born in 1912 in Bamako, where she was schooled at the first French colonial school created for girls. Pursuing higher education in Dakar, she received her diploma as a midwife. In 1931, she started working in Gao and, in the course of the 1940s, became more and more active in the independence movement launched by other representatives of this first generation of African intellec-tuals trained in the French colonial school. Her career in the US-RDA party since the 1950s culminated in her becoming the first female deputy in Mali's preindependence political history (in 1959). President Modibo Keita's fall from power in 1968 put an end to her political career, but until her death in 1980, she remained the—widely respected—grande dame of the generation of African political activists who had led the country into independence.

POSTCOLONIAL LITERATURE IN MALI

Especially in the last decade of the colonial period (shaped by political struggle and unrest leading to political independence in 1960), as well as in the early 1960s, Malian writers and intellectuals were generally held in high respect. In this period of late colonial rule and early postindependent politics, the success of a writer was linked to his political commitment. His status was prestigious but also ambiguous because, as an intellectual, he was exposed to charges of intellectualism and arrogance.

Among the Malian authors who made their mark during the 1960s, two deserve special mention: Yambo Ouologuem, who received the Prix Renau-dot in 1969, and Seydou Badian Kouyaté. Born in 1928 and a medical doc-tor by training (in Montpellier, France), Kouyaté published the novels *Sous l'Orage* (1957) and *La Mort de Chaka* (1961) under his pseudonym Seydou Badian before embarking on a political career in postindependent Mali, as Minister of Economic Affairs (until 1966). His role as a key thinker of the socialist agenda of Mali's first government under President Keita showed in his authorship of the national hymn and his "Les Dirigeants africains face à leurs Peuples" (1964). Imprisoned after President Keita's fall from power (1968) and liberated in 1975, Kouyaté was exiled to Senegal, from where he published the novels *Le Sang des Masques* (1976) and *Noces Sacrées* (1977). He returned to Mali after the political opening of the early 1990s to pursue his political interests under postauthoritarian conditions.

Whereas Kouyaté's political writings received recognition mostly within the sphere of Francophone West Africa, Yamba Ouologuem rose to international fame when his first novel, *Le Devoir de Violence* (1968, published in English as *Bound to Violence* in 1971), won the Prix Renaudot. Born in Bandiagara and schooled in Bamako, Ouologuem studied in Paris in the 1960s. His *Devoir de Violence* offered a harsh settlement of accounts with African nationalists and their idealization of a golden African past. In 1969, Ouologuem published *Lettre à la France nègre,* a collection of incisive essays on the postcolonial situation, and, under the pseudonym Utto Rodolph, the erotic novel *Les mille et une bibles du sexe.*

In response to allegations that he had plagiarized passages from Graham Greene's *It's a Battlefield* and from *Le Dernier des justes* (1959), a novel by the French writer André Schwartz-Bart, Ouologuem turned away from the Western press. After his return to Mali in the late 1970s, he led a reclusive life in the region of Mopti, not too far from his native town Bandiagara. In spite of the controversy surrounding his *Devoir de Violence,* numerous critics still consider the novel a hallmark of African postcolonial literature. Several of Ouologuem's poems have been anthologized in *Poems of Black Africa* (ed. Wole Soyinka, 1975) and the *Penguin Book of Modern African Poetry* (1984).

The 1970s were marked by the work of Massa Makan Diabaté, as well by the theater of Gaoussou Diawara, whose most important contribution to the emergence of a Malian theater resided in his combination of traditional Bamana theatrical genres with topics and presentational stylistics borrowed from European theater.

Massa Makan Diabaté, born in Kita in 1938, came from one of Mali's most illustrious jeli families. Raised in Congo, Guinea, and France, Diabaté received his diploma and doctorate from different educational institutions in Paris that prepared him for a career as a researcher and a high-ranking official in the Malian state educational system. Diabaté was a prolific writer and won international acclaim for his various theater plays and novels (*Si le feu s'éteignait,* 1967; *Kala Jata,* 1970; *Janjon et autres chants du Mali,* 1970; *La Dispersion des Mandeka,* 1970; *Une si belle leçon de patience,* 1972; *L'aigle et l'epervier, ou la geste de Sundjata,* 1975; *Le Lieutenant de Kouta,* 1979; *Le Coiffeur de Kouta,* 1980; *Le Boucher de Kouta,* 1982; *Comme une Piqûre de Guêpes,* 1980; *Le Lion à L'Arc,* 1986; and *Une Hyène à Jeûn,* 1988). But one of his last novels, the *Assemblée des Djinns,* also earned him much resentment, and even rejection within his own family, because of its biting portrayal of the conflict-ridden relations among the jeliw of Kita, his native town. The early 1980s were also marked by the publication of works by Ibrahima Ly, Modibo Keita, Moussa Konaté, and Doumbi-Fakoly.

The first generation of writers and intellectuals, many of whom simultaneously engaged in politics, had considered literary creativity a means of social education and of enlightenment of fellow citizens. As postindependence politics progressed, however, the intellectual orientation and political ideals of these writers met with growing distrust. Authors tended to stress their duty to improve the social and moral life, yet their writings were often considered an affront not only by the political elites but also by major parts of the urban and rural populations. To this date, writers in Malian postcolonial society occupy relatively marginal social and political positions. Because of the Western school training most of them received (though in varying degrees), they are often associated with intellectualism and an elite status. They are regarded with skepticism and distrust by many older people, not only in the countryside but also in town, because their lives are considered to be withdrawn from the everyday realities and concerns of most Malians. After the transition from President Keita's single-party rule to the military regime under Moussa Traoré, writers no longer regarded themselves as an intellectual elite related to the political leadership. As practices of political corruption expanded under Traoré's single-party rule, writers felt that they should act as interlocutors between intellectuals and political leaders on one side and Malian society on the other. A notable example of this politically critical literature is the novel *La Nièce de l'Imam* (1994) by Mandé Alpha Diarra, which denounces, though in an indirect, subtle manner, the political corruption and clientelism that increasingly infested politics under President Traoré and gradually undermined even intimate relations among kin and friends.

Although the critique of these writers about the excesses of political power, tradition, and religion were certainly pertinent, they provoked the ire of both political leadership and conservative forces of society. Many older people took offense with authors who attributed responsibility for the social ills of Malian society not to colonialism but to the new political leadership, to social conventions, and to the prerogatives of patriarchal family authority.

Starting in the early 1990s, and closely related to the political changes that brought Malians multiparty democracy, authors no longer highlighted their roles as educators or as promoters of political and social reform. Instead, they presented themselves as defending merely individual and personal viewpoints on the foundations of personal liberty and on the possibilities of confronting certain social ills. Regardless of these significant changes in the self-understanding of Malian writers and in the political circumstances under which they write, authors continue to face major obstacles to their literary creativity, such as a lack of wider recognition and of material resources.

Starting in the late 1980s, with the death of three towering figures of Malian literature—Massa Makan Diabaté and Ibrahima Ly (in 1988) and Amadou Hampâté Bâ (in 1991)—literary creativity moved into a state of dormancy for a number of years. The only international prize awarded to Malian literature in this period was the novel *Amakoullel, L'Enfant Peul* by Hampâté Bâ in 1991. Also, the period noted a significant increase in publications and in new authors, but the majority of these authors published only one novel. No innovative rupture with traditional forms of writing occurred, as was the case in other African countries at this time.

The 1990s considerably improved the conditions for literary creativity with the proliferation of private press publications and the creation—or reopening—of several private publishing companies, such as Jamana ("homeland"), Editions-Imprimeries du Mali, Donniya ("knowledge"), and Le Figuier. As a consequence of these initiatives, for the first time in history, Malian authors have the possibility to publish with a choice of Malian publishing companies. These companies are also importantly involved in producing a certain amount of what could be called educational literature in various national languages, particularly Bamanakan and Fulfulde. These brochures and pamphlets are most often commissioned by and used in the context of development work aiming at alphabetization, the acquisition of skills of calculation and business administration, and the improvement of people's living conditions.

Although this development-related instructional material offers an important source of income for Malian publishing companies, they face persistent difficulties of financing, as costs for the import of primary print materials are high, and most readers (who form about 31 percent of the population) cannot afford to buy books. Also, in spite of the mushrooming of private printing presses, only a few of these organs cover new literary productions. Nor does an established culture of literary criticism exist. Book reading is still intimately connected to school education and identity of pupils, students, and teachers.

Since 2000, owing partly to the newly instituted Festival Étonnants Voyageurs, a number of younger Malian authors have emerged on the scene whose publications in international publishing companies offer glimpses of hope for a revival of Malian literary production.

In the works of this new generation of authors, the conflicting values of modernity and tradition and confrontations between the urban and rural worlds remain important topics, but the lines of conflict are no longer defined by reference to colonialism. Also, although the ignorance of urbanites toward village life and ethics is denounced, the ultimate message of this work is not to idealize village life but to plea for a mutual respect between villagers and those residing in town.

Books are mostly accessible to a well-to-do and literate urban elite. This mobile public library seeks to overcome these limitations by providing wider access to books and journals. (Courtesy of Ute Roeschenthaler.)

Much of the recent Malian literature remains silent about the hopes that the political opening of the early 1990s generated initially. The reflections of this new generation of writers are characterized no longer by a critique of political power and of the ways it affects society and morals, but by authors' presentation of themselves as free, self-determined artists who do not necessarily define themselves as Malians but as cosmopolitan Africans. These writers' silence on politics reflects on their skepticism and fear of new disappointments about multiparty democracy. Their literary production continues to suffer from a lack of recognition and social status.

Although women figure largely in many novels (as representatives of a position of submission to or of revolt against patriarchal traditions), women writers are still a minority in Malian literature. Women writers face several difficulties. Not only does society tend to refuse women the status of authors, that is, of someone who may devote her entire life to writing; they also need to write against very conservative and patriarchal views of women's role in society. Women writers face the additional dilemma that their reading public consists mainly of men, as fewer women are interested in reading. (Of the 6,368 visitors who visited the Bibliothèque Nationale in Bamako in 1995, only 302 were women. Since then, the number of female visitors has slightly increased, with 716 women out of 12,180 visitors in 1999.)

In view of these challenges to female literary creativity, the existing, though scarce, work by women writers deserves even more attention. An early and notable literary work by a female writer is Aoua Kéita's autobiography (1975), which offers important information on the conditions for women's political action under French colonial rule. In addition to Shaïda Zarumey's poetry (*Alternances pour le Sultan,* 1982), only Aicha Fofana won recognition as a female writer until the late 1980s. Her *Mariage, On copie* (1994), the first novel written by a Malian woman, probes conventional views of the role of women in Malian society by juxtaposing voices and experiences of different women with respect to marriage. Since the 1990s, more women writers have appeared on the scene. Among them are Aida Mady Diallo (*Kouty, Mémoire de Sang,* 1999); Fanta-Taga Tembley and her novel *Dakan* (1999); Oumou Diarra and *L'Afrique un défi au féminin* (1999); M'Bamakan Soucko and *Comme un message de Dieu* (1995); Aicha Fofana with her second novel, *La fourmillière* (2002); and Fatoumata Fathy Sidibé (*Une saison africaine,* 2006). Also represented with shorter essays are Aminata Dramane Traoré, the former Minister of Culture, and the wife of ex-president Alpha Konaré, Adame Ba Konaré. These grandes dames of the Malian political scene articulate a critical distance to, but also a partial embracing of, Western feminist ideas. Women writers often call into question conventional norms regarding women's status and proper behavior. They also address different forms of violence, directed against women and other weaker members of society, such as orphaned children. M'Bamakan Soucko's "Comme un message de Dieu," an account of a handicapped child's exposure to denigration and abuse by society, won the First Prize of Short Stories launched by the Fondation Culturelle ACP-CEE and the Journal *Le Courrier.*

Mass Media

Printed Press

The Malian press dates back to the colonial French Sudan, when the newspaper *Le Soudanais,* created by the French colonial administration for a Francophone reading public, coexisted with newspapers run by the parties leading the anticolonial struggle. *L'Essor,* for instance, the official publication of the US-RDA, first appeared in 1949. The circulation of these newspapers was limited to a tiny, literate, and urban elite. Dailies such as *L'Essor* directed themselves toward highly educated Africans who, regardless of their employment in the colonial administration, staunchly supported the anticolonial political struggle. *Le Soudanais* addressed the same African reading elite yet also a French expatriate community of merchants and administrators, all of whom were strongly oriented toward French society, its lifestyles, and modes of consumption.

After independence, the number of Malian dailies dropped drastically as most of them were either prohibited or faced bankruptcy. *L'Essor* became the official organ of Modibo Keita's single-party rule and, after his fall from power and the subsequent CMLN military regime, remained under governmental control. After the return to civilian rule in 1979, *L'Essor,* tightly associated with the new ruling UDPM party and its news agency, the Agence Malienne de Presse (AMAP), benefited from the widest circulation. But its news value remained very limited because it mainly covered local events and government decrees and speeches.

With the new freedom of the press guaranteed under the new constitution of 1992, numerous newspapers were created in addition to *L'Essor,* which, managed by the Ministry of Communication, displays a certain independence from governmental policy in its news coverage. Since the early 1990s, daily newspapers (in French) such as *Le Républicain, Les Échos, Nouvel Horizon,* and *Info Matin* have been instrumental in creating a critical platform for political information and exchange among readers. Still, newspapers continue to be far less effective in spreading information than radio. Their circulation is limited to literate segments of the urban population and to those who can afford them on a regular basis.

Radio and Television

Since its creation in 1957, Malian national radio (which was then called Radio Soudan and renamed Radio Mali after independence) has remained the country's most important mass media institution. From the outset, national radio was conceived to serve the autocratic and hierarchical profile of a highly centralized state. As an institution under close control of the ruling party, national radio has a strong legacy of disseminating governmental policy and of educating the masses. In addition to news broadcasts and general information, it offers educational programs, as well as entertainment, cultural, and religious programs. In addition to its main languages of broadcasting—French and Bamanakan, the lingua franca of southern Mali—it offers short weekly programs in other national languages. Because of this language policy, but also because its culture programs tended to privilege musical and oral traditions from the south, national radio has been an important motor in representing southern traditions as cornerstones of Malian national identity. Also pivotal to this skewed representation of the national community on Radio Mali was its years-long limited coverage of the national territory. Because until the early 1990s local relay stations only existed in some regional capitals, reception of national radio was limited to certain, privileged areas of Mali and to certain seasons. In those areas where national radio could not be received,

Local radio stations in rural areas often operate on a very low budget and with minimal equipment. They nevertheless enjoy great popularity among listeners because of their proximity and accessibility and also because they feature local-language programs and musical traditions. Becoming a radio speaker on local radio grants young men and women great prestige and privilege. Here is a community radio station in Mali's rural southwest. (Photo by the author.)

international radio channels broadcasting in national languages, most notably Radio France International, Voice of America, and Deutsche Welle, often played an important role.

The mushrooming of local radio stations after 1991 that feature local languages and music has attenuated (but not fully reverted) national radio's uneven representation of Mali's regional diversity. The challenges that the new private radio stations pose to national radio has led to a revision of the programming policy of national radio and to the creation of a second radio channel, the Chaine 2, whose coverage, however, remains limited to Bamako and its immediate surroundings.

National television was created in 1983 to form part of the national broadcast station Radiodiffusion Télévision du Mali (RTM) that, in 1992, was renamed Office de Radiodiffusion Télévision du Mali (ORTM). Because it covers only urban areas and their immediate surroundings and broadcasts

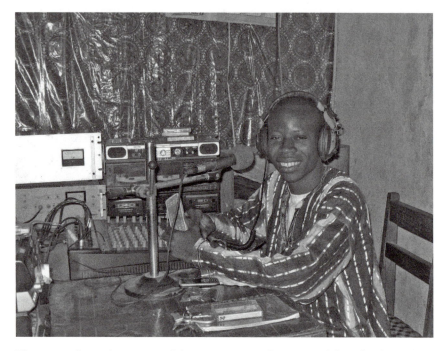

This image shows the interior of the community radio station. (Photo by the author.)

almost exclusively in French, ORTM's reach and effects are limited. Still, the spread of television and video-recording technologies since the late 1980s, supported by the massive influx of low-cost technical infrastructure from Southeast Asia, has facilitated television consumption among broader strata of the urban populations. In its programming structure, contents, and news programs, national television is conceived largely as complementary to national radio. Apart from its—highly popular—music talent shows and other programs, only a few of its entertainment programs are nationally produced. The many foreign television series, produced mainly in France, Brazil, Mexico, Germany, and the United States and dubbed in French, are highly popular, even if their language can be understood only by certain segments of the urban population. Important national productions include a weekly program featuring Mali's diverse local cultures and traditions and a television serial depicting daily family life in town. Several international television programs, among them TV5 Monde Afrique, BBC, and al Jazeera can be received via satellite.

One of the most significant changes brought by the political liberalization of the early 1990s has been the granting of civil liberties and thus of journalistic freedom and independent media institutions. Apart from a thriving printed press, these changes have been most palpable in the emergence of a heterogeneous landscape of national and local radio broadcasting. The renaming of the national broadcast station to Office Radiodiffusion Télévision du Mali signaled its transformation from an exclusively state-financed institution into an office that generates its own revenues. Since 1992, local radio stations, all of them serving towns and their immediate surroundings, have grown steadily in number, with varying longevity and program quality. From 20 local radio stations officially registered in early 1994, the number steadily rose to more than 80 local radio stations in 1997 and then to more than 150 operable radio stations in January 2011. Since 1996, the number of local radio stations in the northern areas has increased considerably, with new radio stations being created in Kidal, Gao, Menarka, and Timbuktu. But to date, there are considerably more local radio stations in the southern triangle of Mali than in the northern regions. In the radio euphoria of the early and mid-1990s, numerous undocumented radio stations existed in addition to the local relay stations of national radio and other officially registered radio stations. These stations were run by young men who, with a minimum of equipment, broadcast music, debates, and local news to the general acclaim of their local audiences. Although these unregistered radio initiatives had a short life, they illustrated the great excitement with which local radio broadcasting was received in many locales. Today, local radio stations fall into two categories, commercial and noncommercial ones, but except for the few radios that receive international donor support, they resemble each other in their program structure. Their deficiencies in topical and listener-specific programming, as well as their financial and technical constraints and lack of professionalism, make many of their programs repetitive and of limited quality.

There are also political constraints that prevent local radio stations from realizing the democratic potential that many Malian intellectuals and outside observers attributed to them in the first years of their existence. So far, the supremacy of state media has not been undermined. State administration has successfully restricted the endeavor by private entrepreneurs to create unions or other organizational structures for the representation of their interests. The Ministry of Communication uses a heavy hand in controlling the nongovernmental media market through the Conseil Supérieur de la Communication, a governmental commission in charge of allocating frequencies. The restructuring of the national broadcast station and its program formats in response to a more competitive market situation disadvantages local radio stations with their budgetary constraints and lack of professional expertise. The authoritarian and controlling prerogatives of the central state have remained in place and prevent the existing legal framework from guaranteeing the emergence of a diverse and truly competitive media landscape.

In spite of the limitations and challenges local radio stations face, they enjoy such wide popularity among urban and rural listeners that the Ministry of Communication and program directors of national radio have readapted their broadcasting formats to align them with the more participatory program structure and language policy of local radio stations. Important reasons for the overwhelming success of local radio stations are that, by broadcasting local languages and oral and musical genres, they enable forms of communication that are in continuity with established forms of socializing and exchange in unmediated settings. Local radio stations also thrive because of the new social and political context of the 1990s and the first decade of the 21st century, in which claims to local identity and belonging are enjoying an ever-growing appeal. The most significant political import of local radio stations may therefore reside not in the politically critical content they disseminate but in their creation of a space for creativity and self-expression for illiterate consumers. In a sociocultural context where music and the spoken word are highly appreciated for their aesthetic appeal and sociable nature, local radio stations appear as ideal platforms for the articulation of listeners' changing understandings of their own place in a national political community. Thus, in spite of the multiple restraints local radio stations face, their formats and contents make them likely candidates to challenge the top-down and autocratic legacy of state media.

NOTES

1. Dianne Oyler, "Re-inventing Oral Tradition: The Modern Epic of Souleymane Kanté," *Research in African Literatures* 33, no. 1 (2002): 75–93.

2. Other important authors of the French Sudan were Moussa Travélé and Mamby Sidibé.

4

Art and Architecture

ART

ART IS A concept foreign to traditional Malian societies. Even within the Western world, understandings of African art have changed over time, with changes in the economic and sociocultural context of its consumption and most recently with the intensification of transnational circuits of selling and consuming authentic African cultural artifacts. Many artifacts that people in Europe and the United States consider as traditional African art, and that are placed as objects of contemplation and aesthetic appreciation in the exhibition spaces of museums and art galleries, have a particularly close connection to ritual and religious practices. Their primary function is not to invite distanced contemplation but to immerse viewers and listeners into religious ritual or into forms of leisure and entertainment. The concept of African art thus does not correspond to Malian traditional understandings of the use and value of these objects. Still, precisely because of the role some of these objects play in ritual contexts or for purposes of entertainment, they often unfold an immense aesthetic and sensual power that makes them a perfect vehicle through which people act and reflect on their social, religious, and political environments. Malian objects of art, rather than simply constituting a passive, reflective element of culture, are the creative means through which to rework and change the world.

Malian material art includes utensils, cloth, leatherwork, pottery, terracotta and wooden sculptures, masks, puppets, and iron and bronze objects.

Different ethnic groups specialize in various kinds of arts and art objects. Some of these objects are designed for use in movement, for instance during masquerades, dances, or other kinds of performances. These objects are thus meant to appear in combination with an elaborate bodily and gestural apparatus and together with other materials, such as fabric, feathers, and pearls.

Creativity and innovation are central characteristics of Malian artistic production. This does not mean that all Malian art objects are beautiful and pleasing. To the contrary: the preoccupation of Western notions of art with beauty and pleasure sometimes makes it difficult to appreciate an opposite framing of the function of these objects as something made to arouse feelings of dread and aversion. Another difficulty relating to the ways in which Malian and, more generally, African art has been treated conventionally is that early scholars of art history, archeology, and anthropology, as well as art connoisseurs, have not considered sufficiently the social and semantic contexts within which individual art objects have circulated historically. As a result, we have very little knowledge about the ways in which certain objects have been received and consumed within and across different locales.

For a long time, the dynamics of Islam in West Africa, as it affected and was shaped by the artistic traditions it encountered, have been neglected. Only recently have scholars illustrated the intense interaction between Muslims and those who practice traditional religions and how the basic pragmatism that informed these encounters also extended to art making. Thus, in contrast to common assumptions about Islam's repressive and destructive effects on African art, the relationship between Muslims and local traditions of figurative arts was more complementary, engendering immense cultural creativity and persistent innovation. The relationship between Muslims and practitioners of other religions was often shaped by mutual accommodation and tolerance and by a shared concern with divination and harnessing the powers of the occult. Their relationship of complementarity translated into a range of cultural artifacts whose distinctive Islamic or traditionalist character is difficult to establish. A good illustration of this merging of Islam with local religious conventions are certain masking traditions whose mixed religious purposes and stylistic elements demonstrate that Islam does coexist with West African figurative traditions.

Traditional Arts

Although the distinction between traditional and contemporary arts is a common one, Malian artistic production sometimes makes it impossible to neatly distinguish between these categories. Mali has been famous for its archeological findings, especially the ancient terra-cotta objects and jewelry from Jenne-Jeno (or old Djenné), neighboring the modern town Djenné situated in the inland Niger delta. The settlement Jenne-Jeno emerged in the third century BC and became an important urban center between the fifth and the ninth century AD. The numerous terra-cotta figurines, intact vessels and jar inhumations, and other cult objects that were found in the graves confront those engaged in cultural heritage management with considerable difficulties. Because of the high value of objects from this archeologically rich zone of the Middle Niger on the art market (up to $100,000), they have been easy prey to looting. Almost all terra-cotta figurines owned by museums outside of Africa today have been obtained from earlier looting. Because international private collectors are still willing to pay exorbitant fees for these archeological treasures, practices of faking these objects are expanding. But looting, too, continues, a trend that is supported by the fact that the European Parliament has not passed a law similar to the 1993 U.S. ban on the unlicensed sale or import of Malian antiquities.

Sculptures/Masks

Historically, masks and sculptures in Mali were fabricated to serve as containers of supernatural forces and thus to help people get into touch with, and ensure harmony with, a universe beyond the visible world.

African arts have become virtually synonymous with visual arts and even more narrowly with sculpture. But there is need to recognize the importance of orality and aurality in masquerade performances. In Mali, as in other African societies, historically the visual has rarely stood alone without its accompaniment of sound and movement. There is thus ample reason why we need to move away from a narrow focus on material objects of art and from sculpture as art item par excellence. Song and dance are as important to the masquerades during which a mask or sculpture is presented, as is the mask itself. Another important component is the costumes accompanying a masquerade; separated from the whole ensemble of visual and oral materials, as so often happens in Western display and scholarly analysis, the mask makes no sense for people who use it in religious ritual or for general entertainment. Also, many masks and sculptures were intended not for public view but only for settings with restricted access, settings characterized by different degrees of secrecy and demarcated by different degrees of initiation.

It is often difficult to date the age of masks because written sources are rare that give us information about the historicity of certain types of masks, about their circulation, and about social, political, spiritual, and economic structures in which they are embedded and used. There also exists considerable difficulty with respect to classifying masks as belonging to an ethnic group. In Mali, ethnic boundaries are easily penetrated by members of other ethnic groups, as a person's identity is defined as much by her regional, historical, and social origin as by her patronym. As individuals move around, both in geographical terms and in terms of social affiliation, families realign themselves to forge new political and economic alliances and thus generate configurations of people that scholars call ethnic groups. As a consequence, the internal structure and composition of ethnic patrimony are highly flexible and constantly shifting. This also affects the uses, designs, significance, and movement of masks and sculptures across ethnic boundaries and wider geographical areas. Rather than representing a timeless, static essence of Malian traditions, masks embody their malleability, mobility, and ever-changing nature. There are indications that certain individuals and socioprofessional groups played a special role in translating the use and significance of certain masks from one social and ethnic context to another. Merchants, itinerant craftspeople, hunters, and military groups were all agents of transmission who, in their attempt to adapt to their new situations, would seek supernatural competence through the manipulation of ritual objects.

Hunters of the Mande-speaking societies in southern Mali are known for their expertise in handling the forces of the wilderness and for the various sculpted devices they employ to enhance their supernatural competence. They are in league with Muslim spiritual specialists who rely on their own power objects to harness forces that are invisible to the human eye. The hunters' association does not possess masking traditions on its own, but many hunters are members of the Komo secret society, which uses certain types of masks. Although initiates of these societies are bound by the strict tenets of secrecy, it is likely that hunters, with their rugged individualism, passed on information about the Komo society and thus contributed to a traveling of the Komo institution and its masks across geographical distances.

Bamana sculptures illustrate the restricted, secretive context for which masks were and are often made, and also the flexibility of sculptural elements and associated meanings as they traveled from one context of use to another. Historically, Bamana mask and sculpture carving has been related to the Bamana initiation or secret societies (*jow*) that had an enormous significance for social and religious life. The rituals and objects of the initiation societies offered a way to address various physical and emotional afflictions and misfortune. Today, initiation societies are still relevant to the resolution of local political conflicts, but their influence has been limited by the influence of Islam and state institutions. The initiation societies and their rituals centered on masks and other ritual objects. In secret societies like Ciwara, Kono, and Komo, initiates would gain secret knowledge by traveling around and becoming the apprentice of a well-known connoisseur of the forces of the occult (*soma*). Initiation societies were unequally distributed across a region, with some villages having several *jow* and other villages having none. Bamana initiation societies only allow men to become initiates, but women, too, may solicit the help of supernatural forces through sacrificial offerings. Women may also perform certain ritual functions in a *jo,* without being initiated into the society's secrets.

Sculptures and ritual objects are key to the management of invisible forces on which Bamana cults and initiation societies center. The most powerful objects need to be hidden from view, and access to them is carefully guarded and restricted. When they are not in use, they are hidden away within the shrine houses or sacred groves of certain institutions as part of a complex matrix of power-laden ritual objects. Notable examples are the power objects (singular, *boli*) that are covered with sacrificial material and used in rituals of men's initiation societies. Other examples are iron and wood staffs to be carried during initiations and funerals and placed strategically around dance arenas.

Cultic practices of the initiation societies fall into categories of secretive and easily accessible ones. The most secret rites, conducted by no more than three or four initiates who are well advanced in age and secret knowledge, are held at night, illuminated only by straw torches. In the public elements of the rituals, all members of a village may participate, by accompanying the arrival of a mask or a mask performance through singing, dance, and sacrificial offerings.

Notable Bamana initiation societies are the Jo, Komo, Kono, Ntomo, and Ciwara societies. Conventionally, initiation into these societies took prolonged periods of instruction during which boys had to live apart from the rest of the community, very often in the bush, and to undergo preparatory rituals. The Komo and Kono societies form political networks that stretch beyond individual villages. Initiates into these societies communicate with the Komo and Kono supernatural being through masks and power objects that are believed to symbolize initiates' pact or association with this invisible being. Komo sanctuaries, traditionally in the hands of blacksmiths, yielded considerable political weight. In recent years, Komo initiation societies seem to have gained in importance, with Komo sanctuaries spreading throughout Mali, southern Mauritania, eastern Senegal, northern Côte d'Ivoire, Guinea, and western Burkina Faso. Komo sanctuaries show strong influences of Sudanese-style mosques and thus illustrate that this cult, rather than constituting a static tradition, is characterized by innovation and adaptation to new religious and stylistic influences. Characteristic of the Komo masks is their horizontal sculptural form. They are worn horizontally or on a strong diagonal, use helmets to fit on the dancer's head, and have long snouts or mouths projecting forward from the helmet. In contrast to Komo masks, whose decoration with horns, teeth, and feathers inspire feelings of dread, masks associated with the Kono society have a pleasing, simple-shaped appearance. The Komo mask, mounted by male initiates, exists in two styles. The first, an oval-shaped mask, bears between 4 and 10 horns on top and is often decorated with cowries. The second style bears a protruding mouth, a ridged nose, and vertical horns to which a figurine or animal is attached.

Ntomo masks are either female (bearing an even number of horns) or male (with an odd number of horns). They are worn to be publicly seen while announcing a ritual or a puppet masquerade.

Other masks intended for public display and performance are those related to initiation societies that ensure a balance between humans and nature. The most famous example of this type of Bamana initiation society and related masquerade is the Ciwara, whose activities relate to agricultural fertility and, through symbolic extension, to human and social reproduction. The masks are stylized representations of the antelope, the mythical character believed to have taught the Bamana agriculture. The Ciwara antelope masks appear in three distinct styles that vary with respect to their vertical and horizontal shapes and different levels of abstraction. Ciwara masquerades are annually performed at the harvesting time.

Dogon Masks and Masquerades

Masks sculpted by Dogon artists have gained similar fame as Bamana wooden carvings have, primarily because of the spectacular performances during which they are displayed. Beyond these public masquerades, Dogon masks and sculptures are usually hidden in special sanctuaries or in individual family houses to keep them away from the public. Here again, the fabrication and symbolic significance of these masks are cloaked in secrecy.

Dogon sculptural forms comprise a broad range of representations of human actors performing daily chores that manifest the long-standing interaction between the Dogon and the cultural and religious influences of other peoples. These sculptures reflect Dogon beliefs and practices surrounding the veneration of mythic primordial ancestors (the Nommo) and of deceased family members. According to Dogon cosmogony, the Nommo were created by Amma, the supreme god. Family shrines are altars where figurines are placed that serve as containers of a family's real ancestors. Certain masks are intended for keeping at bay the spirits of deceased family members after the mourning period has come to an end. Other masks are worn by young adult members of Awa, the men's masking association.

One of the most famous Dogon mask types is the Sirige, which has a tall, flat projection above the face and measures several meters in length. Dancers wear it in combination with spectacular, black apparel made of fibers. Because of the height and weight of the mask, dancing with it—a dance that involves jumping and turning the head in rotating movements—is extremely physically demanding and therefore mostly limited to young men. The Kanaga is perhaps the most widely known Dogon mask. It has a short pole on top, with two parallel, perpendicular blades attached to the pole. At the ends of each pole, two small flat boards are attached that point into opposite (upward and downward) directions. A crown of unbending red or yellow fibers encircles the face of the mask.

There are different meanings associated with the Kanaga mask that depend on the degree of initiation. Both masks are employed, together with other masks, on ritual occasions requiring the intervention by supernatural forces, such as when, as in the case of the Kanaga masquerade, the passage of the deceased into the realm of the ancestors needs to be facilitated. Kanaga dance performances are very spectacular, partly because of the sheer number of performing masks. During these performances, dancers make rotating semicircular movements with the mask while sliding its upper part on the soil. Another Dogon mask is the Satimbe, a rectangular face that recalls, in its projecting and receding forms, stylistic elements of Sudanese mosque facades. It is surmounted by the figure of a woman whose mystical powers are meant to facilitate the communication with the invisible world.

Puppet masquerades are a very popular form of entertainment in certain Bamana regions, such as around Segu. Some puppet masquerades date back at least to the 19th century. The puppets consist of wood carvings with clothes and represent different mythological figures as well as other characters, some of them intended for social parody. The puppets, and the masquerades in which they appear, can be classified into various types (see chapter 8).

Pottery and Textiles

The making of pots, such as water jars and vessels, has a long-standing history in the region, and there exist clear aesthetic standards and expectations concerning the surface design of pottery. Although the tools and materials for pottery may appear to be rudimentary, the technical know-how necessary to successfully form and fire is highly complex. Pot making is thus a craft one needs to acquire through long-lasting apprenticeship. The potters are women whose pottery production techniques reveal distinctive, regionally specific combinations of sophistication, conservatism, and innovation. These women are often, but not everywhere, the wives of blacksmiths. Their craft illustrates the important role of women in the creation and maintenance of artist identity in contemporary Mali.

Textiles present another significant example of a long-standing, highly aesthetic Malian craft. Some of the oldest textile fragments in West Africa were found in the Bandiagara escarpment. They have been dated to the 11th century and attributed to the Tellem, the people who preceded the Dogon in this area. Handwoven textiles, especially blankets, played an important role in life-cycle rituals and sometimes also in religious ceremonies. The cotton or wool is woven into strips of cloth that are then sewn together to form variously sized cloths or blankets. Most textiles can be identified according to their different regional and ethnic origins, their sizes and shapes, the manufacturing techniques and materials that go into their production, their social and ritual significance and use, and the symbolism of their designs. Characteristic of traditional Fulani woolen marriage blankets, for instance, are their delicate motifs. Soninke cotton textiles, in contrast, impress through their spectacular arrangements of horizontal stripes in white and different shades of blue.

Weaving is generally done by men who in some ethnic groups belong to a group of specialized artisans. The Fulani weavers, for instance, are renowned for their richly patterned wool blankets and tent furnishings and practice their craft as an occupation linked to their social origins. Bamana and Maninka weavers, in contrast, weave cotton blankets only as a side product of their agricultural activities and thus after the harvest season. Although weaving is a male profession, women play an instrumental role, too, by preparing and carding the wool and spinning the thread. They are in danger of losing their former role, though, because of the growing import of commercial cotton thread from China and Europe.

In spite of the high artistic value of these traditional textiles, today they are gradually disappearing, to be replaced by low-cost, industrially produced and imported fabric. Still, some of the older pieces, as well as newly handwoven blankets, persist as valuable family heirlooms, passed on from one generation to another and used on ceremonial occasions. More and more weavers migrate to the cities, where they fabricate new shapes and patterns in response to new consumer preferences and an ever-growing tourist clientele. In addition to traditional plant-based, hand-dyed reds, yellows, blacks, and whites, new commercially produced colors—such as reds, oranges, blues, and blacks—are used. This process implies a gradual move of a long-standing form of handicraft toward a modern aesthetic and a new function of certain textiles that are now used to indicate the owner's modern and cosmopolitan consumerist orientation.

A prominent example of traditional textile with a signature type of ornamentation is the Bamana mudcloth (*bogolanfini*). One regional origin of mudcloth production lies in the Bamana region north of Bamako, the

Beledougou. Until the 1980s, mudcloth tended to be associated by many urban dwellers with a backward, "animist" Bamana, rural background. Since then, mudcloth has become a key element of trendy local outfits for urban men and women, as well as a key item of an international fashion scene and tourist market.

Mudcloth has been conventionally fabricated by women for various ritual and ceremonial purposes, such as the marking of major life transitions. Women rely on men to weave their hand-spun cotton and to sow together the cotton strips to create panels that measure between 33 × 50 inches and 44 × 72 inches. Women are the artists who decide on the designs and who apply diverse and distinctive techniques and styles of preparing the cloth that they pass on to their daughters. The basic technique of mudcloth fabrication involves soaking the cloth in a suspension made of crushed leaves from the cengura (*bogolon*) tree. This suspension prepares the fabric for absorption of the mud dye and gives it a yellowish color. Women then apply the mud dye itself, made from iron-rich mud (with iron oxide as active ingredient), by drawing various designs on the cloth, with the help of reeds, sticks, cardbox templates, and other tools; they only cover the background with the mud dye while sparing the design itself. Nowadays, not only traditional textile production is of great value and symbolic significance to Malian consumers. Also widely appreciated is the practice of dyeing imported cotton fabric (the *bazin*) to be used, by men and by women, for high-prestige outfits (see chapter 5).

Artists

For a long time, Western observers and art connoisseurs considered African art as the expression of a people or tribe, rather than attributing it to individual artists, their innovative creativity, and personal skills. Art historians, in particular, focused on the art object and its context of use. There are authors who question whether *artist* is the right term to describe the creator of ritual objects that are exhibited as art in Western museums. But the identity and context of artisans who create certain ritual objects for different ethnic groups, such as Bamana/Maninka sculpture, suggest that the label *artist* is appropriate, even if it refers to a social context of artistic production that differs significantly from what Western observers often have in mind when speaking of an artist. All these sculptors and artisans hold a specialized knowledge that, learned through years-long apprenticeship and augmented by individual experience, is transmitted from one generation to the next. A notable example of these experts of artistic creation are those who were born into a family of professional specialists (*nyamakalaw*), such as the blacksmiths and potters (singular, *numun*), leatherworkers (singular, *garanke*), and experts of the spoken and sung word (singular, *jeli*). Blacksmiths make ritual and medicinal sculpture in wood and metal and are often in charge of the powerful Komo initiation society and its cultic sites and objects. The experts of the word work as praise singers and public speakers on behalf of the powerful (see chapter 3). Common to all these craftspeople is that they are all considered to deal with processes that involve the danger-ridden handling of materials (such as iron, but also turning unspoken knowledge into spoken words) and that therefore require special, initiate knowledge. These special functions and knowledge define their distinctive place in society. They are separated by endogamy (i.e., only marrying among each other) and occupation from the rest of society, and their interactions with people of other social origin follow certain preconceived notions of purity and danger. This organization of professional specialization is widespread throughout Mali, but there are also areas where artistic occupations such as wood carving, iron working, and pot making are the responsibility of another group of specialists.

In addition to artists who were born into a socioprofessional artisan group, there are also people who, while of different social origin, were trained as artists at one of the state professional schools, such as the Institut National des Arts in Bamako. There are also some musicians who, regardless of their social birth as *jeli* or freeborn people, make music their profession. Notable examples are the world-famous singer Salif Keita (who comes from an aristocratic family from the region south of Bamako) and guitarist-singer Habib Koité, who emphasizes his identity as an artist and who considers his *nyamakala* origin to be of secondary importance to the kind of music he performs.

Contemporary Art

Clear-cut boundaries between traditional and contemporary art are difficult to draw because, as we have seen, traditional art itself has been subject to considerable historical transformations and also because contemporary art draws strongly on aesthetic conventions and techniques of traditional artworks. The blurring of traditional and contemporary art forms is most evident in wooden and iron sculptures produced for a thriving international consumer market. Many of these newly produced objects are intended for tourist consumption, but some are also produced for sale at high-class art galleries in South Africa, Europe, and the United States.

Painting

Paintings constitute an art form that is of a very recent nature and lacks roots in conventional techniques and historical visual and artistic conventions. Some variation exists with respect to artistic style, inspiration, and artistic self-understanding. Predominant in the national market are naive depictions of African traditional life that are sold to tourists and are put up for decoration in the houses of urban middle-class families. The painters of this naive style often understand themselves as preservers of African traditional culture. There are also a few painters who choose topics that identify them not as Malian or African painters but simply as artists whose work reflects on their engagement with very different aspects of the contemporary world.

Cinema and Photography

Since the colonial period, Mali has generated several outstanding film producers. Cheick Oumar Sissoko and Souleymane Cissé both gained world fame with their films, which acquainted international audiences with the complexities of social life and the rich historical and cultural heritage of Mali. Souleymane Cissé was born in Bamako in 1940 and trained in Dakar and Moscow before embarking on a career as filmmaker and playwright in Mali. Cissé was jailed for one of his earlier movies, *Den Muso* (Daughter), which was banned by the Malian Ministry of Culture. His most famous films are *Baara* (Work, 1978), *Finye* (Wind, 1982), *Yèlèn* (Light, 1987), and *Waati* (Time, 1995), all of which won or were short-listed for international awards.

In recent years, Bamako has become the site for several international cinematic events. Here is an advertisement for a retrospective of 50 years of African cinema organized in 2010. (Photo by the author.)

Cheick Oumar Sissoko, born in 1945 in San and trained in France received several international awards for his movies *Guimba* (The tyrant, 1995), *Le Genèse* (Creation, 1999), and *Battù* (2000, based on a novel by Aminata Sow Fall).

Photography in Mali has a long-standing and strong tradition in Mali. For years, Bamako has hosted a biannual photography activity, African Photography Encounters. Photography in Mali reflects no uniform and distinctive cultural style but reveals the personal agendas and preferences of individual photographer-artists. Since the 1930s, a group of professional urban photographers emerged in then colonial French Sudan. Some of these photographers established themselves in the capital Bamako as well as in the towns of Segu, Mopti, Bougouni, and Gao, and they became avid documenters of the changing faces and modalities of urban life. Photography was and is keenly consumed by a relatively small (mostly urban) segment of the Malian population, but consumer expectations often do not fully match the self-understandings and artistic visions of photographers. Many people are keen on purchasing portraits of themselves and their beloved ones but show limited appreciation of the range of photographic motives and also of the truly artistic value of some photography. Two notable representatives of photography in Mali who, for a long time, struggled hard to gain recognition as artists in Mali's national arena are Seydou Keita and Malick Sidibé.

Seydou Keita is often referred to as an eminent representative of studio photography in Mali, yet his work covers many more styles and subjects. Born in 1921 in Bamako (and died in 2001), Seydou Keita was a self-trained amateur whose ingenious use of props and studio technique earned him some popularity among urban middle classes of the 1940s and 1950s. Characteristic of Keita's signature photographic style is his impressive ability to portray his subjects as urbanites with all their dignity, dreams, and fantasies. Yet, although Keita enjoyed a certain recognition as a photographer, the genuinely artistic value of his work was acknowledged by national and international audiences only late in his life, in 1977.

Malick Sidibé, the other internationally acclaimed Malian photographer, was saved from this fate. A native of the small village of Soloba, where he was born in 1935, Sidibé moved to Bamako in 1952 where he graduated from the École des Artisans Soudanais in 1955. Working as an apprentice of French photographer Gerard Guillat, he bought his first camera in 1956. Sidibé opened his own Studio Malick in 1958, at a time when a fashionable clientele of middle-class youths turned the streets of Bamako into popular dance venues. In contrast to other studio photographers, Sidibé used his lighter 35mm camera to move around in town and document the festivities and family events of the new urban elite. He thus created an immensely rich collection of portraits and vivid depictions of street scenes, capturing some of the insouciance and spontaneity that energized Bamako's nightlife in the late 1950s and early years of postindependence.

Starting in the late 1980s, when his work gradually gained an international reputation, Sidibé presented himself more and more at international venues, attending conferences and exhibiting his photographic oeuvre. In 1995, the Fondation Cartier pour l'Art Contemporain in Paris hosted Sidibé's first monographic exhibition. Today, Sidibé still works from Studio Malick, doing studio photography and repairing cameras. He received the Hasselblad Award in 2003 and, in 2007, the Lion d'Or at the Venice Biennale.

ARCHITECTURE

The adaptations of Mali's populations to the climatic conditions and vegetations of the country's different regions, and to the different, sedentary, nomadic, and seminomadic lifestyles that accompany them, are reflected in the characteristically great diversity of building structures and materials of Mali. In many cases, these buildings illustrate the mutual influence of Muslim and various local architectural styles of different regions. The connection is most evident in mosques and in structures associated with local religious traditions, such as sanctuaries and ancestral gates.

About three-fourths of the population is rural. In the southern savannah and Sahel regions, the majority of rural people are sedentary agriculturalists. They typically live in thatched dwellings grouped together in villages of between 120 and 600 inhabitants and surrounded by grazing lands and cultivated fields. The regionally diverse building structures and materials displayed in these villages reflect as much on different cultural conventions and on the availability of building materials as on the climatic conditions and requirements of each zone.

Until recently, the nomadic populations of the Sahara and Sahel did not opt for permanent building structures but preferred to live in temporary dwellings, such as tents made of a combination of wood and animal skins. But French colonial administrative policy and the attempts by the postcolonial state to control the movement of transhumant segments of the population have seriously affected this nomadic lifestyle. The periods of drought in the 1970s and 1980s and, more recently, the civil war of the 1990s, further contributed to an alteration of former nomadic ways of life.

The area of the Niger Bend and the Voltaic Basin, stretching across the savannah belt of Mali and its adjacent countries, is shaped by the physical infrastructure and social and trade activities and mobility of the Mande-speaking people and their neighbors, as well as by the northwestern trade routes linking the Niger emporia to Kumasi and the Guinea Coast. This area was historically distinct from the area to the east, where Hausa state formation, the Fulani jihads, and the commercial activities surrounding the northeastern trans-Saharan trade routes generated a different form of architectural expression. The specific architectural style found in the western savannah belt is generally referred to as Sudanese architecture. This term is derived from the name of the colonial territory, the French Sudan, in which it was located when European travelers started writing about it. The medieval towns of Mali—among them Djenné, Timbuktu, Gao, and Segu—are, though to different degrees, built in the Sudanese style of architecture. The most famous example of Sudanese architecture is the mosque of Djenné, the largest mud building in the world, which together with several other mosques attests to the successful merging of Muslim faith and religious practice with local aesthetic conventions. Other towns, among them Kayes, Kita, San, and Bamako, owe their historic buildings to the times of French colonial occupation. These former sites of colonial administration were designed in a way that a central business district, dominated by the historical colonial buildings, is surrounded by residential districts.

Mud Architecture

Among the arts of sub-Saharan Africa and of Mali in particular, sculpture, music, and dance have received widespread attention and appreciation, whereas architecture has remained a relatively neglected field of study, often relegated to the realm of anthropology or archeology. There are several reasons for this neglect. For a long time, the widespread perception was that building styles in sub-Saharan Africa should not be considered architecture in the proper sense of the term but, at most, building technology. Abodes were seen primarily in terms of the techniques that their builders commanded and not in terms of their aesthetic value and creativity. Another reason for the tendency to underestimate African architecture is that many conventional building technologies are based on materials of short durability. This applies especially to the architecture of Mali. Stone constructions exist, but they are few. Mud constitutes the most important building material for sedentary peoples. Many Western observers and scholars did not consider mud a respectable architectural medium because of their own cultural preconceptions that associated monumentality with permanence.

Mud is used in many different ways, and indigenous building, diverse in both its forms and in the functions it serves, manifests a broad range of types. The fact that in all these buildings mud bricks serve as a basic element suggests that this technique has a very long history in this region.

At one end of the range of building types constructed with mud bricks are the flat-roofed, rectangular houses, often replete with pierced parapet walls and crowded into tightly nucleated villages. At the other end are clusters of circular roundhouses that are capped by their thatched-roof bonnets and dispersed over the arid landscape. Intermingled with this range of sedentary buildings are the various nomadic, transient abodes made of thatch, woven mats, or skins, whose occupants used to live in a relationship of exchange and mutual dependence with their sedentary mud-building neighbors. From this range of building types, with their attendant, distinct technology, the Sudanese mosque architecture appears as a unified and easily recognizable form throughout the area, even if it comprises several distinct building styles that can be loosely identified with certain ethnic or regional identities.

Mosques

In other areas of the Muslim world, Islamic architecture often comprises tombs and palaces in addition to mosques. In the area of contemporary Mali, the mosque has been the primary physical manifestation of Islamic presence. Other kinds of Islamic buildings existed only in certain historical periods, such as in the times of the empires of Ghana, Mali, and Songhai, presided by Muslim ruling dynasties at whose seats in the urban centers the sites of palaces and tombs were to be found. In these times, a thriving long-distance commerce fed into the growth of urban centers and of a wealthy and powerful elite.

The Sudanese mosque architecture reflects strong influences from Muslim North Africa. But it is also unique in its adaptation of translocal architectural and ritual requirements (reflected in the physical and social organization of sacred space) to local conventions and aesthetic preferences. Formal modifications pertain to size and scale, structure itself, finesse of construction and detail, definition of plane surfaces, and the degree of verticality, as well as to the deviations from the standard plan layout for mosques. Other forms of modification and adaption relate to local climatic conditions, available building materials, and the existing construction techniques and skills. Also decisive are the location of the mosque in an urban or rural milieu and the religious actors who supported its introduction in the area. Thus, to comprehend the impact of Islam on indigenous building forms, one needs to consider the various historical patterns and actors through which Islam spread in this area of West Africa and what processes of synthesis between Muslim religious conventions and local social and cultural practices occurred.

The Sudanese mosque architecture is essentially mud architecture. Mud as a building material permits great flexibility in the treatment of plane surfaces

but imposes major limitations on potential structural form. As a consequence, a number of basic variations regarding the formal arrangement of
minarets, stairs, and inner courtyards emerge that can be loosely associated
with mosque buildings in Timbuktu, Djenné, Mopti, San, and some towns
in the Voltaic Basin. The first type of Sudanese mosque architecture, represented in the Djinguereber and the Sankore mosques of Timbuktu, as well
as in the tomb of Askia Muhamed at Gao, corresponds to the first phase
of Islamization in the Western Sudan under the influence of Arab-speaking
Berber traders and clerics from the areas of present-day Mauritania. Because
Islam was then rooted in an urban culture, Islamic buildings were limited to
a few urban entrepôts of trans-Saharan trade. Characteristic of this architecture are its massive, heavy scale and its minarets, built of solid mud, that are
pierced by projecting timbers. These timbers provide permanent scaffolding
for the necessary, regular maintenance of mud wall surfaces and serve to concentrate the seasonal cracking of walls—an unavoidable outcome of rapid
changes in humidity and temperature—along prescribed lines. Other types,
such as the one typical of the Sahelian city of Djenné, are characterized by
a more refined, carefully balanced interplay of wall surfaces, in parapet construction, and through the use and placement of wooden dentils obtained by
cutting trunks of the fan palm. The symmetry of its facade, composed of three
major minarets rhythmically interspersed with absolutely vertical buttresses,
achieves a sense of verticality unrivalled in this part of the world. In contrast
to the massive Timbuktu type, the Djenné mosque generates a sense of spatial
enclosure. The minarets are not built up of a mass of solid material but rather
enclose an ample set of spiral mud stairs that leads upward to the roof. This
incorporation of the minaret as an integral element of the facade itself marks
an innovation in mosque design. Other types of Sudanese mosque architecture are represented by the mosques of Bobo Dioulasso and Kong, which are
much smaller in scale and lack the monumentality that characterizes both
the Djenné and Timbuktu types. The mosques of Bobo Dioulasso and Kong
correspond to another historical period and organization of religious identity
and practice. They indicated the growing influence of Muslim Mande traders
in the areas of what are now the northern Ivory Coast, northwestern Ghana,
and the southern Upper Volta. Both mosques thus reflect a politico-religious
structure vested in small Muslim agglomerations surrounded by communities that practiced traditional religions; this structure contrasts with the earlier
large mosques that symbolized the concentration of religious erudition and
political power in cosmopolitan Muslim city centers.

Local populations invest great efforts into preventing these buildings from
disintegrating during the rains by adding a new layer of clay to the mud
structure. All inhabitants of Djenné come together once a year after the rainy

season to repair the mosque by covering its facade with a new layer of mud. For this, people climb on the wooden spikes sticking out of the walls that, apart from their aesthetic value, serve as permanent scaffolding.

Defense Structures

Traces of the periods of political turmoil and insecurity following the breakdown of centralized polities in the 17th to 19th centuries can be found today in the remnants of fortified structures called *tata, tara koko,* or *diin* in various Bamana and Maninka settings of southern Mali. These fortress-like structures, made of mud bricks and surrounded by additional protective walls, were built by local communities to defend themselves against the attacks and razzias of bandits who formed veritable military and economic enterprises, the so-called war houses, in search of slaves and other booty. A considerable number of *tata* are to be found today in the areas around Bougouni and Sikasso in southern Mali, where Samori Touré waged his war in the 1860s and 1870s. The defense structures gained fame as objects of repeated sieges, such as the *tata* of Sikasso, which successfully resisted Samori Touré's nine-months-long siege, as well as that of the French colonial troops, whose eventual victory in 1898 was only due to their use of heavy artillery. Apart from their military protective functions, many fortresses also played an important role in maintaining control over the trade routes between north and south.

To secure a city with a fortress, an enormous amount of manpower was needed. So the city's entire population and that of adjacent villages had to participate in the *tata*'s construction. Mud, the basic building material, was mixed with other substances, such as gravel, dung, and scoria, and then stacked layer after layer in a weeks-long process. Once the desired height (about 6 meters, approximately 20 feet) was reached, it was covered with a rendering made of a mix of mud, dung, and shea butter to insulate the wall against water. In spite of their historical significance, today most of these fortresses are steadily falling into pieces, crumbling because of exposure to weather and to people's misappropriation as a low-cost building material.

Colonial Architecture

French colonial architecture imitated certain stylistic elements of Sudanese mud architecture and is therefore commonly referred to as neo-Sudanese. These buildings are found in towns that served as centers of French administration and commercial activities, such as Kayes, Kita, Bamako, and Segu. Kayes was the first entry point and headquarter of the French colonial troops that arrived from the area of present-day Senegal, and it became an important stopover for the railway construction linking Bamako to Dakar. Together with the adjacent town of Medine, Kayes displays today some of the most eminent examples of colonial architecture, all of them built in the period between 1880 and 1923. These are heavy, three-story buildings with large verandas and archways that ensure constant aeration. In spite of their historic significance and the fact that some of them house state administration and extension services, these buildings suffer at present from a lack of maintenance. Other instances of colonial physical infrastructure are the fortresses built in the Niger and Senegal basins between the early 18th century and the late 19th century. The most impressive French fortress is the one located in Medine (near Kayes), a massive, two-story building built in 1855 under Governor Faidherbe, which comprises several adjacent structures, among them a powder magazine, a prison, and a school building and is surrounded by a formidable defensive wall.

Segu hosts a number of colonial buildings from the period between 1928 and 1952 that served the colonial irrigated rice production project Office du Niger. Twelve of these buildings grant a certain stylistic coherence to the present-day city center of Segu.

Other Historic Buildings

Another building type of great historic and cultural import is the vestibule, that is, a rectangular or circular edifice that comprises several doors and is built of solid mud. Some vestibules house extended families and constitute the symbolic core of family continuity and cohesion and of patriarchal authority. Other vestibules have ritual functions, such as the famous Kamabulon of Kangaba (located southwest of the capital Bamako), whose origins are said to go back to the political endeavor of Sundjata Keita in the 13th century. The septennial reroofing ceremony of this round-shaped, thatch-roofed *kamabulon* is an occasion of great ritual and social significance to families who trace their origins to the legendary Mali empire founded by Keita. In spite of its modest size and shape, the Kamabulon of Kangaba constitutes a symbolic site of great cultural and political importance that has been recently added to the UNESCO list of world heritage cultural sites.

Rural Settlements

Types of rural settlements vary with the region, vegetation zones, mode of livelihood, and degree of influence from urban areas. Building shapes and architectural styles vary, too, reflecting the influence of an Islamic urban culture and Sudanese architecture. Pastoral groups living on the fringes of the Sahara and throughout the Sahelian zone live in easily transportable tents made of thatch and animal skin and settle individually or in loosely arranged agglomerations.

Until a few decades ago, most Tuareg were seminomadic. They lived in rural communities that ranged from temporary camps of 5 to 10 nomadic tents that moved around to graze their herds, to hamlets that, in their mix of adobe houses and tents, were best adapted to their semisedentary, gardening and herding subsistence activities, and finally, to immovable hamlets where people lived off horticulture. A household unit corresponded to a tent, owned and occupied by a married woman. The droughts of the 1970s and 1980s, as well as periods of unrest and civil war, forced many Tuareg to adopt more sedentary lifestyles. Their present residential structures range from compounds of tents to more permanent structures and mud houses that are considered the property of men. Sedentarization has therefore triggered considerable shifts in the distribution of responsibilities and property between men and women. The Moor populations who live in the northwest of Mali, and who traditionally also led a nomadic lifestyle, have undergone similar sedentarization processes and effects.

Although many Fulani have turned more forcefully toward livestock production and sedentary settlement in the late 20th century, Fulani settlement patterns still range from a traditional transhumant lifestyle to various modes of sedentary life. Those with a nomadic or seminomadic lifestyle live in season-specific settlements: dry-season and wet-season camps. Households are patrilocal, with sizes ranging from one nuclear family to extended families encompassing over a hundred members. The wet-season camps are the primary site of family residence. Very often, only the young men are sent away to the dry-season camps, where the majority of family cattle is kept during the dry season.

The sedentary populations of the Sahelian and savannah zones, in contrast, live predominantly in villages composed of compounds and also of some isolated houses. This also applies to many Bozo and Somono of the middle Niger belt region, who subsist mainly from fishing and who live, depending on their socioeconomic standing, in semipermanent and permanent buildings. In areas with a predominantly agricultural population, there are hamlets located outside the village and in closer proximity to farmlands that may over time turn into permanent settlements.

While traditionally houses in Mali were built out of mud and timber, today many people prefer, if they can afford it, to build houses of a mixture of earth and cement.

House roofs are either thatched conical roofs or they consist of timber beams that support a flat terrace (made of mud bricks) on which inhabitants sleep during the hot season. In rural areas, it has become a sign of affluence and success to cover one's houses with roofs made of sawn timber and corrugated iron sheets rather than of the relatively short-lived materials wood and thatch. However, this is an expensive and uncomfortable option because iron sheets retain heat much longer at night.

Depending on the area, houses are rectangular or circular mud buildings that, grouped in circles or semicircles, encompass a spacious courtyard that forms the social and spatial core of family life. A kitchen and a circular, thatched storage house complete this cluster of one-to-two-room houses that together form an extended family's residential unit. In addition to these family residences, there exist in most villages a number of buildings that are of communal interest and use, such as a building with an adjacent large lobby used for village meetings, a mosque, or a round, thatch-roofed sanctuary where ritual objects are kept.

Depending on the region, ethnic composition of a village, and personal taste of individual family members, these various buildings may bear various kinds of abstract or anthropomorphic decoration painted in plant-based red, brown, yellow, and black colors.

The construction of sanctuaries and other buildings with ritual functions requires special preparation and knowledge. Before the construction is even launched, oracles need to be consulted and protective sacrifices need to be performed to ensure a smooth building process and a successful use of the site. Village mosques are usually of modest proportions and stylistic elaboration. They basically consist of a rectangular building to which a minaret has been added. In villages in close proximity to town, or on the main roads, more and more mosques are found nowadays that feature architectural and stylistic influences from mosques in North Africa and the Arab world and thus reflect the aesthetic and doctrinal orientation of their foreign-based sponsors.

Urban Housing

The influence of Western-style architecture is evident in towns, particularly in those that served as centers of French colonial administration. As a result, Malian towns exhibit a juxtaposition of styles, including houses made of a mixture of mud and cement, concrete houses and high-rise buildings, villas modeled on European mansions, as well as official structures and mosques built in the Sudanese style. Whereas historic towns such as Timbuktu and Djenné have retained much of their ancient appearance and charm, towns such as Segu that similarly pride themselves on a long-standing history have changed to modern-style towns that display a variety of building types and architectural styles. Bamako, the capital city and largest urban center, has many structures built with concrete and steel.

In town, many people live in homes made of cement and covered by corrugated roofs. These houses are climatically less adapted, but their attractiveness stems from their stability, longevity, and identification with modern lifestyles and consumerist orientations. Most buildings, apart from mosques and colonial buildings, are of relatively recent origin. However, there exist traditional houses, some of them palace-like buildings, in towns with a notable political history. In Segu, for instance, the capital city of the ancient Bamana kingdom, there are several massive buildings with intricately shaped facades, a style that was practiced in various areas of southern Mali. Other traditional-styled houses in town distinguish themselves from their rural counterparts by the facade facing the street, which is distinctive in its architectural elaboration.

Many towns in Mali have housing problems. Bamako and several other towns have grown enormously after the Second World War, benefiting from the governmental investments in improving urban sanitary infrastructure and housing. With increasing migration toward Bamako and other towns, and partly in response to the droughts of the 1970s and 1980s, urban real estate has become a major source of contention among urban populations and between citizens and the state administration.

Mali's medieval towns, such as Timbuktu and Djenné, did not have any defensive structures and walls. Still, similar to other historical towns located in the area of present-day Mali, they constituted the material and symbolic core of political power. They were the site where the ruler, as well as his followers and military forces, resided and from where they launched attacks on and raids of neighboring polities. With the spread of Islam, the town became a center of religious power and erudition whose glamour appealed to the urban higher classes yet also extended to the surrounding areas. The political and the religious powers remained spatially separate (symbolized in the structures of the palace and the mosque) while blending in actual politics. The mosque, with its attached institutions of learning, formed the key site of knowledge transmission and religious erudition and also the heart of social and cultural life. Traders (who were most often Muslims) resided in a separate neighborhood, in residences characterized by their impressive, elaborate facades and decorations. Urban neighborhoods and settlement patterns also reflected ethnic divisions and professional specialization in town. Many inhabitants made a living from cultivating the surrounding lands and raising livestock. For this, wealthier families relied on the labor of slaves.

Under French colonial rule and after independence, Mali's historic cities expanded. They often benefited from infrastructural developments initiated by the French administration and, as in the case of the famous Djenné mosque, from the French efforts to restore historic sites and buildings. Recent

architectural developments in the middle Niger region point toward a sim-
plification of architectural forms and facade decorations as a consequence of
changing building techniques. The mixing of mud and cement helps improve
the stability and longevity of traditional-style homes and opens up new opportunities for innovation of architectural forms, but it also invites a process
in the course of which some traditional forms are abandoned.

5

Cuisine and Dress

Ere aqqiman war-t-ikayyad ere iglad.
A traveler must not be disappointed by his host.

—Tuareg proverb

CUISINE

THE AVERAGE MALIAN family spends more than 50 percent of its family income on food consumption. As in other cultures, food and eating in Mali is not simply about satisfying one's hunger. Rather, food-related practices—such as cooking, eating, and inviting others to share a meal—are important expressions of social status and of ideals of sociability. Food and its consumption make manifest culturally specific norms of hospitality and friendship, of being together and sharing, and thus of generosity. Food and eating also serve as metaphors for social and political hierarchies and the ordering of social and political relations. For instance, among the rural Tuareg residents of northern Mali who seek to hold on to the patron-client relations that once constituted the backbone of rural society, different food products, such as milk, corn, and millet, are used as metaphors to explain and present as naturally given social divisions among people of free birth, socioprofessional specialists, and descendants of former slaves. The particular qualities and textures of individual food products are taken as an illustration of the innate personality features that, as people maintain, characterize individuals of different social origins.

Food is also of central importance to many Malians because of its immediate, existential, and material functions. In a society where daily food is not
a certainty for everyone, the availability of sufficient or large food quantities
is an object of daily concern and of sustained effort. Eating well and eating
in abundance are associated with the consumption of meat and heavy, greasy
sauces.

The strong connection between food consumption and sharing is manifest in the fact that people in a family eat the main meals together from large
bowls in which the food is offered. For this, family members are separated
into groups divided according to age and gender so that women and men
eat from different bowls. Eating with forks and spoons and from individual
plates is practiced only among a relatively small intellectual elite. Many Malians feel that consuming food with the help of eating utensils deprives them
of the pleasurable, sensuous experience of touching and feeling the texture of
food.

Norms of commensality are also reflected in other rules regulating the
preparation and consumption of food. Those who cook are expected to prepare more than is needed so that one is always in a position to invite surprise
visitors to join them for a meal. Such a family will be favorably looked at and
praised by neighbors and friends for its generosity toward neighbors, friends,
and strangers. The norm of sharing is also evident in the rule, taught even to
children, that one may never eat in the presence of others without inviting
them to join the meal with the standard phrase "join me in eating" (*na du-
muni ke* in Bamanakan). Reversely, it is thought highly improper to flatly refuse such an invitation and gesture of politeness, for instance with the words
"no thank you." Rather, whoever wants to decline the invitation to join a meal
should say that he or she is not hungry (*n'fara,* "I am full" in Bamanakan).

All these conventions highlight the communal nature of food consumption and the strong social expectation, even pressure, to share whatever food
one has with others. The counterpoint to this strong obligation to share food
consists in the practice of eating aside (in Bamanakan, *dunduguma,* literally,
"eating on the floor"), a notion that refers to legitimate individual (sometimes surreptitious) food consumption. That is, people distinguish between
basic staple food (*suman* in Bamanakan), which should be shared and comes
mostly in the form of the main meals on one side, and additional food for
pleasure (*nègèlafen,* literally "things to satisfy one's cravings") purchased for
individual consumption on the other. All kinds of snacks but also soft drinks,
cigarettes, tea, and cola nuts enter into the category of pleasurable, individually consumed food. Whereas everyone may rightly claim to receive a share
of the staple food prepared daily for the family, purchasing and consuming
pleasurable food is a matter of individual initiative and luck. A person may

share her pleasurable food with friends, visitors, and neighbors, but no one is obliged to do so.

Eating is closely associated with home as the sphere of intimacy, and there is a strong tendency—and expectation—to eat at home. In recent decades, under the growing influence of Western leisure-time activities, partly introduced by returning labor migrants and expatriates, eating out at a restaurant (mostly at night) has become more frequent, but it is practiced mostly by a small urban business elite. In town, many small eateries exist, for travelers and employees in the state administration who do not have an opportunity to return home for lunch or dinner. In Bamako and other large cities, many women turn the preparation of lunch and dinner dishes for the working middle classes into a professional occupation and sell these meals at their little food stands placed next to administrative buildings and commercial centers.

Food preparation in the family is considered the exclusive domain of women. Women who excel in cooking are highly appreciated, not only by their husbands but also by their wider social entourage. Even though women are in charge of preparing all food for the family, in recent decades, cooking for private households has also become a (paid) profession. Because it can be a lucrative occupation, more men are moving into this occupational sector, serving mostly as cooks of the well-paying expatriates working in the development sector.

The broader ramifications of food consumption and food preparations for social life are best illustrated by discourses and struggles surrounding the preparation of the daily sauce. A good sauce has multiple, material, sensuous, and symbolic meanings. In an immediate sense, eating a good, richly savored sauce is a source of considerable sensuous enjoyment. Husbands often take it as an indication of their wife's willingness to invest time and money into the preparation of food and thus as an indication of her affection. In town, the term sauce price (*nasòngò*) denotes the amount of money a husband gives his wife to prepare the daily meals. But many women spend additional money to purchase ingredients for the sauce, either because they feel that the sum provided by their husbands is insufficient or because they want to do him a favor with a particularly well-prepared dish. The quality of a sauce thus often has manifold material implications. For instance, a husband may reciprocate the affection his wife showed him through her good sauce with gifts or other signs of affection. A good sauce is also the means by which a woman may gain the upper hand in her competition with co-wives over their husband's affections.

Over the past decades, with worsening living conditions among many middle and lower-middle-class households in town, disagreements between husband and wife over the sauce price have increased. Reports on "struggles over the sauce price" (*nasòngo kèlè*)—that is, marital and intrafamilial disputes over the amount a husband should give his wives for the daily meals—are the central subject of everyday conversation. In households where men struggle to make a living and to earn a regular income, these fights over the sauce price capture the growing inability of husbands to provide for their families. Here again, we see how food and eating relates to the broader social order of Malian society and how talk about food serves to express concerns about social change and what is perceived as a degradation of a former moral order.

Staple Foods

The most important Malian staple foods are millet, rice, corn, and *fonio,* a cereal found mostly in West Africa. Varieties of millet and sorghum are prepared in the form of porridge, soups, and couscous and dished out with various sauces. In the farming areas and among rural populations more generally, the amount and richness of meals vary significantly with the seasons, depending on the availability of crops and vegetables but also on a family's monetary means to purchase the ingredients for the sauce. In the agricultural societies of Mali, farmers have a special name ("period of makeshift solutions," *periode de soudure* in French) for the season in which the family granaries are almost depleted but the new season's crops have not yet been harvested. That period is the hardest time for the farming populations because it coincides with the time of the highest labor input. Depending on the size of the preceding harvest, this period may last between several weeks and more than two months. It is this period that threatens farmers with the risk of hunger or even famine.

Depending on a family's economic standing and location of the homestead, people eat one or two main meals consisting of a huge bowl of staple food and the accompanying sauce. In addition, a soup-like porridge made of corn, millet, or rice and (if available) mixed with sugar and fresh or powdered milk is served for breakfast. The consumption of bread (modeled on the French baguette) is usually done as an addition to the breakfast porridge but only by people who can afford this extra expenditure. Poor families can only afford one main dish (if at all); for the rest of the meals, older children and adult members of the family need to fend for themselves while mothers struggle to find food for their younger children.

Strong Moroccan tea, made of green Chinese tea and large quantities of sugar and served in small glasses, occupies the place of the national beverage that in Europe and the United States is taken by coffee and tea. The tea is consumed in the form of three (sometimes four) consecutive brewings, with the first one being the strongest, most concentrated serving and the last one consisting mostly of sugar. Because the preparation of the tea requires large amounts of sugar, it is considered a luxury in rural areas. Here, its consumption is limited mostly to festive events and other occasions of social-izing and to visits of guests. In town, many adult Malians consume this tea after or in between meals, and there are many who, similar to coffee drinkers in Europe and the United States, confess to being so addicted to tea that they cannot start their working day without it. Black coffee is not very widely con-sumed. Those who do consume it (mostly intellectuals and other members of the urban middle or upper-middle classes but also travelers at small road-side coffee places) drink it in the "nescafe" form. For this, small quantities of instant coffee (usually less than half a tablespoon) are mixed with strongly sweetened milk concentrate or, if this is not available, with milk powder and large amounts of sugar. Black tea is called Lipton tea, after the company pro-ducing the tea bags, the standard form in which black tea is prepared in Mali. Lipton tea is consumed in analogous ways to coffee, mixed with several table-spoons of sugar and, if available, served with a lemon slice.

Malian cuisine differs from region to region, but it does not offer as wide a range of dishes as is the case in some neighboring West African countries.

Millet and sorghum are the major crops grown by the majority of the farm-ing population. Both millet and sorghum are said to fill the stomach more ef-fectively than rice, so it is these two crops that are preferentially eaten among rural populations. Rural people save rice dishes for special occasions, such as festive events. In town, many households, whenever they can afford it, tend to replace millet with rice, or they alternate between daily plates of rice and of millet. Here, rice makes up 40 percent of the daily food intake, whereas sorghum and millet make up 35 percent of daily consumption. No single na-tional dish exists, but millet or sorghum porridge (*to* in Bamanakan) is widely consumed among the different ethnic groups, especially among the farming populations. Certain ethnic groups have a special liking for specific dishes. The Soninke, for instance, frequently eat millet couscous (served with a sauce made of leaves or with milk and sugar). The Minianka show a stronger pref-erence for corn as a staple food than other ethnic groups. Among the cattle herding populations, milk is an important element of daily food consump-tion and an important source of protein.

Rice is grown in several regions in Mali and also imported. Rice dishes come in two variants. The main form in which rice is consumed on a daily basis is the *kinin,* that is, plain white rice accompanied by a sauce. The sec-ond variant, the *riz au gras* (fat rice, *zaamè* in Bamanakan), is more costly in its preparation because its ingredients include oil, *maggi* (bouillon) cubes, and tomato paste. For this reason, *riz au gras* is considered something special, to be reserved for extraordinary occasions or the visits of special guests.

Depending on the region and ethnic culinary specifics, sauces are made on the basis of protein-rich baobab leaves, other leaves, or peanut or okra. Standard ingredients of sauces are tomato paste, salt, peanut oil, and the ubiquitous *cube maggi*. Sauces may also contain components that correspond to regionally or ethnically specific preferences, such as the *sumbala*, a spice made of a local plant and whose unmistakable flavor is characteristic for the sauces prepared by many rural Soninke. Depending on a family's economic standing, different kinds of meat may be added to enrich the sauces, such as beef, goat, sheep, chicken, fish, and, in rare cases, game. In rural areas, the slaughtering of domestic animals is limited to special occasions. For instance, a chicken may be slaughtered to celebrate the visit of an honorable guest or to perform a sacrifice. If an animal is slaughtered, every part of it will be used for consumption. Regular meat consumption is a sign of status and wealth. So whereas well-to-do households in town eat meat or fish every day, these additions may be a rare luxury for many lower-class households, in town and among rural populations.

Vegetables such as tomatoes, peppers, eggplants, carrots, cabbage, and onions are added to sauces and usually eaten in thoroughly cooked form. Also popular, though not regularly eaten, are plantain, yams, and sweet potato. Raw vegetables, in the form of a salad, are considered a recent innovation and a luxury addition to regular food. Culinary influences from other West African countries, such as Senegal and Nigeria, are evident in dishes such as *poulet yassa* and *foutou*.

Fruit such as orange, lemon, banana, grapefruit, and mango are considered a snack, not a regular (that is, stomach-filling) meal. Other delicious snacks exist, such as roasted or salted peanuts, roasted corn, brochettes of grilled meat, doughnuts made of millet or ground beans (called *furufuru*) or millet doughnuts (*farini*), sesame crackers, and homemade ice cream.

Most people drink plain water along with their meals and also during the day. Bottled soft drinks, such as Sprite, Coca-Cola, Pepsi-Cola, and Fanta, are a rare luxury accessible only to well-to-do households. Very popular are locally produced soft drinks, such as the *jenjenbere* (made of ginger root, lemon, and sugar) and the *dableni* (made of hibiscus, vanilla, and sugar). But for the majority of the population, their consumption is limited to festive occasions, such as weddings and baptizing ceremonies.

Alcoholic beverages are not widely consumed in this predominantly Muslim society. Those who do consume alcohol do it mostly in the form of industrially produced beer. They drink beer not so much during regular meals but as an accompaniment to socializing activities. Regular consumption of alcoholic beverages is looked down upon, and excessive drinking is strongly discouraged and denigrated. In certain rural areas where non-Muslims form a significant share of the local population, the consumption of millet beer is widespread. Here, the production of millet beer (frequently done by women) constitutes an important income-generating activity.

Eating Routines

The act of eating is divided into several steps, each of them regulated by a set of rules and routines. Eating starts with the arrival of the meal, usually in the form of a large bowl containing the staple food and one or two smaller bowls containing the sauces. When the family head or senior is present, the meal is formally posed in front of him by the female cook (or by her daughter or another female junior who helped her with the food preparations) with the words "here is the meal." Family members and visitors will sit down on chairs and stools to form circles around the large bowls (one bowl for adult and adolescent men, a separate one for women, adolescent daughters, and small boys and girls). The cook or her assistant provides a bowl with water, often also soap, which each one in turn will use to wash his or her hands. The most senior person then arranges the food in the bowl by pouring the sauce (and the vegetable and meat or fish it may contain) over a portion of the staple food, proceeding from the center of the bowl. He (or she) then signals the start of the common meal by taking the first handful of food and pronouncing a *bissimilah* ("In the name of God"). Eating is done with the right hand only. Proper eating requires that one touches the food with the upper part of the fingers only, forms it into a small ball, and dips it shortly into the sauce. While taking handfuls of food from the bowl, one should not venture with the hand into other areas of the bowl but stick to the spot right in front of oneself.

Silence should reign during the entire meal, and everyone should keep his eyes focused on the meal in front of him. It is also considered extremely impolite to take a new handful of food while still chewing on the last one or to pick a piece of meat or fish, rather than waiting for the senior person to do so for himself. Those who are done with eating should turn away, wash their hand in the water bowl, and then express their gratitude through the formula (in Bamanakan) *a barika* ("Thanks"), to which the host and the cook should respond with *a barika ala ye* ("Thanks to God").

Ceremonial Food

The close link between food and its ritual dimensions can take several concrete forms. The preparation of a special dish may indicate a special social event, and its consumption may set the tone for an atmosphere of sociality. In such cases, the religious dimension of a particular dish may not be prominent. Examples of ceremonial food are dishes such as the *riz au gras* that are considered a luxury because of the more expensive ingredients that go into their preparation (oil and, if possible, meat or fish). These dishes are often prepared to mark the arrival of a particularly honored visitor. Special dishes

are also prepared for the celebration of life-cycle rituals, such as naming ceremonies and weddings. The food consumed during these ceremonies thus
creates and reflects feelings of sociability and enjoyment. The slaughtering
of domestic animals, such as a chicken, a goat, or a sheep, on these occasions
may highlight even more the atmosphere of commensality that the hosts seek
to create. The slaughtering of bigger and thus more costly animals, such as
cows, is limited most often to funeral ceremonies, when the children of a deceased person seek to honor her or him one last time by showing generosity
and hospitality to all visitors.

A second, closely related type of ceremonial food is the one prepared and
consumed to mark special events of importance to the broader community,
for instance, when the *nyamakalaw* from a certain district or region celebrate
the nomination of their leader, the *nyamakala kuntigi.*

A third type of ceremonial food serves to mark a change in status. For instance, the *dègè,* dried millet couscous that is mixed with milk and (if available) sugar, has a centuries-long history as a ceremonial food. Because dried
millet couscous can be easily stored for a longer period of time and is prepared as a delicious dish within minutes, this makes it an easy-to-keep snack
that every woman in rural areas will try to store in smaller or larger quantities to be able to demonstrate her hospitability. In contrast to contemporary
convention that makes *dègè* a token of generous hostship, in the 19th-century
societies of southern Mali, to drink the *dègè* was the ritual of submission par
excellence. If a military leader accepted to receive the *dègè* from the winning
opponent in a military confrontation, this gesture signaled the act of accept-
ing the opponent's victory and hence a recognition of the inferior status he
was to occupy henceforth. For instance, Samori Touré—during his empire-
building war expeditions that were to bring vast areas of southern Mali under
his control in the second half of the 19th century—made his enemies drink
the *dègè* to mark their subjection and their new status as vassals to his rule.

A fourth category of ceremonial food refers to the slaughtering of sacrificial animals. Animal sacrifice (or, as a kind of substitute sacrifice, the pouring
of cereals or milk) has a long history in Mali; it is still important in the procedures performed by ritual specialists in their effort to harness occult forces
for special purposes. For instance, a ritual specialist may diagnose a person's
illness as having been caused by an ill-wishing neighbor. In a second step, the
ritual specialist might offer to slaughter an animal as part of a ritual aiming at
generating a protection for the afflicted. Much more widely celebrated nowadays is another animal sacrifice: the ritual slaughter of a goat on the occasion
of the Muslim Feast of the Sacrifice (*Eid al-Adha* in Arabic)—a ritual that
every observant Muslim is expected to perform in commemoration of Abraham's willingness to sacrifice his own son.

Regardless of these very different rationales for slaughtering sacrificial animals, in each case, the repartition of meat among the recipients is a serious affair. This is so because the person who is responsible for the sacrifice (and thus its owner because he financed the sacrificial animal) distributes meat of lower and higher quality to certain family members, friends, and influential persons, depending on their prestige and social position. Here again, food, and its distribution and consumption, is used to reconfirm—or create—specific social hierarchies and power inequalities. Food serves not only as a metaphor for the ordering of the social and political universe but also as a means to reproduce or rework it.

DRESS

As in the case of food consumption, the significance of dress and other modes of adorning the body extends far beyond the immediate function of body coverage. The choice of dress styles and cuts reflects on a society's moral standards but also on the extent to which individuals comply with, or seek to challenge, these standards. Dress standards are usually gender- and age-specific, prescribing different zones and degrees of body coverage for men as opposed to women. In Mali, gender-specific prescriptions for bodily coverage also vary significantly from region to region. For instance, the (often indigo-blue) turban that an adult Tuareg is expected to wear to cover face and hair contrasts with dress conventions in some regions of the south where men, at least conventionally, were not expected to cover their heads at all. A person's compliance with dress codes varies with her educational background, socio-economic status, her exposure to Western school education; it also depends on whether her homestead is located in a rural or urban environment.

Dress, clothing, and related forms of adornment mobilize various forms of bodily perception, such as vision, touch, and locomotion, among wearers and those who view them. The texture of fabric, of jewelry, leather, and other materials making up dress leaves a sensual impression on the skin that may be enhanced or complemented by perfumes and other additional means of elaborating on a person's embodied appearance.

Dress is very important in Mali. Malian fabrications of textiles and dress constitute a veritable art form. Many Malians, even those with a low or irregular income, are ready to invest considerable sums of money into a new outfit to be worn on the next important social occasion. Dress and related modes of bodily adornment serve as important sources for the purposeful performance of a dignified and self-respecting social persona. Dress forms a highly valued domain of cultural creativity and individual inventiveness on the part of consumers and of those who fabricate dress and its constitutive elements—the tailors, dyers, and weavers. What matters importantly about dress is the way people don it, exhibit it, and walk and move with it. Regardless of the particulars of a dress cut, dress should be worn in a particular way, that is, with dignity and self-respect expressed through slow, self-constrained body movements and, for women, a controlled yet evocative movement of the torso.

The copious, beautifully ornamented, eye-catching costumes of men *and* women that are such a typical feature of everyday life in Mali accentuate the movement of the body and the dignified body posture taken as a sign of personal respectability. Dress can thus be seen as an extension of the body and of the bodily enactment of a certain social persona—of claiming personal status, a position within the family, with regard to one's immediate social entourage and vis-à-vis the society at large. The choice of a particular apparel, and specific forms of wearing it on the body and displaying it, are thus practices essential to the purposeful assertion—or disclaiming—of a social identity or political position. For this reason, sartorial choices and practices are deeply influenced by, and reflect back on, broader societal and political processes and debates. In Mali's urban and rural areas, dress practices are a principal mode of daily practice by which individuals, men and women, situate themselves within hierarchies of socioeconomic and status difference. The social message of dress practices is of particular significance during life-cycle ceremonies, such as baptizing and wedding celebrations, and other social events.

Not only dress but textiles, too, may carry important symbolic meaning. This applies to the fabric used for the standard, male and female ceremonial dress, the *dloki ba*. Regionally specific traditions of weaving, dyeing, and ornamentation style exist that endow a *dloki ba* made from this traditional fabric with particular meanings. The most widespread and well-known dyeing method in Mali is the one using the color indigo, made from the plant with the same name. Traditionally, other colors, too, were fabricated on plant basis. Today, the import of industrially produced dyeing colors has expanded the range of possibilities for ornamentation.

The symbolic meaning expressed through the texture, mode of ornamentation, colors, and shape of a cloth is also of primary import in the case of textiles traditionally fabricated for certain ritual contexts and purposes, such as life-cycle ceremonies. The shape, appearance, and aesthetics of these handmade textiles vary significantly from region to region and sometimes also with the ethnic identity of those who fabricate and wear them. Some significances of the cloth, and related styles of ornamentation, have changed over time, illustrating the active incorporation of new aesthetic influences and uses by artisan producers and by consumers.

Tie-dyed textiles are popular in several regions. The world-famous mud cloth (*bogolan*), made of handwoven cotton fabric, conventionally had ritual meanings and uses in the Bamana heartland of southern Mali before it became popularized as an emblem of authentic Malian culture (see chapter 4). In the Sahel and the northern regions of the country, textiles intended for ceremonial use are often woven of camel and sheep wool. Good examples are the Fulani wedding blankets, made of sheep wool and offered as a contribution to the dowry during wedding ceremonies.

Hand-painted textiles display patterns of ornamentation and designs that have specific names referring to events, proverbs, individual artists, or ritual purposes. Older ornamental patterns sometimes include numbers and letters in the Arabic or Roman alphabet, whereas more recently invented designs incorporate allusions to the industrial age and the world market, in the form of cars, trains, telephones, and dollar signs.

Conventional Dress Cuts and Styles

Most women and men in Mali have a clear preference for conventional, non-Western dress cuts and styles. Western-style pants, skirts, blouses, and other accessories are popular mostly among younger segments of the urban population.

The regionally diverse, conventional dress forms and styles in Mali have been subject to substantial change over the last 150 years. Thus, although one could label these dress forms as traditional dress, one needs to keep in mind that they do not express a timeless and unchanging custom but manifest the substantial social, political, and economic transformations effected by the different peoples of Mali since the late 19th century. Of particular relevance to the great regional diversity in dress style is the influence that different religious traditions, most notably Islam but also different local African religions and Christianity, had on standards of proper dress. In the northern regions of Mali (where Islam has been practiced by significant segments of the population for centuries), extensive body coverage, practiced in the form of loosely cut, expansive robes and trousers, has had a long history. In the southern areas of Mali, in contrast, Muslims constituted—if at all—a small urban minority for centuries. In towns with a significant Muslim presence, people had been acquainted with Muslim ideals of more extensive coverage, but they continued to dress more sparsely, very often covering only certain parts of the body. In addition to cotton fabric, they used raffia and other grass-based textiles for fabricating dress. In most rural areas of southern Mali, the transition from a relatively scanty body coverage (very often leaving the torso of both men and women naked) to extensive body concealment was closely tied to the Islamization process of the past 150 years. The influence of Christian missionary efforts on clothing practices remained limited to those areas where they established a significant presence. Body coverage, whether initiated under the influence of Muslims or Christians, came to be associated with a civilized outlook and education. These trends were reinforced under the influence of French colonial administration and the Western school system it established. The traditional outfits worn preferentially by many Malians today are thus a good illustration of the recent nature of seeming age-old cultural forms and traditions in Mali.

Many textiles of which these attires are made are imports from neighboring African countries, China, and Europe. Other textiles are the products of COMATEX (*Compagnie Malienne de Textiles*), a state-owned enterprise privatized in 1993. The most prestigious fabric is the *damas* or *bazin,* of which several qualities exist. The *bazin riche,* imported from Germany, has the highest value and prestige. Also popular among men, especially for dress worn on festive occasions and during ceremonies, are garments sown from the highly prestigious, locally produced cotton fabric made of multiple stripes of hand-spun and handwoven cloth. The various patterns of these textiles, achieved by different colors and arrangements of stripes, reveal regional and ethnic varieties.

The three most widespread types of male attire are these: First, the *dloki ba* (*Grand Boubou* in French), an often richly embroidered three-piece combination tailored out of 5 meters (ca. 16 feet) of cloth, which comprises loosely cut trousers, a men's shirt, and a poncho. This garment signals prestige, power, and wealth and is the preferential ceremonial dress for men. The second type of male attire is the *pipau,* a one-piece, ankle-length caftan. The third type, the communist (*le communiste*), consists of khaki-colored, Western-style trousers and a shirt with short sleeves. Modeled on the simple apparel of Chinese party functionaries, the communist was popularized by the political and administrative elite of Modibo Keita's socialist regime. A popular variant of the communist is the so-called three pockets (*trois poches*), a similarly cut combination of shirt and trousers. In contrast to the *pipau,* which, when made of low-quality fabric and lacking any ornamentation, may indicate the owner's low-class background (and minimal formal education), the communist and the three pockets are generally associated with a middle-class, Western-oriented, intellectual identity. Both variants are frequently worn by state officials as well as by teachers and university professors. Business suits are considerably less common among men than these three types of male dress. They are mostly worn by members of the political elite, lawyers, and businessmen who maintain commercial networks with the United States and Europe.

The social significance of a particular kind of male attire often emerges from the combination of different items and forms of adornment. For instance, the *pipau,* when combined with a cap and a long beard, signals the owner's specific Muslim identity—that is, his orientation toward and support of interpretations of Islam that are associated with Sunni-Salafi-inspired intellectual trends in the Arab-speaking Muslim world. It may also indicate the owner's identity as a (Muslim) businessman with connections to these areas of the Muslim world.

Women's attire encompasses a range of traditional outfits that follow standards of decent female dress and use industrial textiles, with varying degrees of elaboration. Western-style business suits do not enjoy great popularity; they are worn mostly by younger, unmarried women.

Women's outfits that demand greater expenditures are purchased mainly by urban middle-class women who receive a regular salary or can count on that of their husbands to cover their expenditures. Although lower-class women do not have the means to purchase such fancy outfits, they occasionally receive such a robe as a gift from friends or family members so that they, too, have a set of city clothes they may wear on festive occasions.

Of the different qualities of printed cotton of which many everyday female outfits are made, wax-print batiks (the *waxi*) imported from Nigeria and the Gambia are the most expensive ones. Cheap quality cotton is imported from

This woman is wearing a simple outfit made of imprinted cotton. (Courtesy of Ute Roeschenthaler.)

Germany, Holland, and, lately, China. The exact value of the fabric of a dress and of its degree of ornamentation is astutely discerned and eagerly discussed during their daily socializing activities by many women, who relate individual outfits to the owner's social status and economic position. In this way, women's selection of diverse dress elements allows them to claim, attribute, but also question social excellence and moral perfection.

Women who purchase the *bazin riche* for a dress make a special point to have it dyed according to their personal preferences, often after extensive discussions with friends and neighbors of the most fashionable colors. Since the 1980s, this high-prestige fabric has competed with the industrially dyed *bazin sinois* from China, which, because of its lower price, is frequently bought by low-income groups of Mali's urban and rural populations. But the *bazin riche* still enjoys greater prestige because of its superior quality and also because its dyeing leaves women with many possibilities to design a unique apparel by modifying color and style, often by borrowing from international fashion trends.

The most popular dress cuts for women are the *dloki ba,* a full-length, poncho-style robe, as well as different varieties of the camisole (*Grand Dakar*). Like male dress, the cut and ornamentation of these robes vary from region to region, but they are all combined with ankle-length wrappers. They are made of *bazin* or printed textiles and are worn by professional women, such as employees in the private sector, politicians, and high-ranking members of the state administration, whose enthusiasm for these dress cuts makes them differ from professional women in many other countries in East and West Africa. The latter have long since showed a preference for Western-style female dress (e.g., combinations of knee-length skirts and jackets). Still, even in Mali and in spite of the strong preferences for traditional dress cuts and forms of ornamentation, over the last 20 years there has been a notable turn toward the incorporation of various international and cosmopolitan dress styles and trends. This development is reflected in the growing popularity of fashion shows and beauty contests through which Western-style dress and also beauty ideals have become more predominant.

Another conventional, widely popular outfit among women is the combination (*combinaison* in French), which girls and women wear during their daily chores and which comprises a 2-meter-long (6.5 feet) square cloth (*pagne*) tied around the waist and a diversely cut blouse. The value of individual *combinaisons* and of other robes varies with the quality of the fabric and the ornamentation of the piece. Many dress cuts and embellishments are directly taken from the apparel of Malian female pop stars (or from soap opera heroines), whose televised performances and fancy display of recent fashion trends are eagerly followed by fashion-conscious urban women.

A combination (*combinaison*) is worn by professional women at work. (Photo by the author.)

Because women with lesser financial means cannot purchase costly and trendy outfits, donning an elaborate and high-priced robe serves to express high social status and economic power.

Turbans, which indicate a woman's married status, are popular items to manifest one's hip status and knowledge about the newest fashions.

Regardless of their diversity, women's dresses all respond to the norm that a woman should show self-respect by dressing properly, that is, by covering her body and concealing exact bodily contours. Most women do not doggedly conform to this standard of dress, but they make sure that their legs (and arms) are widely covered.

Breast-feeding women have no qualms about doing so in public; others like a large décolleté that allows them to casually expose their exquisitely shaped shoulders. Those who consider themselves as particularly fashion-conscious wrap their turbans in spectacular ways that, again, borrow from the appearances of Malian female pop stars.

All this shows that while dress is often measured according to the decency and dignity it might bestow on its owner, it is not the dress cut alone that counts but the ways in which a robe is worn and displayed. For numerous

Female dress typically worn by female farmers on everyday occasions. (Photo by the author.)

women, their wish to prove their sophistication by dressing exquisitely is so strong that they pay exorbitant fees that frequently exceed their income. Trendy outfits fetch prices starting at 20,000 CFA francs and going up to 200,000 CFA francs (1,000 CFA francs = U.S. $2.20, with a primary school teacher's monthly salary not exceeding 70,000 CFA francs). The sum of money that went into the fabrication of a dress often constitutes the object of considerable debate among women when they meet and socialize. Because only few women would be in a position to cover the expenses for such a sophisticated dress in their entirety, ownership of such a dress hints at the financial assistance a woman received from her husband, family members, or friends and thus, ultimately, at her social connectedness, popularity, and capacity to mobilize the support of others. In this fashion, fancy outfits allow women to claim amiability and social connectedness.

Among younger segments of the Malian population, especially among the urban youth, Western-style clothes have been highly popular since the 1960s. At that time, jeans and miniskirts were the rave of the day until their use was discouraged and even officially repressed in the later years of President

This kind of female dress requires more work and additional material and is therefore a costly affair. In this photo, it is worn by a woman attending a wedding celebration in town. (Photo by the author.)

Keita's rule. Since then, T-shirts with imprints of world-class soccer teams or pop stars, and Western-style (knee-length) skirts, pants, and blouses have continued to be highly cherished consumer items among girls, boys, and younger men in town. A striking illustration of their selective incorporation of Western-style dress is the enormous popularity that white wedding gowns enjoy among girls and young (unmarried) women (see chapter 6).

Over the last 15 years, certain dress items borrowed from the U.S.-European West, such as baggy trousers, large T-shirts, and baseball caps, have become emblematic consumer articles of a local, urban (mostly male) hip-hop culture. At present, many young consumers express subtle differences in status and cosmopolitan orientation through their preference of imports from Europe and the United States, as opposed to the cheaper, lower-quality imports from China. Their consumption practices reveal not a simple borrowing from or aping of Western forms of consumerism, but a selective appropriation of certain items and symbols in an attempt to construct for himself an identity as a modern, cosmopolitan, African consumer who remains connected to his own sources of cultural creativity.

Adornments

Embroidery is the most widespread form of ornamentation used for male and female dress. Additional forms of aesthetic elaboration may consist in beads or other materials sown onto garments. Traditions of embroidery in Mali go back as far as the 11th century. They show great regional specificity and variation, within the national borders of Mali and across West Africa. A typical factor of variation in embroidery patterns across West Africa is the use of colors. Soninke embroidery is particularly striking in its broad range of colors—a range made possible by the long-standing implication of Soninke merchants in trans-Sahara trade.

In the case of the *dloki ba,* embroidery often centers and elaborates on the neckline and décolleté. In the case of a male *dloki ba,* it also embellishes the contours of the breast pocket. Because embroidery is work-intensive yet also a particularly spectacular form of ornamentation, it is an enormous additional cost factor in the fabrication of an outfit. A copiously embroidered *dloki ba* is the sign par excellence of the owner's extraordinary spending power and conspicuous consumption. The richly embroidered *dloki ba* outfits of President Moussa Traoré and of people in his immediate entourage who sought to imitate his lavish spending are still legendary today. In popular memory, they are often contrasted with the far more modestly embroidered gowns of Traoré's successor, President Alpha Oumar Konaré.

Gold and silver jewelry worn in combination with a dress are also important means to impress on viewers a person's stylish self-presentation, attractiveness, and wealth. Different forms of jewelry can be easily associated with different ethnic or regional origins. In addition to their leather pendants, the Fulani, Moors, and Tuareg historically used silver pendants as a means of storing wealth. This custom changed dramatically with the periods of drought of the 1970s and 1980s, when many women and men were forced to sell their heirlooms. Among these rural populations today, semiprecious stones are a widespread form of pendants, which, however, do not bear the same symbolic and economic value. Necklaces, bracelets, rings, and earrings are highly popular among urban women. Here, the display of gold jewelry, purchased with the help of a suitor or given as a gift by a relative, serves as proof of the wearer's popularity, attractiveness, and social connectedness. Jewelry, rather than merely embellishing the surface of a person, helps bring out her inner qualities and social capabilities.

Other accessories worn along with a particular outfit are meant to cover parts of the body and to render it invisible. However, some of these items may look very spectacular and thus, paradoxically, attract enormous attention through the very fact of covering a body part. A striking illustration of this mix of concealment and heightened visible attraction is the headwrap or turban that a woman is required to wear in everyday life, so as to prove her status as a self-respecting woman who covers her hair. Many women are highly inventive with regard to the ways they tie their turban and often signal sophistication and worldliness by coming up with a new, spectacular outlook. Notable illustrations of this are the elaborate and trend-setting headwraps of the female pop stars who perform on national television and radio and whose innovative ways of tying their turbans are keenly commented upon and imitated by female consumers and fans. Other female dress accessories used for additional body coverage are the different head coverings used by strictly observant Muslims, such as the additional prayer shawl that they wrap around head and shoulders or the hair nets and caps that allow them to fully hide their hair. The male equivalent of these protective hair coverings is a cap whose specific shape and ornamentation shows its inspiration from the Moroccan fez. Men who wear this type of cap signal their identity as an observant Muslim. If worn in combination with a long beard and loosely cut trousers,

Especially in town, many women spend much time and energy on bodily adornment and on discussing the latest fads of the beauty industry. This photograph shows a typical shop where beauty and other toiletry articles for women are sold. (Photo by the author.)

Having one's hair braided is a time-intensive affair that, in the case of elaborate hairdos, may take an entire day. (Photo by the author.)

this cap indicates its owner's support of Sunni reformist understandings of Muslim religious practice.

Shoes and handbags, made of leather or richly decorated with plastic beads and gold and silver strings, are a must among fashionable urban women. Rural women only rarely use handbags (if at all); instead, they prefer to carry money by tying it into their wrappers. More voluminous items are often wrapped into a rectangular cloth and transported on one's head.

Traditional forms of body adornment meant to complete dress and accessories comprised various kinds and degrees of face scarification. In some ethnic groups, they were applied as permanent marks that often indicated an individuals' change in age and status. Today, certain of these traditional forms of body embellishment are practiced less and less. But other forms of bodily adornment, such as the application of elaborate drawings made on the basis of henna plant powder, continue to play an important role.

Ceremonial Dress

Dress made for ceremonial occasions often carries special symbolic weight. Its ceremonial use may consist exclusively in it being given as a gift, not in the

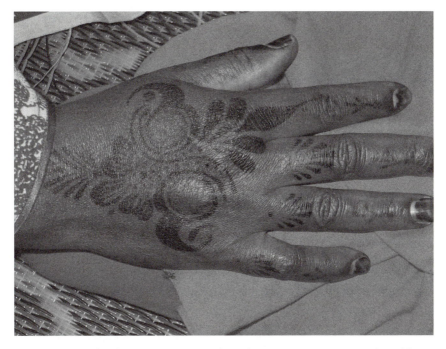

In preparation for festive occasions such as baptizing ceremonies and weddings, women like to embellish hands and feet with elaborate decorations for which the plant color henna is used. (Photo by the author.)

act of wearing it. Other dresses and dress accessories are made explicitly for ritual occasions. Good illustrations are some dress items worn by women who act as the ceremonial mothers of a bride during wedding ceremonies. Particular variants of the *dloki ba,* usually those made of hand-spun cotton ribbons dyed in white and blue, may also assume ceremonial functions during life-cycle ceremonies. Patterns of arranging these cotton stripes often hint at the specific regional and ethnic origin of a *dloki ba* and its ritual significance.

The shirts worn by the hunters in the Bamanakan- and Maninkakan-speaking societies of southern Mali illustrate the regional and ethnic specificity of ceremonial dress, its appearance, and its functions. Hunters wear these shirts during special ceremonies and gatherings. The shirts, made of white or mud-dyed cotton stripes sewn together with vertical seams, differ from ordinary shirts by the great number of ritual objects and materials that are attached to their surfaces and that are said to enhance their owners' powers to harness the occult forces of the wilderness the hunters are said to control. The fact that it would be dangerous for anyone else to don such a hunter's shirt shows that, in this case, the function of dress is purely ritual. With the commercialization of traditional textile production for an international tourist market, some dress items that were originally intended only for restricted, ritual use have lost much of their ethnic specificity as they have been turned into key emblems of a national, Malian culture.

Refashioned Traditional Fabrics and Dresses

Recent developments in national Malian fashion have led to a revalorization of fabrics and dress cuts conventionally associated with rural traditional dress styles. These developments have been strongly supported by a governmental politics aiming at promoting what it conceived of as key elements of traditional culture. The most successful example of the revalorization of traditional fabric was the undyed cotton fabric, made of woven cotton bands sewn together, and its variant, the mud cloth fabric *bogolan*. The origins of the *bogolan* are in the heartland of the Bamana ethnic group that occupied a central place in postindependent politics and in the evocation of a national identity and culture. As part of this cultural policy, dress items, fabrics, and styles associated with Bamana tradition have been presented as emblems of an authentic national identity and history.

Starting in the late 1980s, the *bogolan* also became famous in the international fashion scene. Decisive for the mud cloth's move to global celebrity was the creative work by the Malian fashion designer Chris Seydou. Since the early 1990s, while Seydou worked in Abidjan (Ivory Coast), his imaginative recombination of various, European-style robes and dress cuts with traditional African textiles, geometrical designs, and ornaments irreversibly changed the fashion scene in West Africa and also left a long-lasting imprint on productions by Parisian fashion houses. Until his precocious death in 1998, Seydou's efforts to revalue African materials and aesthetics by integrating them into a cosmopolitan consumer culture resonated well with the agenda of the ADEMA-party government of President Alpha Konaré (elected in 1992) that aimed at promoting and revalorizing Mali's authentic traditions. In the 1990s, during official ceremonies and holidays but also during the concerts of Malian music stars, *bogolan* costumes were often worn to mark the owner's pride in Mali's prestigious cultural heritage.

Thanks to Chris Seydou's efforts, the *bogolan*—which formed the emblematic cornerstone of his fashion—also became an essential element of an international authentically African dress style associated with the African American diaspora. Chris Seydou's inspired mix of African and occidental design allowed him to develop a characteristically African aesthetics in which various traditional fabrics as well as African-style decorations, colors, and dress types, were innovatively juxtaposed with fashion elements and industrially fabricated textiles (such as viscose, polyester, wool, and silk). Seydou thus re-made traditional *bogolan* into an emblematic element of a cosmopolitan African American identity, thereby prompting an unprecedented, international approval of this fabric that, until then, had been tied to the allegedly unchanging, traditional, and also somewhat primitive life in Mali's rural south.

Following the elevation of the *bogolan* to the status of an international fashion symbol, its links to its original social contexts, uses, and social significance became tenuous. By integrating the *bogolan* into international and national fashion industry, the locally specific, ritual meanings of the cloth were lost. In their stead, new symbolic content was associated with the *bogolan,* marking it as an authentically African textile that reflects the dignified identity of its owner as someone who is a sophisticated consumer and who, thanks to his spending power, partakes in an international fashion market.

Interestingly, Chris Seydou's *style bogolan* became a success among Malian consumers only after it had won wide acclaim in Dakar (Senegal) and Abidjan (Ivory Coast), the centers of the Francophone West African fashion scene that also serve as a hub to a global African American consumer market. The majority of consumers of *bogolan*-style dress items in Mali are from the upper-middle and middle classes in town.

Outside of Mali, *bogolan*-based African fashion has been exceedingly popular among cosmopolitan-minded West African professionals and intellectuals as well as among consumers of different socioeconomic backgrounds in the African diaspora. International commercial structures, and also media institutions and images, have played a decisive role in promoting *bogolan*-style fashion as a venue for asserting genuinely African emotional and aesthetic attachments. Malian aesthetics of dress and body adornment have thus become a driving force in a transnational fashion industry, to be staged and marveled at on the catwalks of New York, Brussels, London, and Paris.

6

Gender Roles, Marriage, and Family

Tella-hin tahit tazzar i-adar.
The foreleg always stays ahead of the hindleg.

—Tuareg proverb

Bamunanfini ye fila ye: bangebaga be min kè ka den ncininman bamu, ani den be min kè ka bangebaga kòròlen ta.
There are two kinds of cloth that help tie an individual to one's back: the one used by the mother to carry her child on her back, and the one that a child uses to carry his parents at an advanced age.

—Bamana proverb

THE FAMILY IS at the heart of Malian social life. Everyday routines are molded by values, ideas, practices, and discussions relating to the family. As is the case for Western industrial societies, the family in Mali is the central institution and site where relations between men and women and between members of different generations are regulated and expressed. However, whereas the symbolic and economic significance of the Malian family comes close to that of the family in many other cultures, the exact form it takes in Mali differs from the nuclear family model that has become predominant in the Western world since the 18th century.

PRINCIPLES OF FAMILY AND SOCIAL ORGANIZATION

Malian families are organized hierarchically in terms of gender, age, and generation. This means that the position, status, and rights of each family member are defined according to whether they are female or male, whether they belong to the generation of parents or of their children, and finally, whether they were born before or after their siblings. Closely related to this rule of Malian family organization is the principle of male gerontocracy: family authority and decision-making powers rest in the hands of the older generation of men, and the oldest brother of the older generation of men is the head of the extended family. The strong prerogatives of the older generation of men in traditional Malian societies manifest themselves in the fact that they decide on important family matters, such as the marriage of daughters and sons, and also on how the family income will be used and distributed. Their decision-making powers do not preclude, however, that older women often assume an important role behind the scenes in influencing family decisions.

Similar to the institution of the family in Western industrial societies, the exact form and internal organization of the Malian family is subject to regional variation and to changes over time. Hence, rather than representing an unchanging and static element of traditional Malian culture, the family in Mali illustrates the fluidity and variability of Malian family life across regions and different historical periods.

The prerogatives of older men, and their control over family decisions, have been weakened in the course of the last century under the effects of economic and political change. Among some rural populations, such as certain groups of Tuareg, Moors, and Fulani pastoralists, the traditional form and ideology of patriarchal family authority have suffered severely not only from ecological degradation and concomitant migration, but also from subsequent periods of political crises that turned numerous people in the north into (temporary) refugees starting in the early 1960s. The consequences of the 1963–64 bloody repression under Modibo Keita's government of the secessionist efforts of certain Kel Tamasheq groups not only meant that numerous family fathers were killed and that their wives had to replace them as household heads. For the families who survived, the destruction of their livestock by governmental troops meant that they had nothing left to live off. This prompted many people in the regions of Gao, Timbuktu, and Kidal to move to Mauritania, Niger, Algeria, and Libya. They were followed by others during the 1970s drought period. These migratory processes radically transformed power relations between men and women and also between the older generation and their children. In other areas, especially in towns, younger people and many women have gained a greater say in family decisions. In spite of these variations and qualifications, it is safe to say that in ideology— and, depending on the economic situation of a family and on its geographical location, also in practice—the opinion and decisions of the male household head remain very important.

In rural and urban courtyards, women of different generations live together and need to divide the daily household chores among themselves. (Photo by the author.)

Another feature that distinguishes many families in Mali from their Western counterparts is that they are polygynous, which means that a husband is simultaneously married to several wives. Malian family life is also organized around the rule of virilocality, which prescribes that after marriage, a woman will move to and reside in her husband's parental courtyard.

Among the rural and farming populations, the characteristic family form is the extended family comprising not just one father, one mother, and their children, but also the parents of the father as well as his different brothers and their wives and children. People of different generations, therefore, live together in one courtyard. A typical family courtyard in the countryside may host between 20 and 40 people. The situation is slightly different among peoples who lead a nomadic or seminomadic life. Still, even here, a family homestead often comprises more people than the nuclear family does in Western society. In town, many courtyards house extended families, too, but the overall tendency over the last 50 years has been toward smaller family units. Here, divisions and competition within the family translate more frequently into a visible, spatial segregation of the different wives' realms of domestic influence.

Courtyards are composed of different houses (*so* in Bamanakan) with two or three rooms (*bon* in Bamanakan) built by the husband to provide separate accommodations for each of his wives and a shared veranda. Ideally, women of the same house should use the same externally built kitchen by taking turns. They are responsible for cooking during the two days that their husband should sleep in their room at night. Whether the ideal of equally divided nights and a shared cooking space is put into practice very much depends on the relationship among the co-wives, a relationship that is often a result of their husband's (im)partial treatment. Because in rural society there is stronger social pressure to conform to this expectation, there are fewer occasions for the conflicting parties not to follow the norm.

Depending on the economic success of a family, rural courtyards vary in size, in the number of houses, and in the quality of infrastructure. Only a small number of courtyards comprise fewer than three houses. They either indicate a family's impoverishment in economic and human resources or constitute recent offspring of an old, much larger courtyard from which the new nuclear family left because of lack of space. Separate from the houses, most often in the middle of the courtyard, stands the most important symbol of family prosperity, cooperation, and joint submission to elderly authority and control: the granary in which the product of joint production on family fields is stored and redistributed by the family head. The granary is a small, round

Older women enjoy great respect and influence in most families, especially if they can rely on sons in family decisions and on their daughters-in-law for taking care of the daily household chores. (Photo by the author.)

hut covered with a traditional straw roof and a small entrance wide enough only for children to slip through and collect parts of the stored wealth. Chicken stalls and a fenced-off area, in which part of the family cattle is held, hint at a family's prosperity and capacity to quickly cash their livestock assets. Ownership of a donkey cart (*wòdròn* in Bamanakan) is another indicator of (if only moderate) economic standing. Enclosures of varying material separate courtyards from each other. Mud brick walls are more work-intensive yet are also efficient enclosures that connect the different houses or rooms of a courtyard and shield it from the sight of passersby. Enclosures made of wood are less work-intensive (yet, at least in town, also cost-intensive) forms of physical separation. Rudimentary forms of enclosure, or their complete absence, are among the most striking and appalling signs of a family's lack of means. They indicate a lack of regular income and the absence of support by migrant children.

Similar patterns of spatial arrangement exist in town—even if the size of the family has been reduced and a strict division of financial obligations and responsibilities (between the sexes and the generations) can no longer be realized. Only some families live in courtyards they own; they often accommodate remote relatives, foster children, and additional (paying) houseguests. In the lower-class neighborhoods of Bamako, courtyards are often large but are rented out to several families or individuals who live in separate rooms, often with between two and four people sleeping in a room of not more than 8 square meters (ca. 86 sq ft).

Marriage is of primary social and symbolic importance in Malian society. This is so because marriage allows a family to establish matrimonial alliances with other families and thus to extend its kinship ties or to reinforce already existing kin relations to another family. Marriage is also important because it sanctions the procreation of children and the formation of a new family unit within the extended family. Marriage thereby ensures the continuity and, as family members hope, the expansion of the extended family. Kin relations that emerge from the forming of matrimonial alliances are called affinal ties. In contrast, all kin relations that are based on birth (blood ties) are referred to as consanguineous relations.

CLAN AND DESCENT

Descent and ancestry have enormous symbolic and material weight in Malian society. The importance of ancestry comes out clearly in the great significance of a family's clan identity. Clan identity and clan membership refer to the fact that members of different branches (lineages) of a very large family network or tree trace their descent back to the same (often mythical) ancestor.

The name of a clan (that is, its patronym) and its identity often go hand in hand with certain food restrictions and also with rules regulating the interaction with members of other clans.

Similar to the dominant model of kinship reckoning in North America and Europe, ethnic groups in Mali classify their kin relations according to the patrilineal principle. This means that they trace their descent through the father (in contrast to a matrilineal kinship reckoning, in which descent is traced through the male members of the mother's family). The strong emphasis that Mali's different ethnic groups place on patrilineal kinship ties is coupled with a strong tendency to justify power inequalities between male and female family members by reference to a patriarchal gender ideology. Nevertheless, it is important to distinguish patrilinearity (a term that denotes a system of kinship reckoning, or tracing one's ancestry through the father) from the principle of patriarchy (which refers to the organization of power relations between men and women, indicating that men exert full authority in the family and in society). Moreover, it is important to keep in mind that wherever a patriarchal organization and justification of gender inequalities exist, this form of regulating gender relations is not pervasive. In Mali, it is frequently challenged by women, if only on an individual basis. Although many Malian men are certainly in charge of important, intrafamily and public negotiation and decision-making processes, adult women may also have a say in decisions, in particular if they can rely on their grown-up sons as informal channels of influence.

EXTRAFAMILY NETWORKS

The central symbolic and material significance of the family and the clan, as modes of organizing social life and economic production, is reflected in the existence of various cultural conventions that enable the inclusion of non-kin people into one's family. These extrafamilial social networking strategies rest on diverse practices of incorporation and association, such as patron-client relations, long-term affiliations between slaves and their former masters, and various modes of taking in other people's children or an (adult) stranger for foster care, adoption, or even marriage. The practices also comprise the use of classificatory kinship terms for non-kin, for instance, by respectfully referring to friends and strangers as older brothers or sisters and becoming the member of a certain clan by taking over its clan name and attendant ritual obligations and interdictions. All these practices and institutions allow people to extend their family ties based on blood and matrimonial alliances in flexible ways to include strangers and newcomers. For centuries, these different forms of making family ties and of actively creating kinship have given people inhabiting the area of present-day Mali enormous opportunities for geographical and social mobility. In turn, the characteristically high mobility of the Malian peoples has created a web of social relations and commercial networks based on—fictive and consanguine—kinship, matrimonial alliance, and common regional origin. These ties of social kinship crisscross the country and increasingly transcend national borders.

Other forms of extrafamilial networking consist in treating members of certain other clans as cousins with whom one exchanges standardized jokes and taunts. This practice is widespread among the peoples of southern Mali and referred to as a joking relationship (*senankuya* in Bamanakan). A joking relationship defines and sanctions relations of mutual reliance and connectivity between members of certain clans and sometimes also of different ethnic groups. Many Malians are convinced that joking relationships are important in helping to minimize ethnic strife in Mali because they grant a legitimate realm of mutual tease and ethnic stereotyping and thus offer a playful outlet for potential social antagonisms.

FAMILY AND HOUSEHOLD ECONOMIES

The family constitutes the basic unit of production in Mali. But the modes of production and income generation in town differ significantly from those pursued by sedentary and nomadic populations in Mali's rural areas. Even among the rural populations, the exact composition of a family and the organization of family production differ from one ethnic group and its residential patterns and mode of livelihood to another.

Among rural populations that engage primarily in subsistence farming and in cattle herding, children participate in the family production from early on, very similar to other rural societies in and outside of Africa. According to recent estimates, more than 50 percent of all children aged 10 to 14 help their parents in their daily subsistence production activities and, in town, in other income-generating activities.

In rural areas, women are not only responsible for food preparation, the care of children, cleaning, and water and wood supply. They also contribute importantly to agricultural production and, although to a lesser extent, to cattle herding. Men are more expressly associated with the realm of the wilderness and the area of agricultural production. In town, women are omnipresent in the streets and the market, but they preferentially go out in groups of married women or, in the case of girls, of peers, with the accompaniment of a younger male relative. A woman who shows an interest in being on her own raises deep suspicion. As expectations are strong and generally accepted that a decent woman should spend as little time as possible outside the family, it is relatively easy for a husband or mother-in-law to reprimand a woman for freely wandering around (*yaala* in Bamanakan), that is, for spending time outside the courtyard without any rationale, a reproach that implies the charge of promiscuity.

The Bamanakan- and Maninkakan-speaking farming populations of southern Mali are patrilineal and virilocal and live in nucleated villages. Their villages tend to be made up of different wards, each of them inhabited by members of a distinct lineage or of different social origins (that is, by freeborn or noble people, by socioprofessional specialists, or by descendants of slaves). Depending on the specific settlement history of a village or conglomeration of villages, the lineages are made up of one or several households, each of which constitutes an autonomous unit of production. Each household produces staple food on its collective field. All members of a household are expected to contribute to the cultivation, and everyone is entitled to the consumption of the jointly produced staple food that is stored in the family granary. Individual household members (such as married women and younger, unmarried men) may also cultivate additional crops on individual plots and earn an individual income from this labor. In addition to the consanguine and matrimonial ties that link the different households of a village, younger men, girls, and married women may also organize themselves in working groups to assist each other in the cultivation of their individual plots.

Among the Tuareg of Mali's north, too, long-standing social distinctions— but also divisions according to gender and age—play a role in regulating economic production, in a gender-specific distribution of tasks and functions, and also in establishing extrafamilial networks of work cooperation. The traditional distinction between people of freeborn or noble origin, people of a servile background, and professional specialists, such as blacksmiths, still constitutes an important element of social classification. People continue to frame the relations between people of different social birth as a matter of mutual dependence and as a form of patron-client relation between noble and freeborn Tuareg and their former slaves and other dependents. Herein are strong parallels to the system of social stratification and of legitimizing distinctive behavioral norms that characterize the different societies of southern Mali.

Historically, family life was organized according to the specific nomadic or sedentary lifestyles practiced by these different social strata of traditional Tuareg society. The specific kinds of services and goods that were—and are—exchanged among them reveal distinctive elements of a desert and oasis economy. They also reflect the interlocking of the sedentary and agricultural lifestyles of people of servile background with the nomadic livelihoods of their freeborn Tuareg masters. In the late 19th century and until the 1970s, people who lived at the oases were primarily of servile origin. The freeborn or noble Tuareg lived a nomadic life. They owned the majority of livestock, especially cattle and camels. They were entitled to receive a part of their clients' labor product that they harvested around oases. Nobles also had the right to access the oases and enjoyed certain privileges while being there, such as consuming the harvest of the date palms located in the oases gardens, where the people of servile origins cultivated millet and wheat. Groups of people of servile status and other clients practiced different degrees of nomadic and sedentary lifestyles. They engaged in domestic services, livestock herding activities, or gardening activities on behalf of their noble masters. Until the gradual breakdown of these arrangements during and following the droughts of the 1970s and 1980s, the noble Tuareg and their servile clients referred to these special privileges of the nobility, and the division of labor on which they were based, as a sharing of harvests, not as a tribute to be paid to the noble masters. Other groups of clients, such as blacksmiths, fabricated tools for everyday consumption and also provided services that required technical expertise or social negotiation skills. For instance, Tuareg women of noble origin considered it expedient to call on a blacksmith woman to style their hair and to perform important tasks during life-cycle rituals. In return, blacksmiths and other clients could approach their masters and legitimately ask them for a gift or material support given in the form of foodstuff. These donations of food constituted both material and symbolic gestures through which noble Tuaregs could display their social status and generosity vis-à-vis their dependents. Family life among the sedentary Tuareg populations was therefore organized in ways similar to those of the sedentary Bamana and Maninka populations of southern Mali, not only with respect to their agricultural production but also in their reliance on clients who specialized in tasks of social and political mediation and other services.

As a consequence of the political crises and droughts in the northern regions, Tuareg populations in the Kidal and Gao regions experienced drastic changes in their modes of livelihood and in intrafamilial repartition of responsibilities and work. The many women who had lost their husbands during the wars were forced to migrate to neighboring countries or to stay and engage in a daily struggle for family survival. Still today in the regions of Gao and Kidal, these women are single-household heads; they own a few sheep and goats and conduct small commerce from their homes.

For the Songhai population of the Gao region, the situation is similar. There are many women whose husbands migrated to Ghana and Libya after recent periods of low harvest and who alone are in charge of providing for their families. In their case, too, the social transformations triggered by recent ecological and economic crises have increased the responsibility and decision-making power of women, a change they very often experience as a burden rather than as empowerment.

A different model of intrafamily organization and of family subsistence production exists among the Fulani pastoralist groups in central Mali that have maintained a more or less traditional pastoral economy. Traditional Fulani society was composed of a tripartite social hierarchy comprising the freeborn or noble Fulani, socioprofessional specialists who worked as the clients of noble families, and finally people of servile status who were in charge of agriculture and other heavy manual labor. Fulani families of free descent were in charge of any work related to cattle, and their activities thus bestowed additional prestige on a freeborn or noble Fulani.

The Fulani pastoralists practice a seminomadic pattern of livelihood based on transhumant cattle keeping. The Fulani seminomadic lifestyle requires people to live in relatively small social units during most of the year. These households, run by older men, are the basic units of social, economic, and political life. Where this mode of organizing economic life is still intact, women play a central economic and social role, too, because they maintain the social networks that are indispensable for the great mobility of individual family units as well as for their transhumant mode of cattle keeping. The central place held traditionally by women in economic and social life was reflected in the existence of special, female-headed or women-centered economic units, the so-called hearthholds, the economic core of which consisted in women's control of the milk economy. Each hearthhold was of central importance to the social and material well-being of the members of a household. Because it served as a point of articulation between different spheres and forms of material transaction, for instance by regulating the circulation of material goods relating to marriage, the hearthhold and the women who sustained it were eminently important for the making of matrimonial ties and thus of kin relations.

The traditional Fulani pastoral economy has come under stress following the droughts of the 1970s and 1980s, forcing certain groups of Fulani pastoralists to minimize or even abandon their own geographical mobility and, though to a lesser degree, their transhumant cattle keeping. Cultivation is still considered degrading for freeborn Fulani. Yet most of them have become more dependent on their own agricultural production over the past decades, a development that supported these Fulani families' integration into, and dependence on, the market and cash economy. By the mid-1980s, more than 60 percent of the herds of the Fulani cattle owners of central Mali had perished. Fulani men felt compelled to switch increasingly to grain production to ensure their families' survival. These alterations in the social and economic organization of Fulani pastoralist livelihoods have affected women in ways that jeopardized their formerly central role in the making and maintenance of social networks. Because of the loss in cattle, the milk production on which pastoralist women once relied for their informal influence and networking activities dropped drastically. Women have lost a central source of material and symbolic power because they are no longer in a position to establish and maintain the social alliances that formerly tied different families together.

CHILDREN, YOUTH, AND SOCIALIZATION

As in other societies, adult men and women in Mali strive to raise their children in such a way that they come to respect certain moral values and rules of behavior. These core values and rules center on life in large households and the extended family, on the importance of tradition and family history, and on the role models provided by older family members, women and men. Sociability, solidarity, and respect for others are values that are highly cherished in a society where many people live together and interact in a spatially restricted realm. Children are taught to obey the directives of older family members, to treat their mothers with special respect, and to consider the interests of others in all kinds of daily settings and social interactions. These rules of behavior were—and are—often challenged by younger people, who do not embrace them wholeheartedly or without partly revising them. In this fashion, cultural values and rules that adults consider essential to the functioning and continuation of social and moral life are at once passed on to and partly reformulated by the next generation of (future) adults. Children and youth, in their readiness to learn but also to question values and rules, are therefore of crucial importance to the partial adaptation and perpetuation of traditions.

In traditional society, a number of institutions and practices aimed to socialize children into these values and rules and thus to gradually teach them the code of conduct necessary for becoming a fully responsible, adult member of society. Children would learn these rules while observing their parents and other grown-up relatives in everyday life. Occupational crafts, too, were learned through observation and learning by doing. In addition, there also existed specifically designated periods in childhood during which children between approximately 8 and 12 years old received special instruction. Traditionally, these periods of instruction, meant to prepare boys and girls for their future life as adult men and women, preceded the age of puberty. For several months, boys and girls led a secluded life (in same-sex groups) separated from the rest of village society. Very often, this preparation period ended with a special initiation ritual that in many societies of Mali is linked to female and male circumcision.

Children are considered the wealth and sign of social and economic success of a family. (Photo by the author.)

Schooling since colonial times and compulsory school education for girls and boys since independence have changed these traditional forms of learning and initiation for children, even if their school enrollment remains limited and numerous children, especially girls, never finish primary school. Circumcision continues to be widely practiced today, but very often, it is not tied to a preceding period of preparation and spatial segregation. Also, circumcision for girls now often happens at a very early age.

Because of children's important contribution to family economies, but also because opportunities are limited to find a job even with a formal school degree, many parents are reluctant to send their children to the modern school (modeled after the Western institution). These reservations and concerns are widespread among parents from the different farming and cattle-herding populations and from the urban lower classes. Parents' reticence is even greater with regard to girls' school education. Mothers expect their daughters to help them with their daily household chores. Many fathers see the advantages of schooling girls, but they also fear that by granting their daughters a certain level of education, they risk raising daughters whose independent-mindedness and willfulness minimize their desirability as marriage partners.

Because many parents in rural areas feel that Western school education produces boys and girls who no longer respect family authority and tradition, they prefer to send their children to traditional or reformed Islamic schools where, they feel, children learn to submit not only to God's will but also to the directives of family elders. Among the educated urban classes, in contrast, there exists strong awareness about the importance of granting their children education in a modern school. But because school education offers no guarantee for future employment, there are also many educated parents who consider an Islamic school education as a morally superior and thus more acceptable option of raising dutiful, disciplined, and fairly educated children.

Traditionally, youth marked a relatively limited period of in-between-ness for male and female adolescents. *Youth* referred to the period in which adolescents were no longer closely supervised by their fathers, mothers, and other older relatives and simultaneously lacked the credentials of full adulthood because they were not yet married and, for male juniors, had not yet received from their fathers the financial means for establishing an independent homestead through marriage. Over the past 30 years, the period of youth has come to stretch over a considerably longer period of time, especially for younger people in town. Since the structural adjustment measures of the mid-1980s, opportunities have been shrinking for young men in town to find employment, even if they learned a trade or obtained a higher educational degree. Their continued economic dependency on their parents makes it almost impossible to marry a woman and move out of the parents' courtyard and thus to establish themselves as independent adults. Conversely, girls and young women in town have great difficulties in finding a marriage partner. Only motherhood within a marriage makes a woman a complete moral persona. For this reason, female adolescents, too, are unable to meet the requirements for becoming a full-blown, adult member of society as long as they cannot get married. Many girls from the urban middle and lower-middle classes go to school and enjoy greater autonomy from the obligations toward their families. At the same time, they are afraid that they will be morally sanctioned by their relatives and neighbors for their striving after greater independence. Because love relations are built more easily but are of a more transient nature, many girls experience the current, more liberated life situation in town as precarious and threatening. Well aware of young men's difficulties to find an independent income, young women fear that they will end up without a husband able to offer them secure living conditions and an independent dwelling.[1]

Young women and men reflect on the dilemma in which they find themselves, and on the tensions between aspirations and restrictions, through different forms of cultural creativity and expression, such as songs that are in varying degrees inspired by traditional musical styles and international hip-hop music.

FAMILY DYNAMICS AND TRANSFORMATIONS

Because of the centrality of the family to the economic and social organization of Malian society, the structure and dynamics of family life reflect most clearly how the rules and customs regulating social life have been changing over the past hundred years. These changes have been triggered by the political and economic transformations effected under French colonial administration and by the attendant, gradual integration of Mali's peoples into an international market economy, following the forceful imposition of taxation under colonial and later postcolonial rule. Changes in the rules and customs regulating family life become particularly evident in three domains. One change relates to the forming and celebration of marriage and to the transfer of economic and symbolic goods required for the constitution of a successful marriage. The second kind of change affects the relations between men and women within a family and also the norms and ideals of masculinity and femininity that structure everyday interactions between female and male family members. Third, changes in family life also stand out starkly in the relations between family elders and the generation of their children. Already since the early 20th century, the relations between male elders and their sons have been strongly affected by the tendency among younger people to migrate—seasonally or for a number of years—to faraway places in the French colonial territories in search of paid labor to be able to cover the taxes imposed by the colonial administration. These different forms of labor migration have generated radical transformations in the economic basis of family production and reproduction.

Nowadays, many men from rural areas engage in labor migration, either during certain seasons or for several years. Until the late 1980s, they migrated to Bamako, Abidjan (Ivory Coast), Libreville (Gabon), and other industrial centers that offered lucrative wage-labor jobs. In recent years, these earlier routes of temporary labor migration have been partly abandoned in favor of younger men's (and increasingly younger women's) migration to Europe, especially to France, Belgium, Spain, and Italy.

The migrants use the income they earn for their personal needs but also to cover family expenses for marriage arrangements, education, taxation, and health expenses and to purchase agricultural equipment, dress items, and consumer goods such as bicycles and radio recorders. For this reason, the remittances sent home by these migrant workers have become an essential contribution to Malian household economies. Many rural families, especially those residing in remote areas that have suffered from prolonged periods of drought or from ecological degradation, depend strongly on the money their migrating children send back home on a more or less regular basis.

One implication of young men's money remittances is that they have significantly altered the authority divide between the older and younger generations. New intergenerational struggles have emerged over the control of the money generated by younger family members (who want to keep part of the money they earned), over marriage decisions, and also over occupational choices. Until recently, young men who migrated abroad in search of a lucrative job were often reluctant to return to the village and to take up the time- and labor-intensive work on family fields. Instead, they envisioned staying in town and making a living there. This tendency among young labor migrants has been reverted since the late 1980s with the shrinking of job opportunities in town and in overseas locations. Many young men are now ready to return home to their villages of origin and to initiate new cultivation strategies and crops. At the same time, these initiatives generate new conflicts with the generation of their parents.

All of this suggests that labor migration and the contributions of a younger generation of men (and of some women) to the survival of their family back home generate not only family wealth, but also new conflicts over the amount of money sent back and over its distribution and use. Most Malian families are thereby firmly integrated into a global economy of labor migration. Reversely, one can observe that the transnational networks that most Malian families maintain feed in complex ways into intrafamily and wider societal dynamics even in remote rural Mali.

MARRIAGE

Marriage, and the matrimonial alliances that issue from it, is among the most important institutions in Mali. Marriage allows members of a family to perpetuate and expand their kinship ties, through matrimonial alliances with other families and by adding new household units. Because marriage sanctions biological reproduction, it is in several respects foundational to the regeneration and growth of the lineage. Among the rural farming and cattle-herding populations, a family's prosperity was—and is—considered to manifest itself in plentiful offspring. Wealth in people, rather than wealth in material things, was the most desirable form of prosperity, partly because successful agricultural and livestock production depends on great manpower. Marriage is mandatory for any adult member of society. As much as a woman needs to have given birth to a child in order to be recognized as a proper woman, it is only marriage that confers respectability and status and sanctions childbearing.

Men, too, are expected to marry and procreate lest they be looked down upon and denigrated for their failure to become a family father.

Marriage in Mali differs from Western institutions of matrimony in several respects. In Western industrial societies, marriage refers to the union between two individuals, who in the majority of cases freely and deliberately chose each other as marriage partner and whose choice is informed by the ideal of a romantic relationship that emerged in 19th-century European bourgeois society. In Mali, in contrast, especially in more tradition-bound settings, marriage is first and foremost an alliance between two extended families (and lineages) whose heads agreed on uniting their children in matrimony. Even though arranged marriages are becoming less frequent in town, here, too, individuals most often give great consideration to the feelings and wishes of senior members of their extended family when it comes to choosing a marriage partner. A side effect of the strong influence of family elders on matrimonial arrangements is that in case of marital conflict, the support and intervention of the extended family become very important in stabilizing and preserving a marriage. For many women, this stabilizing influence is a double-edged sword. Marriage stability offers them security, yet those who wish to quit a burdensome marriage resent the strong pressure on the part of their parents to remain in it. Until recently, divorce was strongly discouraged, especially among agricultural populations, where it conferred a stigma on women, disqualifying them as quarrelsome and recalcitrant spouses. In town, family pressure to uphold a shaky marriage against all odds has lost influence over the past decades, which has led to a rise in the number of divorces. Even though the dissolution of marriage has gained broader acceptance, divorced women and men are still under enormous pressure to remarry.

The collective significance of a marriage, and of its stability and continuance, for the extended family comes out clearly in the role that senior family members (who are considered to represent the interests of the family vis-à-vis the outside world) play during marriage negotiations and the marriage ceremony itself and also in the resolution of conflicts that might emerge between the marriage partners or between them and their new in-laws. The identity of the daughter and male junior family member on whose betrothal the household heads agree is less important than the alliance between the two families. Romantic love and affection form the basis of a conjugal relationship mostly among the more educated classes of urban society. Among the rural populations, very often the future bride has been chosen not by the groom himself but by his father and uncles. Traditionally, age at first marriage used to be very early for girls, but it has been fixed by Malian state law at 15 (18 for boys). Although marriage without formal consent on the part of the bride has been rendered illegal by changes in national legislation, this practice is still widespread. This means that when family elders offer one of their daughters as a potential bride, neither the girl in question nor her mother are formally asked for their consent. Still, although household elders are in charge of finding a wife for a junior and of conducting the marriage negotiations, mothers may also play their part in initiating a successful marriage. Their role is usually invisible, effected through confidants who act as mediators and negotiators. The male household head who successfully asked another family for a bride for one of his junior family members will pay a bridewealth in return, to compensate the family for the working power they lost with the daughter they offered for marriage. Marriage is thus a multilayered material transaction conceived of by both parties as an exchange of a bride against material compensation. Another distinctive feature of marriage in Mali consists in the marriage procedure itself. Whereas in the West marriage refers to a singular and clearly identifiable event, in Malian society, the different steps, procedures, and negotiations that bring a marriage into existence may span years. Traditionally, the protracted nature of the marriage negotiations and act was considered normal and even purposefully cultivated because it helped sustain the image of a long-lasting friendship between the family of the wife-giver on one side and that of the wife-receiver on the other.

In each ethnic group in Mali, marriage rules and prohibitions exist. This means that—similar to Western industrial societies, in which a marriage between brother and sister is forbidden and a marriage between cousins of the first degree is strongly discouraged—matrimonial rules in Mali prescribe whom one may marry, whom one should marry preferentially, and with whom a marriage is prohibited. Among the rural Bamana populations, for instance, parallel cousins or children of a father's different co-wives are not allowed to marry. Nor are freeborn people expected to marry members of certain other ethnic groups or people of different social origin, such as descendants of former slaves (*jonw*) or of any group of socioprofessional specialists (*nyamakalaw*).

Traditionally, a household elder looking for a marriage partner for one of his junior men chose among a fixed number of families. Household heads usually explained their choice of a particular family as a matter of the long-standing relationship of trust and the mutual exchange of brides they had maintained with this family or lineage and because in the past, this family had produced well-educated, dutiful, and respectful future brides. Even today in rural areas, most families choose from a limited number of families with whom they feel to be on equal footing. These families may live in faraway villages, but regardless of the geographical distance, families from both villages will always stress their matrimonial proximity and kinship ties. Until a few decades ago, matrimonial alliances between two families worked through a delayed exchange of daughters. A family head who granted another family's request that it give a daughter away for marriage could expect that, at another time, its own asking for a bride would also be answered favorably. This certainty of long-term alliances and exchange has been altered over the last 50 years, along with the partial monetization of bridewealth.

Another significant difference between marriage in Mali and its Western equivalents is the form of matrimonial arrangement. Whereas monogamy is legally prescribed in Western societies, in Mali, marriages may be polygynous, which means that a man is legally entitled to take up to four wives in matrimony, provided that he received his wives' consent to a polygynous union. Polygyny in Mali follows Islamic legal and normative provisions that allow a husband to take up to four wives on condition that he treats them in an equitable manner. In traditional society, polygyny was considered a desirable option by many men because simultaneous marriage to several women would ensure numerous children, a goal many families aspired to. Still today in many rural and urban settings, the practice of polygyny is a symbol of status and wealth and a privilege reserved for wealthy men. Contrary to Western stereotypical assumptions, polygyny is practiced not only by uneducated people. It cuts across all socioeconomic hierarchies. Malians do not agree on the advantageous or reprehensible nature of polygyny. Many women, especially those leading rural livelihoods, point out that sharing the heavy burden of daily household chores with a co-wife has its virtues. Many other women, in contrast, feel that sharing a relatively circumscribed domestic space with another woman and her children is insupportable and that co-wives' competition over a husband's limited monetary means brings discord and distrust to family life. These women comply with polygyny only because norms and traditions, and the older women and men who enforce them, oblige them to accept their fate. Women's approval or disapproval of polygyny also depends on their own position within a polygynous marriage arrangement, that is, whether they are the first wife (who was usually chosen by family elders) or a second or third wife (who were often chosen by the husband himself according to his personal taste and affections). Neither do men agree on the value or desirability of a polygynous marital arrangement. Whereas some men point out that supporting several wives and their children puts too heavy a strain on their financial resources, other men are more insouciant about the material implications of creating another family cell by marrying a second, third, or fourth wife. Although Malian men and women are thus divided about the advantages, difficulties, and challenges related to polygyny, this marriage form is thriving, especially among the rural farming populations, where a polygynous household stands for prosperity and plentiful agricultural production.

Marriage in Mali may entail different marriage ceremonies that may be combined in a sequence. The customary marriage act consists of the exchange of kola nuts between the two heads of the two families. With the spread of Islam throughout the colonial period, this marriage act has in many areas become synonymous with the religious marriage involving the presence of a Muslim religious specialist. The civil marriage act, prescribed by the Malian state, is practiced mostly in urban areas and among some segments of the rural population. But even in town, men (some of them highly educated) may opt for a combination of the religious and civil marriage for their first wife and marry subsequent wives only through the religious marriage procedure (which is less costly yet bears all kinds of insecurities for women). In remote rural areas, most people only practice religious marriage rather than the civil marriage act. To them, the presence of members of the two extended families, and their formal participation in the exchange of kola nuts, is more important and binding than the formal marriage certificate provided by the state. For women, concluding an official marriage ceremony may bring important advantages because it allows them to claim financial support for their children in case of the dissolution of marriage. Yet only few women in rural areas have a chance (or the necessary level of education) to enforce their claims to a civil marriage and marriage certificate.

Considerable differences exist between the different ethnic groups when it comes to the regulation of the start of sexual intercourse in a marriage. Several ethnic groups require observation of a period of several years that should elapse between the customary or religious marriage ceremony and the arrival of the bride in her husband's homestead. Yet the marriage is often consummated soon after the religious marriage, and sexual relations are allowed during the waiting period. In this case, custom sanctions the groom's rights to visit the bride before he and she start cohabitation. Among the Tuareg of the Kidal and Gao regions, in contrast, the bride does not move to her husband's homestead and no rituals confirming the marriage alliance are performed until she has reached puberty. No sexual relations are allowed in the meantime, and it is very important that the bride is a virgin at the time of her marriage. Yet other ethnic groups traditionally performed the customary or religious marriage ceremony at an early age. Bride and groom would start living together at the same site of residence (that is, in the groom's courtyard), but the couple was not allowed to consummate the marriage until the bride reached puberty. Still today, the extreme vagueness of the concept of living together with a man allows parents to subvert the legal prescription of a minimum age for marriage.

BRIDEWEALTH

Traditionally, a marriage in Mali was only considered valid if a series of transactions were effected between the two families who were joined together in the matrimonial union. The family of the future groom was expected to deliver the bridewealth to the bride's family in exchange for receiving their daughter in matrimony. Depending on regional variations and ethnic specificities, these bridewealth gifts were rendered in the form of material objects—of kola nuts, agricultural products, animals, and money—and of labor performed by the future groom on the fields of his future wife's family. With the formal rendering of the first set of these donations, the marriage alliance between the two families was formally recognized and also made public knowledge. Following the initial transmission of gifts, the rest of the bridewealth had to be delivered annually until the wedding took place.

Although giving one's daughter away for marriage was—and is—tied to economic transactions, the economic dimensions of this exchange are generally downplayed. Rather, the two exchanging families highlight in their interaction that giving or receiving presents in exchange for a bride highlights her symbolic value as the future mother of children who will contribute to the prosperity of her husband's family. The bridewealth also serves as a guarantee for the stability of a marriage. Most wife-giving families (who received the bridewealth in exchange for their daughters) are reluctant—or unable—to return the gifts they received in case of a divorce. For this reason, the bride's family elders usually exert great pressure on the bride to remain in the marriage even if she does not get along with her husband or in-laws. In rural areas, most daughters who seek refuge at their parental home in times of marriage disputes are obliged or even forced to return to their in-laws' homestead.

Over the last hundred years, significant changes have occurred in the composition of bridewealth and in the amount of marriage payments, leading to a substantial inflation of bridewealth. These changes affect the procedures through which marriages are negotiated and made and also the stability of matrimonial alliances. Money forms a greater share of the bridewealth, and the amount itself to be offered in exchange for a wife has increased. Even in tradition-bound contexts, many families no longer keep to the families with whom they traditionally exchanged daughters and bridewealth. Nowadays, in a situation in which labor migration has become an important source of income and of prosperity for families in remote rural areas, household heads who seek a wife for one of their juniors among families with whom they used to exchange brides compete with wealthier suitors and families. Less prosperous households find themselves in a situation where their request of a bride will be rejected. Because the reliability of marriage alliances between families is no longer assured, some household heads seek to counteract this uncertainty by making their own offer of a daughter conditional on the promise of a future return of a bride for one of their own juniors. Also, because a major part of the bridewealth is now to be given in money, families discourage a delayed transmission of marriage gifts. This development implies that the exchange character of the marriage alliance has become more evident. Another side effect of the monetization of bridewealth is that extended families cannot act as guarantors of a marriage's stability to the same extent as they did before. Because many household heads now tend to prefer wealthy suitors over families to whom they traditionally entrusted their daughters for marriage, they have fewer possibilities for intervention and conflict mediation in case of marital disputes. Family heads risk losing some of their authority and influence in mending disagreements and in ensuring the continuity of marriage arrangements.

Bridewealth also still forms part of most marriage procedures in town. Yet in urban marriage transactions, the amount and form of prestations are often treated with greater flexibility, partly because many younger men lack (or renounce) the financial support of their extended family in these matters and are therefore not in a position to deliver the traditional bridewealth payments in full.

Historically, many ethnic traditions of Mali prescribed that women who survived their husbands were to be inherited by one of their husband's younger brothers. This practice of widow inheritance is commonly referred to as the levirate. The rationale for the levirate marriage was that it ensured that the deceased person's belongings would remain in their entirety with his extended family; it guaranteed the widow's material security, and also guaranteed that her offspring from her earlier marriage could be smoothly integrated into her husband's kin and homestead. A woman's remarriage with one of her husband's younger brothers sanctioned her new procreative union. It did not necessarily establish the new marriage partners as a new unit of production and consumption. Thus, depending on their new husband's financial situation and his readiness to take an additional wife, the inherited women and their children could find themselves in a financially more precarious position. In recent decades, the practice of widow inheritance has increasingly come under attack. Women's rights groups have struggled to eradicate the levirate marriage, arguing that a widow should be legally entitled to her husband's property rather than being inherited as part of his property. Also, with the AIDS epidemic and a growing awareness of the increased health risks involved in multiple sexual relationships, the government has initiated campaigns aiming to discourage or suppress the levirate marriage. So far, the success of these campaigns has not been evident.

GENDER ROLES AND CHANGING IDEALS
OF FEMININITY AND MASCULINITY

A woman's place (and that includes unmarried women and girls, too) is at home, within the confines of the courtyard, not out in the streets. Men, in contrast, legitimately move around in the outside realm in which politics and economic affairs are conducted. But women's confinement to the courtyard is not absolute, even in areas where a longer-standing influence of Islam may have reinforced the spatial separation of female and male realms of activity. Women's tasks in rural society render the realization of gender segregation more difficult there than in town.

The primary task of a woman is to be a good wife and mother; her social success and moral exemplariness are said to be reflected in her children's success in life. Central to a woman's reputation is propriety in conduct vis-à-vis non-kin males and her elders. Mothers frequently admonish their daughters that a girl should preserve the family's honor by acting respectably. Norms of propriety apply double standards as they blame women for arousing sexual fantasies in men while men are considered to be sexually predatory by nature. However, men, too, are punished for committing adultery—and often more severely than women.

The other side of the coin of the strong expectations toward women is that whenever a woman acquiesces to norms of female behavior, she may exercise considerable influence once her children have grown up. It is only at a very advanced age that women finally identify (and are identified) with their husband's house. The practice of virilocality may be one reason for young women's initial lack of identification with their in-laws. Their daily, often emotionally charged and burdensome interaction with senior in-laws (such as the mother-in-law and the husband's older brothers' wives) gives young wives initially very little incentive to feel at home. In case of divorce, she will have to return to her parents' home while leaving her children behind. The considerable weight in family decisions that women may acquire is a function and the result of their gradual identification with their in-laws in the course of their career as a wife. As a mother, a woman is expected to create an atmosphere of solidarity and mutual understanding and to establish ties of empathy and trust between her and her children. Because of these relations of affection and beneficial mutual dependence, a woman will ultimately exert influence over and through her children. Her influence is felt strongly both in the realm of family socializing and in the bedroom. Most of the time, a woman's informal influence is paired with a submissive attitude toward her husband and senior in-laws whenever they interact in more public or visible arenas of family life. Thus, while patriarchal norms of female propriety render a woman an easy target for admonition and repression, acquiescence to these standards may become a source of influence.

Among the rural agricultural and cattle-herding populations, women have the opportunity to gain an independent income. Marriage endows women with the rights to livestock and with access to small, individual plots on which to cultivate peanuts, cotton, vegetables, and ingredients for the daily meal; marriage also gives them the right to claim labor support from their male in-laws, sometimes also from their own male relatives. Some women grow vegetables in individually owned gardens located inside the courtyard or at other spots with sufficient water supply. Men should provide the staple food (mostly millet, in some areas rice and maize) cultivated on the family fields, as well as (occasionally) meat or fish. No husband has the right to access his wife's personal budget or labor product.

Among the middle classes in town, the husband is expected to come up with all the expenses of the family, including food, clothing, rent, and the payment of articles of everyday consumption. Women and men cite popular adages that invoke the image of a husband who makes the family live by bringing home every month the necessary sacks of rice or other staple food and provides his wives with the daily allowance, the price of the sauce (see chapter 5). Women are expected, yet not obliged, to find some sources of additional income to satisfy their and their children's needs. This division of responsibilities between spouses is an ideal to which men *and* women aspire. Whether they are capable of meeting the norm depends as much on individual factors, choices, and necessities as on external circumstances on which they have little or no influence. Many couples from the middle classes manage to realize the ideal, even though to varying degrees. But with the implementation of the Structural Adjustment measures in the mid-1980s, men's chances of earning a regular income grew smaller than before. As a consequence of the shrinking of the public sector and of the lack of income sources in the formal economy, heads of formerly comparatively prosperous families are no longer capable of living up to the ideal of the main provider. These changes affect common views of male responsibility and traditional ideals of masculinity and femininity.

As many men face a lack of opportunities for securing family livelihood, women are forced to expand their activities outside the ideal realm of female activities. Especially among the lower urban strata, women's financial responsibilities have increased enormously. More and more women turn into the main breadwinners and thus become de facto female household heads.

Women wrestle with the strong normative pressure put upon them by seniors and the social entourage to conform to conventional standards of female obedience and decency. What remain central to the symbolic construction of female identity are a woman's powers of procreation. But because of the shifts in the division of obligations between men and women and between the generations, conventional standards of femininity and masculinity have come under attack; they are subject to contestation, debate, and reformulation.

Regardless of the various challenges that the social and economic transformations of the last decades have brought for Malian family life, and in spite of the new struggles between male and female household members on which these transformations reflect, Malians remain attached to what they consider core social and moral values. They endorse rules of sociability and solidarity and, by emphasizing both the dignity of advanced age and the potential of youthfulness, constantly re-create the foundations for a promising future of Malian society.

NOTE

1. Dorothea E. Schulz, "Music Videos and the Effeminate Vices of Urban Culture in Mali," *Africa* 71, no. 3 (2001): 345–72.

7

Social Customs and Lifestyle

Dinye ye baro ye.
The world is (made by) conversation.

—Bamana proverb

Zanka kan mama lamba dottiijey ga si du ndunnya bayrey.
The child who does not spend time with adult people will not be able to learn (from them).

—Songhai proverb

MOST MALIANS LOVE to socialize. They enjoy hanging out together and spending major chunks of everyday life in each other's company while chatting about recent happenings and future projects, about common aspirations and individual concerns. Malians celebrate family ceremonies, religious festivals, and cultural events with great zest and energy. These events bring people together and allow them to experience sociability and commonality. Friendly and cheerful forms of interaction are highly valued and widely practiced, and people generally treat each other in open, warm, and welcoming ways. Open criticism, direct confrontation, and a straightforward rejection of friendship gestures and entreaties are avoided because these behaviors are feared to create bad feelings and thus to undermine friendship ties and family solidarity. People cultivate playful and joking ways of interacting with people whom they consider to be equal or inferior in status and also with some people whose status superiority commands respect and reserve, such as grandparents and certain other persons of advanced age and authority.

Their great esteem of the values of sociability, solidarity, and reciprocity comes out in everyday life, in the form of mutual visits and invitations, and also on extraordinary occasions such as festive events and community celebrations. Norms of politeness and friendliness are daily put into practice, for instance in the elaborate formula by which people address and greet each other and inquire after the well-being of each family member and of common acquaintances.

Sociability is combined with an elaborate culture of orality. To be sociable means to engage in conversation with others. Good speakers are highly cherished. They are measured by their capacity to spice up their talk with proverbs, metaphors, and onomatopoeic expressions—that is, with expressions whose sound captures some characteristics of the word they designate (such as the Bamana term *munumunu*, to prevaricate). Most people love to engage in debate, whether with family members or friends at home or with complete strangers in public settings, such as marketplaces, buses, and collective taxis. While they might freely address certain topics with people they may have never met before, other topics are hardly broached in conversation except among intimate friends. Establishing physical closeness and direct bodily contact is not discouraged or resented in public places, but personal intimacy and all matters touching on an individual's sexual life are highly protected. It is considered to be extremely impolite and to reveal a person's lack of good breeding if he or she breaches these boundaries of privacy and intimacy in any way, even by just talking about it.

SOCIAL RELATIONS AND INTERACTIONS

The great importance of community and family life, and of an active cultivation of friendship ties, comes out in daily interaction and during the many celebrations that punctuate the different seasons and family life. Closeness and friendship are created and expressed through regular mutual visits that are framed as frequenting and greeting one another. Such a courtesy visit may not last long, with visitors and hosts sitting down and chatting for barely 10 minutes. What matters is not the length of a stay but that each conversation partner finds the time to politely inquire after family members and friends and to deliver the greetings and wishes for well-being a third party might have asked her to transmit. Such a courtesy visit should be reciprocated by the host on another occasion. But as a first gesture of reconnaissance and gratitude, the host will accompany the visitor on her way back by "showing her the way". All these different gestures of reciprocity and sharing underline and create a sense of mutual obligation and empathy, attitudes deemed characteristic of true friendship and of lived, effective kinship ties.

Although one could expect that the recent spread of new communication technologies and formats, such as the mobile telephone and interactive media modalities such as Facebook, has weakened the stress people place on frequent mutual visits, this has not been the case so far. Quite to the contrary: rather than undermining the nurturing of family and friendship ties through frequent interaction, cell phones and interactive Internet formats simply recombine these physical visits with mediated forms of frequenting each other. Whereas before people paid each other surprise visits and could be easily disappointed about their host's absence from home, nowadays people may call beforehand to make sure their hosts will stay put at home. In this respect, the use of cell phones for the purpose of sustaining sociability and friendship is a good illustration of a case in which new media technologies do not disrupt existing forms and values of social interaction but instead serve to strengthen and perpetuate these practices.

Apart from paying mutual visits to each other, people engage in other conventions of socializing beyond the family. In town and in the countryside, friendship is importantly created and maintained through the regular giving and receiving of gifts. Even small donations give friends an opportunity to show off their willingness to share and to reciprocate. In town, quite a number of men (more so than girls and women, who often do not have the time because of their daily household chores) go to another neighborhood at a regular, often daily, basis to spend afternoons or early evenings together with a fixed group of friends. Such a group (the *grin* in Bamanakan) meets always at the same place, in front of a courtyard, shop, or market stand (in the case of men) or in a group member's courtyard (in the case of women). For many unemployed men, this is the place where they spend almost their entire day. It is here that the most important events are discussed. Friends tell each other snippets of scandals and the latest conflicts in the neighborhood, discuss the triumphs of their favorite film actor or pop star, and inform each other about opportunities to find a job. These gatherings also provide room to address family problems and romantic entanglements and to ask friends for their advice on these matters.[1]

For adult women, meeting a group of friends on a daily basis is impossible. But they meet in various kinds of groups (in Bamanakan, *benkadi*), all of which are intended for mutual material and moral support. Among the agricultural populations, women come together in working groups (singular, *ton* in Bamanakan) to help each other cultivate their individual plots of lands. A similar kind of collective working group also exists for young men. In town, the group structures in which women meet have become more diverse, but some characteristics of these groups, such as the principles of solidarity and reciprocity on which they are based, draw directly on their rural counterparts. Since the 1980s, with diminishing opportunities for income generation in town, many women have created credit savings associations. Each member has to pay a monthly (sometimes weekly) fee, and the total of these savings is given in turn to each group member as a starting capital for a new business initiative. The groups in which Muslim women meet to acquire Arabic literacy and basic knowledge about Islamic ritual are another instance of these associations. Group members offer each other moral and also material support in times of crisis and keep each other company at important social and family events. All these rural and urban associations allow group members to realize highly cherished values of solidarity and reciprocity. Even if the groups differ with respect to their goals and agendas, they offer members occasions to meet, to integrate themselves into networks of gift-giving, and to discuss with equal-minded women whatever is on their mind.

CEREMONIES

Ways of celebrating festive events in contemporary Malian society follow a basic distinction between religious holidays and mundane, nonreligious occasions for celebration. This distinction is the outcome of recent historical transformations. It is mostly the result of the spread of Islam in the colonial period and a concomitant, greater political influence of Muslim religious experts and of observant Muslims. Whereas before the distinction between religious and nonreligious events was of minor relevance, now Muslim religious celebrations and entertainment (*njanaje* in Bamanakan) are framed as mutually exclusive opposites. But this contrast does not preclude that elements of entertainment, such as song and dance, have become integrated into the Muslim ritual calendar and revalorized as religiously acceptable forms of venerating God and lauding the Prophet Muhammad. Another result of the separation of religious from nonreligious celebrations is that certain elements of traditional ritual performances, such as particular drumming patterns formerly associated with rituals of initiation societies (see chapter 4), have been readapted to mundane contexts. They have been integrated, in modified form, into public concerts, performances, and celebrations, such as those performed by the youth associations.

Ceremonies are rituals aiming at the marking and celebration of events that are of importance to an individual, a family, or an entire community. Most ceremonies are composed of several ritual acts that need to be performed in a fixed sequence of procedures. In some cases, the different rituals do not take place on one occasion but stretch over a period of several weeks, months, or even years.

The different peoples of Mali celebrate a range of family ceremonies. These ceremonies serve a family to mark and celebrate the different stages each individual member reaches in the course of his or her lifetime. Important steps in a life cycle are birth (marked by, among other rituals, a name-giving ceremony), the passage from childhood to adolescence (very often marked by special initiation rituals, see chapter 5), and the passage from adolescence to adulthood. The last step is usually effected and celebrated through several rituals, among them marriage and the celebration of the birth of the first child. Another final, important step is death, celebrated by funerary rituals that serve the mourning and commemoration of the deceased person and remind family and community members of key cultural values and beliefs they all share. Each of these ceremonies and rituals offers, in varying degrees, an occasion for social celebration and enjoyment. Depending on a family's political status and economic standing, the ceremonies differ in expenditure and elaborateness and also with respect to the number of people they attract for joint celebration.

Name-Giving Ceremonies

Compared to other life-cycle rituals, name-giving ceremonies tend to be celebrated in less elaborate ways. All over Mali, name-giving ceremonies are shaped by the relative simplicity of the Muslim name-giving ritual. Men meet early in the morning for the name-giving ritual proper and to keep the father and male relatives of the newborn child company. Women usually arrive a few hours later; they spend the rest of the day together with the women of the household, chatting, comparing outfits, and consuming lots of soft drinks and food. The atmosphere is joyful, and the air is filled with laughter and smells of deliciously cooked food. All in all, name-giving ceremonies are an important occasion for socializing and for showing social support and connectedness by celebrating together with those into whose family the child was born. Except for the food the host family provides, this ceremony tends not to be overly costly.

Weddings

Wedding ceremonies, in contrast, are very often an expensive affair—for anyone involved. Invitees and visitors may come from far away to greet the two families who enter into matrimonial alliance and to offer lavish gifts, to bestow prestige on the host families and on themselves as generous friends and family members.

Depending on regional and ethnic specificities, and also on the rural or urban environment in which the wedding ceremony is held, different kinds

Wedding ceremonies in town are often elaborate and costly affairs. Equipment needs to be rented to provide sitting space for guests, and in addition, musicians are hired for entertainment. Much of the celebration takes place outside the courtyard, in the streets. (Photo by the author.)

of weddings and different forms of attire and adornment are privileged. Traditional and religious marriage ceremonies (see chapter 5) are rather modest in expenditure. Rural weddings may be a costly affair, with most of the expenditure being spent on the food and entertainment offered to guests. Very little money will be invested in the bride's wedding gown and other consumer accessories. In town, in contrast, weddings increasingly reflect the influence of Western ceremonial conventions. The bride is expected to appear in a white gown, to drive to the civil marriage in a luxury car, and to have many photographs taken of her, as well as of her guests, which will be arranged in albums and distributed to friends and family. In addition to these relatively novel stylistic elements of urban wedding ceremonies, they also draw strongly on traditional conventions. Most notably, the families of the bride and groom will invite family praise singers to laud the accomplishments of the hosts and also to present to guests and the wider public the money and other gifts offered by each family member to the newlywed couple. For this work, family praise singers can expect to receive a generous recompense. But there are also other praise singers who show up on this occasion without being invited, knowing well that praise performances during wedding events are a highly lucrative activity, partly because those on whom the praise is bestowed can hardly refuse to compensate the singer accordingly without risking being shamed for his or her stinginess. It is first and foremost this traditional element of Malian wedding ceremonies—the public praise by specialists of the spoken word—that makes these occasions financially burdensome.

As a consequence, and because of the mix of conventional and foreign-imported elements of urban wedding ceremonies, they have become a very costly affair that creates a headache for many families in town, who risk losing all their savings with this single family feast. But people also welcome these elaborate wedding celebrations because they offer a prime occasion for families to show off their generosity and social connectedness, by inviting many people and hosting them bigheartedly. For weeks after the event, friends and family members who attended the ceremony will discuss details of the ceremony and whether the families of the bride and groom showed sufficient hospitality. The wedding event in itself offers ample opportunities for invitees, women and men, to socialize and to exchange the latest family news and gossip. For women, it is also a prime occasion to show off accomplishment, taste, and economic success by parading the most elaborate dresses in front of other women. A popular pastime among women is to discuss at great length the gowns worn by invitees of particular social standing and compare their own outfits to those of friends and competitors. Weddings thus constitute a core social event in multiple respects. Because weddings are of central import to a family's reputation, video recordings are made of the different steps of the wedding ceremony, in which the gifts and expenditure are presented to public scrutiny and assessment. These video recordings, as well as photographs, are sent to friends and family members who live abroad—in other West African countries, France, and North America—so as to allow them to participate in the event. These migrants, by watching the wedding video recordings, can partake, if only retrospectively, in the actual wedding event and assess whether the families of the bride and the groom lived up to common expectations by making lavish gestures of hospitality. In this fashion, video recordings of weddings help foster and expand family and other social ties beyond national boundaries.

Funerals

Funerals constitute less joyful but similarly important occasions for the celebration of a family's standing in the local community and social connectedness. In the past, prior to the spread of Islam to remote areas where traditional religions and beliefs in an animated natural world were predominant, funerary rites marked the first step toward gradually transforming the deceased person into an ancestor to be venerated on regular occasions. These rites were also important occasions for affirming a family's social and political standing. In most areas of contemporary Mali, in contrast, funerary practices are strongly inflected by the relatively sober and modest Muslim rites. But the burial proper may be surrounded by other rituals and events that serve to celebrate the wealth and eminent position not only of the deceased person herself but also of her extended family. If a person dies at an advanced age and comes from a highly respected family, her funeral may give occasion to a major ceremonial event of which people in the area will continue to talk for weeks.

Community Ceremonies

Community ceremonies often take the form of annual events, such as town festivals and harvest celebrations. Some community celebrations are marked by special masquerades and dance performances. Others center on activities related to the changes in season. A good example of this is the Sanké Mô, the annual town festival in San, a town of approximately 25,000 inhabitants in southeastern Mali. The festival is held each June. It revolves around a big fishing feast in which the entire population partakes to empty a large pond located near town. While the occasion for the festival appears rather mundane, the feast also helps commemorate the mythical origins of the town's three sacred sites: the fish pond (Sanké), the sacred forest (Santoro), and the sacred well (Karantela).

Another famous instance of community celebrations that allow populations to articulate locally specific cultural identities and histories is the Camel Race (Course des Chameaux) and Tende dance festivities organized by Tuareg groups in the regions of Gao and Kidal.

A third example of a widely known local community celebration centering on a mundane practice takes place in Djenné, whose population comes together each year after the rainy season to repair the mosque by covering its facade with a new layer of mud (see chapter 4).

Festivals such as these bear deep social and moral significance for townspeople because they allow them to experience themselves as members of a broader collectivity. Cultural performances held during these festivals are highly cherished because they integrate the broader audiences in a shared framework of values and aesthetic standards.

Some of these festivals have been elevated to the status of a national cultural heritage or, as in the case of the Sanké Mô of San, to that of a UNESCO immaterial cultural heritage.

NATIONAL AND RELIGIOUS HOLIDAYS

There exist a number of religious and state holidays that are celebrated nationally. But as a rule, national holidays are respected in town and in the city rather than in rural areas, where people care little about most secular holidays. Among the most important secular national holidays are New Year's Day, Armed Forces' Day (January 20), Day of Democracy (March 26, celebrating the end of single-party rule), and Independence Day (September 22). Depending on their Muslim or Christian faith, people also celebrate a number of religious holidays. In spite of the small number of Christians, holidays such as Christmas and Easter are commonly recognized as days of special celebration. Because of the Muslim lunar calendar, Muslim holidays do not have a fixed date but move through the year. Among the most important Muslim holidays in Mali are the Mawlud, the celebration of the birthday of the Prophet Muhammad; and the holy fasting month of Ramadan, a period of a moon's cycle during which an observant Muslim is not allowed to eat and drink during the day but is expected to engage in contemplation and supplementary prayer to venerate God and His will. In spite of this devotional intent of the fasting month, it is also a time of great celebration, so normal business hours may not be respected. Because people are allowed to eat only after sunset and before the sun rises again, evenings, nights, and early morning are the time for family celebration and the consumption of great quantities of (often sugary) food. The lunar month of Ramadan ends with the holiday Eid al-Fitr (*zelicinin* in Bamanakan). At times there have been public debates, as in the 1980s and 1990s, about whether restaurants and bars should be kept closed during the entire fasting month, a regulation that would contradict the secular constitution of Mali. The most important Muslim religious holiday in Mali is the Eid al-Adha (in Bamanakan, *zeliba,* literally "the big holiday"). On this day, the global community of Muslims (the *umma*) celebrates worldwide the end of the sacred pilgrimage to Mecca by slaughtering a sheep or lesser animal, in commemoration of Abraham's willingness to submit (the literal meaning of *islam*) to God's will and to sacrifice his son on His behest. On that day, everywhere in town, especially around the main mosque, special communal prayers are organized.

In towns where Muslim religious specialists have had a long-standing presence and enjoyed important political influence, tombs of particularly pious men and women have become centers of regional pilgrimage. People flock to these tombs from everywhere to venerate the holy men and women, to partake in the divinely granted, special blessings (*baraka*) of these "friends of God" (the literal meaning of the Arabic term *wali,* which is applied to these saintly figures) by touching the tomb and other objects associated with these persons and to ask them for their intercession to implore God to grant them their deepest wishes, such as success in business ventures, children (in case of barrenness), or a faithful husband. Although pilgrims may visit the tombs any time of the year, some pilgrimages are tied to specific dates, such as the commemoration of the death of the saint who rests at the burial site.

CHANGING LEISURE: AMUSEMENTS, CULTURAL FESTIVALS, AND SPORTS

In many rural areas but also in town, people enjoy storytelling and plays and speeches held at night. During the dry season, when most agricultural activities have stopped, villagers draw great pleasure from the occasional visits of traveling musicians and storytellers, some of whom belong to the socioprofessional specialists who constitute a separate, endogamous group (meaning that they only marry among each other) in most ethnic groups. Other traveling musicians perform the music of the hunters' associations (see chapter 3). Storytellers relate stories that use human beings, animals, and fairies to teach moral lessons and important cultural values. Good storytellers are able to sustain excitement and attention by including many metaphors and colorful expressions into their narration and also by inserting many narrative turns and twists into the stories they relate. People will listen to them for hours, sometimes until the early morning. Wherever the ambulant musicians and storytellers arrive, they will stay with the village's richest and most influential families, who will take special pride in hosting them generously. Depending on how they are received, the musicians and storytellers will stay for a few days, a week, or even a month and provide entertainment at night, in exchange for food, shelter, and also gifts in grain and cattle. These visits by traveling musicians draw on long-standing structures of patronage that go back to times prior to the French colonization in the second half of the 19th century.

In town and its surrounding areas, people's enthusiasm for oral performances and for listening to them has been transposed to a new medium, radio broadcasting technology. Special programs have been developed on local radio in which stories originally written for and published in newspapers are retold by radio speakers in more elaborate and embellished form. People greatly enjoy listening to these stories and sometimes take such pleasure in a particular story that they request the radio station to broadcast it over and over again.

Since Mali's independence in 1960, its subsequent governments have regularly organized national cultural festivals. The most important of these, the biannual Youth Cultural Festival (Festival de la Jeunesse), brought together young singers, dancers, instrumentalists, and other performers from all the country's regions to compete for the prize of the best regional performance group. The winner was then to move on to a pan-African cultural festival, organized in different countries of the continent. Mali's governments, especially the first single-party government of President Keita, also participated in cultural exchange programs with countries outside of Africa. Still today, musicians and dancers who were once participants in this cultural exchange remember with great fondness these trips to foreign countries and the new inspiration they drew from their encounter with foreign performance conventions.

Since the privatization of the market of cultural and musical production in the early 1990s that followed the end of President Traoré's single-party rule, state funding for national festivals has dried up. At present, several acclaimed cultural festivals are organized by international private enterprises and sponsor structures. Among them are the Festival on the Sand Dunes (Festival sur les Dunes), which takes place every year in the desert near Timbuktu, and the Festival on the River Niger (Festival sur le Niger), organized annually in Segu. World-famous artists perform at these international festivals, but entrance fees are so exorbitantly high that only Malians of relatively privileged economic background have a chance to attend. Apart from these international, high-profile festivals that visitors from all over the world attend, there are many smaller music festivals designed more specifically for Malian audiences and tastes (see chapter 8).

While television is the most important element of evening and weekend relaxation, cinema also has its place in urban leisure-time activities. Although the country prides itself in counting among its ranks several internationally renowned moviemakers (see chapter 3), the consumption of their movies by Malian audiences has been very limited. Partly because of the high entrance fees requested at the movie theaters where these movies are shown, it is mostly the educated urban elite and expatriates who show an interest in the high art movies of these Malian directors. But cinema-going is a popular pastime, particularly among the urban youth. Girls and young women and men have a strong preference for movies that have been imported from Europe and the Far East, such as kung fu movies, action thrillers, and love melodramas. Dancing halls are also highly popular among the urban youth, and the great diversity of places with respect to their infrastructure and music allows clients across the socioeconomic divide to find a discotheque palatable to their music taste and that they are able to afford. At least as popular—particularly among young men, women, and girls—are concerts given in Bamako and other towns by aspiring or nationally renowned musicians.

Soccer is number one on the country's list of popular leisure activities. A common image of everyday life, in the village as much as in town, are the

crowds of boys and young men who meet each and every afternoon on a soccer field in the neighborhood, where they spend hours running around, brav-
ing heat and dust. It is here that the neighborhood's male heroes are spotted
and discussed by girls and that competition among male adolescents over
social standing is fought out. Formally organized competition among soccer clubs at the neighborhood level has become more widespread in recent
years. People in town track the performance of the national soccer team, the
Eagles of Mali, and also that of their favorite team in Europe or elsewhere in
the world. World cups and other international soccer competition events are
closely followed on television and international radio stations and constitute
the favorite subject of daily conversation among many male youth and adult
men, who will discuss for hours the triumphs of their favorite soccer stars.

Whereas soccer is the favorite pastime of many boys and men, regardless
of whether they actively pursue it or simply follow it on the media, women
and girls in town show a strong interest in matters related to fashion and
female beauty. For many years, the national beauty pageant, organized by
the national radio and television station ORTM, has been one of the most
cherished events for many women, surpassed in importance only by the concerts of their favorite female pop stars. Organized annually by employees of
the national broadcast station since the early 1980s, the event is broadcast
live to a nationwide audience via national television. Starting in the mid-
1990s, the winner of the national competition, Miss ORTM, was to move
on to the West African beauty contest, a development that not only increased
the stakes of the pageant but also affected its outcomes. International beauty
standards—such as a strong pressure for thin, tall, light-skinned girls—have
replaced local preferences for nicely rounded women of often darker com-
plexion. These transformations under the influence of international fashion
and beauty trends generate new controversies at the national and local level.
Still, in spite of many Malians' disappointment about the type of women
invited for the national beauty competition, watching these pageants on national television continues to be a popular pastime.

LIFESTYLES: DYNAMICS OF CHANGE AND RECONSTRUCTION

Malian culture has always been in a process of transformation and reconstruction in response to internal dynamics and external influences. Over the
past two centuries, important incentives for cultural and social change came
from the transformation of local economies triggered by changing patterns
of long-distance trade in gold, ivory, salt, and slaves across the Sahara desert
and the Atlantic Ocean. Another motor of change was the gradual spread of
Islam from the urban centers in Mali's north to the rural areas and, in the

course of the colonial period, to broad segments of the southern population. As early as the 18th century, the culture of writing and erudition brought by Muslim intellectuals and religious specialists had a long-lasting civilizing effect on local knowledge cultures and on the ways political power was secured and legitimized. In the second half of the 19th century, missionary efforts to convert people to Christianity brought another set of intellectual influences and institutional and technological innovations that prompted people to reassess and reform conventional ways of life and culture. Finally, French military occupation, colonial economy, and political administration irreversibly changed the conditions for economic and political organization in the area of contemporary Mali. An overarching legal system was created, along with police and military forces capable to enforce it. Western institutions of schooling, sometimes effected through Christian missionaries, were among the most important factors of transforming earlier social and political hierarchies and cultural values. A new political elite emerged that owed its standing, professional expertise, and success to its training in the French colonial school system. Although fiercely opposed by the formerly powerful families, this new elite ultimately gained the upper hand in struggles over influence at the local and national level. This elite was instrumental in leading the country into independence, but it never managed to build a sound economic base for the majority of the population. Today, a major rift continues to divide those in power from major segments of population. Especially the rural populations live under economically modest or even precarious conditions.

Prior to the establishment of the Western schooling system under colonial rule, education and socialization were processes that were largely effected under the control of family elders and parents and of members of the community charged with teaching children key values and norms. Pupils sent to Muslim schools would receive additional training, such as the acquisition of key values and teachings of Islam, the memorizing of the Qur'an, and, at a later stage, literacy in Arabic. These teachings and skills were not considered to be in tension with the values taught at home. Western school education, in contrast, was never concerned with instilling values deemed important to traditional family life and society. Quite to the contrary: an important impetus of French colonial schooling was to relieve pupils from their alleged state of ignorance and primitiveness, by teaching them to adopt Western lifestyle, values, and behavioral norms. Established norms of collective responsibility, of valuing the interests of the extended family, and of respecting elderly authority were seen as impediments to the making of modern Africans and of civilized subjects of the French colonial mission. Because the knowledge taught at colonial schools was indispensable for professional success under colonial rule, Western education became more important as a factor of social advancement than inherited social rank. Colonial French school education has therefore proven to be a double-edged sword. It has allowed students to rise in the political and administrative hierarchy of colonial and postcolonial Mali. At the same time, it has taught its subjects to look down upon their traditions and customs and to treat their cultural roots with disdain. After independence, Western school education was developed into the state educational system. The first government of independent Mali, under the leadership of President Keita, sought to break with the nefarious and alienating legacy of French colonial education by replacing the contents of school materials taught in colonial times. But because of logistical and financial difficulties, these efforts of reforming the school curriculum met with limited success. The formal Malian school system thus stands in clear continuity with the educational institutions introduced by the French colonial administration and supported by Christian missionaries. Muslim schools, in contrast, have remained marginal within this new system. Pupils enrolled at reformed Muslim schools, the *medersas,* may finish school with a degree that at least formally entitles them to public employment. But in practice, partly because of the religious subject matters that the *medersa* curriculum comprises in addition to the regular subjects, graduates from the Muslim schools have fewer options and chances for employment. In addition to a state university and several state professional schools, the Malian educational system consists of a thriving private sector of school education and vocational training.

VILLAGES AND CITIES, OLD AND NEW

Many Malians today, when talking about the ways in which their culture and social life have been changing under French colonial rule and under the influence of Western culture more generally, tend to contrast modern life in town to traditional life in the countryside. In the countryside, so they imply, life is still much the same as it used to be one hundred years ago. The contrast between city and countryside that these Malians posit refers to opposed modes of livelihood, characterized by the different degrees to which Western culture has been integrated into traditional forms of living and being. Rural and urban modes of livelihood are variously judged in positive or negative terms: on the one hand, life in town is portrayed as modern, progressive, but also Westernized and thus distorted by foreign values. Life in the countryside, on the other hand, is depicted as tradition-bound, static, and uncivilized but also as a pristine residue of an unchanging and thus timeless Malian culture.

It is certainly true that life in the countryside differs substantially from life in town. For instance, there exist important discrepancies with regard to the ways family subsistence is secured among the rural populations and with respect to how younger family members and women should behave vis-à-vis

This architecture is typical of a village among sedentary agriculturalists in Mali's south. (Photo by the author.)

family elders. Also, clearly, large towns such as Bamako and Segu, and even smaller towns such as Mopti and Timbuktu, have amenities and opportunities for leisure-time activities that villages lack, such as cinemas, sports facilities, and restaurants. National radio and television can be more easily and regularly followed in town than in the countryside, and the procurement of running water and electricity by the majority of the urban population makes life in these towns a much easier affair than in the village or in a hamlet.

Still, divisions between life in the countryside and that in town are not as sharp as often assumed. There is no static traditional rural culture that has only recently been exposed to social change and to the danger of being wholly altered under the influence of modern or Western forms of life. Rather, rural culture and customs have been constantly exposed to change because of long-distance trade and mobility that already prior to the colonial period connected even remote villages to faraway places. Since French colonial rule, Western school education has acquainted rural populations with new knowledge and forms of learning, and labor migrants, returning back home from extended stays abroad, arrived with new ideas about personal success and advancement but also about agricultural methods. Also, for decades, Western amenities, utensils, and technologies—such as bicycles, motorbikes, radio

Village life in Mali's southwest. (Photo by the author.)

Here is a street scene in Bamako. (Courtesy of Abdoulaye Sounaye.)

The Niger River, locally referred to as Joliba, is considered the stream of life that secures many people's livelihoods. (Courtesy of Abdoulaye Sounaye.)

posts, and television sets—have been made available to people in the countryside, too, particularly to those living in proximity to the main roads connecting rural towns to the capital Bamako. At present, all kinds of activities and personal ties connect people in town to their families living in rural areas. People often move back and forth between the city and the countryside, in pursuit of economic goals but also for reasons of school education and political projects and because of family obligations. For all these reasons, it is important to look behind the apparent stark divide between rural and urban life and to conceive of these livelihoods as ranging across a continuum of lifestyles and of appropriations of external influences and foreign cultural values.

If one adopts this perspective on the great variety and flexibility of rural and traditional culture, one is in a better position to appreciate how much Malians, whether living in a remote rural area or in the capital Bamako, have been able to maintain core values of social and cultural life by selectively appropriating new influences.

CHANGING FORMS OF LIVELIHOOD: FARMING AND PASTORALISM

Depending on regional variation and ecological circumstances, Mali's diverse rural populations have been forced to various degrees to make amendments to their conventional forms of making a living. The pressure for change has been starkest in the areas of the far north and of the Sahelian zone, where repeated periods of drought in the 1970s and 1980s posed serious challenges to peoples who traditionally lived from animal husbandry and practiced a nomadic or seminomadic lifestyle. Among these peoples are many Fulani, Tuareg, and Moors whose nomadic movements used to follow those of their cattle (especially sheep, goats, and cows). Governmental policy, too, has contributed to the fact that these groups have come to adopt a more sedentary lifestyle. Immediately after independence in the early 1960s, the government of Modibo Keita sought to gain greater control over the northern nomadic populations by imposing measures, and to a lesser degree, offering incentives that prompted certain nomadic groups to move to permanent settlements. Among the most important incentives for a sedentary lifestyle were government-run schools and rural development projects providing permanent water supplies and facilitating horticulture and irrigated agriculture. But all in all, the effects of these government projects have been limited. It was mostly the difficult living conditions generated by soil degradation and the lack of water, and exacerbated by the civil war in the north between the late 1980s and the mid-1990s, that forced significant segments of the nomadic populations to adopt more sedentary lifestyles. For many of these peoples, these changes in livelihood are the subject of regret and of nostalgic remembrance of the good old times of greater spatial mobility and nomadic cattle keeping.

Among the many sedentary populations of rural Mali, agriculture has remained the key source of livelihood. But with Mali's increasing incorporation into the world market, subsistence production—meaning the cultivation of grains and other crops that are needed for one's own consumption—has been increasingly replaced with cash crop production, meaning the production of export crops to be sold against hard currency on the world market, such as cotton and peanuts. This shift from subsistence to cash-crop production started in the colonial period, when people's growing need for money to cover taxes and to pay for school and medical fees obliged them to change their patterns of crop production. Nowadays, the need to pay for fertilizers and pesticides is another reason why farmers opt for cash-crop production. While this change certainly brings the advantage of having more opportunities to earn cash, they also bring considerable disadvantages, most notably a heavy dependence on fluctuating world market prices.

Whether farmers produce staple food for their own consumption or cash crops, they mostly rely on the labor force of family members. If seasonal wage labor is employed in agricultural production, this is done mostly by small-scale businesses investing in horticulture and fruit trees. Members of socioprofessional groups, such as blacksmiths, leatherworkers, and praise speakers and singers, practice their craft alongside agricultural production, which constitutes their main source of income.

Large-scale agricultural industries never played the same role in the Malian national economy as it did in other West African countries, such as Ivory Coast and Nigeria. This is due to Mali's ecological and climatic conditions but also to its situation as a landlocked country. In some areas of Mali's Niger delta, rice and, to a lesser extent, wheat are produced in large-scale irrigation schemes that were built under French colonial rule. These irrigation schemes offer wage-labor employment and attract migrant laborers from different regions in Mali. They were once state owned yet, following the economic liberalization measures since the mid-1980s, have been privatized and sold to national and foreign investors. As a result, large plots of irrigated land are now in the hands of international and multinational companies, among them companies controlled by Chinese and Libyan investors. Because this process of so-called land-grabbing concerns areas of irrigated agriculture, water is likely to become a scarce and most fiercely embattled resource in the near future because the water redirected and used for large-scale irrigation is withheld from small-scale farmers.

Although a reliable health care and health infrastructure is of vital importance to people, ambulance cars are still a rare sight in many towns, and are seen even less in the countryside. (Photo by the author.)

Along with the growing integration of rural modes of livelihood into governmental rural extension schemes and into a national and world economic market, the public infrastructure of village life has been changing, too. Road and bridge constructions, funded by the government and by international development aid agencies, facilitate travel and transport from remote areas to urban centers and markets. Dispensaries and schools respond to people's most basic needs for health, hygiene, and social advancement through schooling. Although dispensaries and doctors trained in Western medicine exist side-by-side with traditional healing institutions and experts, they are important elements in contributing to the basic institutional infrastructure.

This infrastructure also establishes new connections among villages at the regional and local level. Along with the creation of local radio stations in many towns since the early 1990s, these changes contribute to a new awareness of local community and identity and foster the expansion of local and regional exchange networks and trade of locally fabricated goods that, in turn, offer new opportunities for income generation. Ultimately, these changes contribute to the transformation of household economies.

In addition to Western medical treatment, which is costly and often difficult to access, many people also rely on traditional medicinal knowledge and plants. This street vendor of medicinal plants uses his motorbike to sell his products directly to as many residents of a neighborhood as he can reach. (Photo by the author.)

Changing Economies and Values

The gradual integration of local economies into a market economy, initiated under colonial rule and perpetuated in postindependence times, has led to a transformation of household economies and internal family dynamics. Under the socialist single-party rule of Modibo Keita, the first president of independent Mali, a complete transformation of rural economies had been attempted, with collective fields, shared storage places, and village party structures that were to realize the allegedly socialist nature of traditional Malian society. Already after a few years, the failure of the party-orchestrated scheme of collectivizing rural production became evident. Under President Keita's successor, President Moussa Traoré, any attempt of reorganizing rural production was stopped; over the years, an alignment with countries and donor organizations in Europe and North America took place. Mali, which had never been an important player in the colonial export economy, continued to play a marginal role as a producer of cash crops. Nevertheless over the years, the country became firmly entrenched in a global capitalist order through the export of a few products, mainly cotton, peanuts, and, more recently, gold. This economic dependence on the terms of trade and exchange of a global market and its effects on opportunities of income generation have been acutely felt by broad segments of the Malian population. Urban household economies in particular have been seriously affected by the implementation of a stern Structural Adjustment Program since the mid-1980s and the concomitant shrinking of the public health and social services sector and the downsizing of the state administration. Rampant unemployment and minor profit margins for activities in the informal economy seriously affect the capacities of adult men in town to provide food and housing for their families. They also limit chances for young people to find regular employment. Women have to assume greater financial responsibility for family survival. All these developments generate new antagonisms and family conflicts, not only between husband and wife but also between the youth and the generation of their fathers and mothers. This means that, along with the transformations in rural and urban household economies initiated under colonial rule and perpetuated with Mali's increasing integration into a global economic order, values of family and community life have undergone radical change. These developments have been reinforced by the new ideas, values, and often individualistic orientations introduced through Western education. Employment in the state administration or in the public health and education sector offers opportunities to gain a regular salary but also a kind of work that differs substantially from the agricultural production and animal husbandry by which Mali's rural populations live. Another factor that shapes economic and social

Most markets in Mali are held in open marketplaces. Very often, sellers arrange their goods in aesthetically pleasing forms. (Photo by the author.)

A market stand sells imprinted cloth as well as various kitchen utensils. (Courtesy of Ute Roeschenthaler.)

Small-scale commerce and long-distance trade remain important occupations in Mali. To transfer goods at low cost across long distances, traders tend to overcharge trucks and other means of transport. (Courtesy of Abdoulaye Sounaye.)

life is the emergent urban industrial sector that transforms working habits, income structures, and people's leisure-time activities. Land tenure and ownership patterns have also been changing with the spread of individual enterprise and industry. Industrial production, by making available new objects and foodstuff for everyday consumption, affects conventional consumer habits and preferences, too. All these changes are reinforced under the influence of media products and images that are imported from countries in Europe and North America. In spite of these changes, Malians remain aware of their own cultural attachments and continue to cherish, and practice as much as they can, the values of community, sociability, and sharing.

A CHANGING POLITICAL CULTURE

Since the French colonial occupation of the lands that constitute the Republic of Mali, traditional forms of political regulation and leadership have been radically transformed so that chiefly families and rulers today no longer have the power they once held over local populations. Prior to French colonial rule, in the 19th century, the area of today's Mali was structured by various forms of political organization. Some regions were under the tutelage of centralized polities. Although these polities are often referred to as kingdoms (in scholarly and press publications as well as by many Malians), they differed from medieval European kingdoms with respect to their administrative and political organization. They were based primarily on warfare, trade, and the redistribution of booty and were characterized by a high degree of instability. Royal and noble lineages and the principle of inherited leadership existed, but established leaders and their successors were often challenged by contending individuals who lived off warfare and the trade of the booty they captured during their raids. Those zones that were outside the reach of these centralized polities were controlled by conglomerations of relatively autonomous village communities, which formed temporary and strategic military alliances against foreign aggressors. In these village communities, powerful families often had large groups of clients, slaves, and other dependents who, in exchange for protection and material support, performed certain services and agricultural labor on behalf of their powerful masters and protectors.

These diverse forms of political organization—and the vertical relations among powerful families, their dependents, and clients that accompanied these political forms—changed gradually under French occupation, with Western education and the employment of people in the colonial administration and the new opportunities for trade and economic enterprise created by the colonial economy. Former social and political hierarchies were not fully abolished but minimized in their relevance to the organization of political life. In order to become a political leader and a party politician, a person no longer had to come from one of the powerful and wealthy families that had formerly dominated local politics. Education in the colonial school system and wealth gained from economic activities were now important factors paving a person's way to political power, even if this person was of lower social origin. At the same time, family members, neighbors, and others remain highly conscious of the social birth of each political leader and hold him accountable for his everyday conduct on the ground. New institutions and rationalities of governance, such as political parties and the practice of voting for a party program and politicians (rather than following a political leader because his father had ruled over the area), gained in force with the independence struggle in the 1950s. After independence, the first government under Modibo Keita and his US-RDA party took over many institutions of colonial administration and jurisdiction, such as collecting taxes, assessing the property and wealth of individual households, and deciding judicial disputes in court. They also created new regulations and structures, such as a state legislation, an army, and a public school system, that were very much in line with what had been implemented by the French colonial powers.

Although the institutions of the colonial and later postcolonial state significantly altered former political structures and rules for accessing political power, Malians have maintained certain elements and values of their traditional political organization. Especially in rural areas, people who descend from formerly powerful families and clans are highly respected in a community, and descendants of their former clients are still expected to accomplish certain services on their behalf (such as marriage negotiations and public praise) and are remunerated accordingly.

In many African countries, colonial administrators presented the ethnic affiliations of colonized peoples as irreconcilable tribal differences and exploited them to keep control over the population, thereby creating political divisions and strife that continue to overshadow national politics today. In Mali, ethnicity has never played a prominent role in political affiliation and conflict. The only exception to this is the revolts launched by parts of the northern population in the 1960s and 1970s and again in the late 1980s. These groups represented their opposition to the central state as a Tuareg resistance, but in reality, there were members of other ethnic groups, too, who joined the ranks of these opponents. Whereas ethnic identity is of weak import to political affiliations and party politics at the national level, people do consider a person's family identity and social descent before they decide to vote for him. They can decipher a person's social identity easily by asking a person (or his social entourage) for his clan name and from which rural locale his family came from originally. Ethnic and regional identities have come to play a more important role in recent decades in town. There, more and more people who come from the same rural locale organize themselves in voluntary associations, with the goal of upholding the customs and traditions of their home community by celebrating important cultural events together and by teaching their children their rural customs. The urban associations are also important in collecting money to initiate development projects in their rural home communities and to support individual members in times of economic hardships. Because members of the associations are very proud of their cultural particularities, they are eager to display their traditions to other townspeople, for instance, by organizing cultural festivities or by inviting the team of the national television to film their folklore performances and broadcast them to a nationwide audience.[2] To many Malians, especially to those disappointed about politics and about what they perceive to be the self-interested doings of individual party politicians, these cultural performances, whether participated in or simply followed on national media, are of considerably greater interest than any political rally. The enthusiasm with which numerous Malians attend these cultural events and respond to individual elements of a performance attests to how proud they feel about their own cultural traditions and local histories—and that this enthusiasm and pride is unlikely to change in the near future.

NOTES

1. Dorothea Schulz, "The World Is Made by Talk: Female Youth Culture, Pop Music Consumption, and Mass-Mediated Forms of Sociality in Urban Mali," *Cahiers d'Etudes Africaines* 168, 42 (2002): 797–829. Dorothea Schulz, "Mapping Cosmopolitan Identities: Rap Music and Male Youth Culture in Mali," in *HipHop Africa,* ed. Eric Charry (Bloomington: Indiana University Press, forthcoming 2012).

2. Dorothea Schulz, "From a Glorious Past to the Lands of Origin: Media Consumption and Changing Narratives of Cultural Belonging in Mali," in *Reclaiming Heritage: Alternative Imaginaries of Memory in West Africa,* ed. Michael Rowlands and Ferdinand de Jong (Walnut Creek, CA: Westcoast Press), 184–213 (2007).

8

Music, Dance, and Performing Arts

Boro kan dirgan bi, a si hunkuna guna.
Whoever forgets about his past will not be able to understand the present.
—Songhai proverb

MALI IS WORLD famous for its music and performance traditions and for a number of highly acclaimed musicians and pop stars. Important musical repertories that are commonly marketed as elements of a national music are the hunters' music, the music performed by *jeli* singers and instrumentalists, *djembe* drumming, *bala* (xylophone) music, and the music of women singers from the Wassulu region. Malian musicians have also integrated a number of musical styles that originated in Latin America, North America, and other regions of Africa, such as samba, salsa, blues, rock, and highlife music. Music production modeled on European classical music is virtually nonexistent in Mali.

In most African societies, different kinds of music making, such as singing, playing an instrument, performing with masks or puppets, and dancing, cannot be neatly separated from each other. In fact, the term *music* as it is used and understood in Western society is rarely found in African societies, where musical sound tends not to be singled out as a separate feature of an aesthetic performance. This situation applies to the societies of Mali in which music, dancing, and other kinds of body movement are closely interconnected and people do not see why these different elements of a performance should be

separated out. Among the Bamanakan- and Maninkakan-speaking societies of southern Mali, for instance, the literal meaning of the term for *song*
(*donkili*) means "call to dance." This shows that people view vocal music as
something that goes with dancing and does not exist independently from it.
There are also many overlaps between dance and the forms of embodiment
and performances that in Mali is referred to as theater or ballet. All these connections and overlaps make music an experience and activity that figures centrally in people's everyday lives.

Also widely absent is an understanding of music and of other aesthetic
performances as belonging to a realm of fine arts that exist independently
of their social and political significance and intent. Instead, many people in
Mali feel that music and other artistic activities have a deeply transformative
effect, that music and performances are something not just for entertainment
but also for a person's moral edification. Music, dance, speech, and song are
creative processes that bear diverse and complex social and moral meanings.

IMPORTANT MUSICAL INSTRUMENTS

Mali's different regional and ethnic musical traditions draw on a variety of
instruments.

In addition to instruments that are of local origin, the guitar figures today
as a central element of Malian musical repertories. Introduced in the colonial
French Sudan in the early 20th century, since the 1960s it has become one of
the most widely played instruments in dance orchestras and music ensembles
specializing in popular music performances for concert audiences.

Instruments of indigenous origin are often associated with specific performance occasions and with particular ethnic groups and oral traditions. For
instance, the *bolon,* a calabash harp, was historically played only among the
Fulani, Senufo, Maninka, and Susu (the last live in present-day Guinea). Different ethnic groups of Mali play various types of the frame xylophone (*bala*)
that can be distinguished according to their shape and tuning system. Individual instruments may be associated with a distinct musical repertoire; even
subgroups of one instrument may be tied to different music pieces, such as in
the case of the *simbi* and the *donson ngoni,* both of which are varieties of the
harp played on behalf of hunters throughout southern Mali.

Throughout southern and central Mali, as well as in its neighboring countries, playing different varieties of the harp has been a centuries-long tradition.
Although this instrument is strongly associated with the identity of musical
specialists—such as the *maabuube* and *wammbaabe* musicians and orators
of the Fulani and the *jeli* instrumentalists of the Maninka and Bamana—it
is important to note that some harp varieties may also be played by people

of freeborn or noble origin. The harps come in various shapes and are tuned and played differently, but they all have in common that they are made of a calabash, with a variable number of cords. The *kora* is a 21-stringed harp played by Bamana and Maninka *jeli* musicians on behalf of their masters. The *simbi* or *donson ngoni* is another type of harp, a seven-stringed instrument played for hunters. Depending on its regional and ethnic origins, it takes several shapes and is also tuned differently. Finally, the *bolon* is a three- or four-stringed harp traditionally played on behalf of warriors, to exhort and encourage them to perform extraordinary deeds in the battlefield and to laud them for whatever feat they accomplished. Its Fulani variety, a three-stringed harp played by musical specialists, is called *hoddu*. Some of these harps can be dated back as far as the 17th century, and there are indications that these instruments were played in the area of contemporary Mali and throughout vast regions of West Africa even before then.

The *karinyan* is an instrument tightly associated with a *jeli* identity; it may be played only by women. This instrument is a narrow metal chime that the women hold in one hand and strike with a metal rod held in the other hand. *Bala* or *balafon* is the name of the local xylophone, an instrument built by slats of wood that are placed over and tied to a bamboo frame as part of the resonating body. To add resonance, a small gourd is attached to each slat. These gourds have a small hole on each side that is covered with a thin membrane. The small gourds, when struck, generate a buzzing sound.

Bala fabrication and playing is associated with a blacksmith identity and, to a lesser extent, with people of *jeli* background. In Malian society, blacksmiths work not only with iron but also with wood, and it is the task of the blacksmith to cut the wooden slats for the *bala,* to dry them while keeping the fire on for days, and to finally tie them over the wooden frame. The association of this instrument with blacksmiths is rooted in the legendary origins of the instrument: its mythical invention and initial use by the sorcerer-king Soumanguru Kante, the mystically empowered ancestor of subsequent generations of blacksmiths. The *bala* is often played together with drum ensembles, especially with the *djembe* drum. Today, *bala* music is one of the most popularized musical styles widely heard and enjoyed in many different settings, rural and urban.

Among the Bamana and Maninka populations of southern Mali, three kinds of drums exist: the *djembe,* the *dunun,* and the *tama.* Each of these drums is associated with specific musical repertoires, drumming traditions, and regional histories.

Depending on their regional origin, the *djembe* come in slightly different sizes and shapes. But they share certain key characteristics. All *djembe* are made from one single piece of wood, with an upper part having the shape of a huge bowl and a cylinder-shaped lower part. The diameter of the upper part ranges from approximately 12 inches to 16 inches; that of the lower part measures, roughly, 6 inches, and the height of the entire instrument is about 24 inches. A *djembe* is typically made by spanning a water-soaked animal skin (usually goat) across the bowl-shaped resonance body and by tying it with the help of three metal rings and a strong cord. The tone height and pitch of the drum can be adjusted by tightening or loosening the skin using the cord that holds the skin. In addition, several oval metal plates bearing small metals rings may be attached to the drum. As soon as the skin is struck, these metal rings translate the vibration into a jingling sound that reinforces the drum's sound sensation.

The second type of drum is the *dunun,* a cylinder-shaped drum that consists of two heads or resonating bodies. This type of drum, too, is carved from a single piece of wood, and its resonating body is covered with goatskin. The diameter of a *dunun* measures approximately 12 inches, and they are between 23 and 28 inches tall. In contrast to the *djembe,* which stands in front of the drummer where it is placed slightly between his legs, the *dunun* is typically slung over the drummer's left shoulder. The drummer plays it with a boomerang-shaped stick, which he holds in his right hand. A *dunun* is often played to accompany *djembe* performances.

Similar to the *dunun,* the *tama* (or *tamanin,* if it is a small-sized *tama*) consists of a double resonating body that makes it look like an hourglass held together with strings of cords. The player holds the *tama* under his left arm and strikes it with a bent stick in his right hand. The player may also stroke the vibrating skin with his left hand. The strings that run from one head of the instrument to the other side define the tightness of the animal skins spanned over each head. Depending on whether the strings are pressed down by the player (who holds the *tama* under his left arm) or loosened, the pitch of the *tama* changes.

A wooden flute, a *tambin,* is widely played among many Fulani groups, as well as in areas where other ethnic groups have adopted this instrument from Fulani instrumentalists. The *tambin* flute has three holes and is played as a side-blown flute. Historically used for entertainment but also on certain ritual occasions, the *tambin* flute has been popularized through performances of the national orchestra. Today, it is widely used, along with the *bala,* the *kora,* and the electric guitar, in dance orchestras and during public concerts. Two other instruments widely played in Fulani settings is the one-string lute (*molaandu*) and the *woogéru,* a one-string fiddle. The one-string fiddle also exists under the name *anzad* in Tuareg settings, in the regions of Gao and Kidal, where it is played only by women during evening and nightly community celebrations. The *anzad* is made of a bowl-shaped gourd covered with animal skin (mostly goatskin). The instrument's neck is built by inserting a lean stick of about 13 inches under the animal skin cover. The string, made of horsehair, is attached to both ends of the inserted stick. Horsehair is also used for the arc-shaped bow. Women play the *anzad* while resting it on their lap, holding its neck in the left hand and playing it with the bow in the right hand. The *anzad* is either used as a solo instrument or to accompany a woman's vocal performance. Playing the *anzad* has declined in recent decades, but the instrument still bears important meanings for those who listen to it, reminding them of the heroic traditions and cultural values associated with a past in which the Tuareg peoples were still in a position to roam around freely, without the restrictions imposed on their movement by the colonial and later postcolonial state. The *anzad* and the songs associated with it also symbolize romantic love and youthful aspirations. For some Muslim religious authorities, in contrast, the instrument is associated with illicit entertainment and with giving women a prominence that is discouraged by Qur'anic prescriptions.

Another instrument that is widespread among the Kel Tamasheq of the Gao and Kidal regions in northern Mali is a three-stringed harp, the *tahardent*. It was traditionally played by professional musicians as an accompaniment to their praise performances and genealogical recitations on behalf of their noble patron families. Since the 1960s and 1970s, new genres of *tahardent* music have emerged that are no longer tied to the identities, and heroic past, of specific patron families. These new varieties of the *tahardent* music are nowadays played in urban centers across the West African Sahara and as part of increasingly globalizing genres of world music.

The third principal instrument played among the Kel Tamasheq in Mali's northern Gao and Kidal regions is the *tende*, a mortar drum played during the camel festivals and other public celebrations. *Tende* drumming is considered the music of ordinary folk. Compared to the *anzad* music, which requires years-long apprenticeship, learning to play the *tende* is considered an easy affair. It also figures centrally in healing ceremonies related to spirit possession cults and practices. Made from a single-headed mortar covered by goatskin drum, it is played by male musicians. Women may accompany the playing of the *tende* with songs or by drumming on the *assakalabu*, a calabash upturned in a basin of water that also exists as *jidunun* in Mali's south.

MUSICIANS: DIFFERENT TYPES AND SOCIAL CATEGORIES

In many ethnic groups in Mali, those who specialize in public music making and speech performances are distinguished by birth from other people. Among the Fulani, different groups of professional musicians and family

historians exist, such as the *maabuube* and *wammbaabe,* who act as instrumentalists, singers, and genealogists. Among the Bamana and Maninka populations, these musical specialists are part of the *nyamakala* social group (see
chapter 4). Particularly those *nyamakala* people who were born into a *jeli* or
blacksmith family play an important role in musical performances and have
gained international standing in this domain over the last decades.

Historically, and until late in the colonial period, people of *jeli* origin acted
as oral historians, public speakers, advisers, praise singers, and instrumentalists on behalf of their patrons. Among the Bamana and Maninka peoples of
southern Mali, *jeli* or other families that specialized in music or other arti-
sanal activities (*nyamakala*) lived next door to powerful and rich families for
whom they performed various tasks of social mediation. *Jeli* men and women
with outstanding musical and rhetorical skills spoke for their patron families at public events and praised them. They lauded the accomplishments
of legendary members of the patron family and suggested to other freeborn
people who attended the performance that they should feel gratified to live
together with these models of personal excellence. In this way, *jeli* clients
played an important role in sustaining and enhancing the honorable reputation of their patron family. Those members of *jeli* families who had the necessary psychological and rhetorical skills would be called upon to resolve all
kinds of conflicts arising between families from different villages and to act
as go-betweens, marriage negotiators, and family traditionalists. Depending
on his own economic standing and satisfaction with the *jeli's* service, a patron
compensated a *jeli* for his or her interventions with diverse kinds of gifts, such
as food, cattle, and even slaves. Music performances always followed gender-
specific rules for the roles women and men were allowed to play. Recitations
of a family's history, for instance, have always been the exclusive domain of
jeli men. Public praise songs, however, were—and are—activities reserved for
jeli women. Both men and women could perform tasks of social mediation,
but only *jeli* men were allowed to publicly speak on behalf of their noble
patrons. A similar gender-specific division of labor applies to the playing of
instruments by freeborn people. Women are allowed to play only a few instruments, among them the *karinyan* and the *jidunun* (literally, water drum),
a calabash upturned in a water basin and played by women to accompany
their songs and dance celebrations during social gatherings.

Today, *jeliya,* as a term designating a person's social rank but also the tasks
associated with her or his social origin, still refers to a spectrum of activities
performed by people of *jeli* social birth, ranging from social and political mediation to public speech and song on behalf of their patrons. It is important
to note that an individual *jeli* man may specialize in any one of these activities but, for instance, may only exceptionally become an expert player of an

instrument and a praise singer at the same time. For female *jeli* musicians, the situation is slightly different because a woman may specialize in public praise and, in addition to this, accompany her own song while playing the *karinyan* (see the previous paragraph), a metal chime, which is the one instrument that a *jeli* woman is allowed to perform with.

In town, the praise traditionally performed by the musical specialists of the different ethnic groups has, in recent decades, become a veritable profession. Many people of former client status (*nyamakala*), not just those born into the families formerly specializing in music, make the public praise their main occupation. Contrary to the traditional ideal that a *jeli* should remain the faithful client of one and the same patron family, in exchange for the material recompense he or she received from them, many *jeli* speakers and singers in town now perform for changing patrons. This is so because in many cases, their former patrons are no longer in a position to grant them material support in the form of food, board, and generous gifts. This is the case not only for people of *jeli* origin but also for the specialists formerly associated with specific patron families of the Fulani and Tuareg nobility.

Many *jeli* women in town turn public praise into their main source of income. They show up at weddings and other public celebrations and, without being invited to do so, bestow their praise on patrons whom they may have never met before. As a result, as their critics complain, much of their praise consists of empty speech that lacks the deep meanings and artistic value of conventional *jeli* praise. Moreover, people of free birth often view their public interactions with *jelis* as a mixed blessing. Rich merchants, politicians, or other people of public renown, once they become the object of *jeli* praise, will not hesitate to display their generosity toward the performing *jeli*, whether this praise has been ordered or whether it has been spontaneously bestowed on the patron. In off-stage remarks, however, the person who has just given the singer a generous pay will express his fear of meeting the *jeli* again, knowing well that he would risk losing face if ever he refused to generously compensate the performing *jeli*.

In spite of all these changes, and although many people complain that the times of authentic *jeliya* are over, people still cherish good *jeli* praise and music performances. And they continue to refer to a knowledgeable, rhetorically and musically gifted *jeli* performer as a master *jeli*, a *ngara*, and laud her (or his) capacities to move the audience through compelling music and speech. Also, *jeli* musicians and their music continue to play a central role in Mali's musical traditions. The case is different for the *tahardent* music of the Kel Tamasheq. This music, historically closely associated with the political and social traditions of certain noble Kel Tamasheq clans, has never become a cornerstone of national musical traditions. By contrast, partly as a result of the forced migration of Tamasheq musicians to neighboring countries, *tahardent* music has developed into a new genre of entertainment music, the *tak amba,* which consists of accompanied songs and instrumental solos and is characterized by evocative rhythms. The *tak amba* enjoys great popularity throughout West Africa and is increasingly marketed at a global stage as the expressive forms of an authentic Tuareg culture.

The fact that a number of musical instruments and music genres are closely tied to a *jeli* identity does not mean that anyone who plays a music instrument or makes music in Malian society must be of *jeli* or *nyamakala* origin. Moreover, varieties of one and the same music instrument may be linked in varying degrees with the endogamous socioprofessional specialists. Whereas the 21-stringed harp, the *kora,* is played exclusively by *jeli* instrumentalists, playing the *bolon,* another variety of the calabash harp, has not been subject to hereditary restrictions. The question of whether someone may play a certain instrument is sometimes tied to the public or more secluded nature of the performance. For instance, among the Fulani of the Macina in central Mali, the three-string lute is played by musical specialists on public occasions. The flute and a one-string lute (*molaandu*), in contrast, may be played by any young (unmarried) man of free birth, as long as these players restrict their performances to nonpublic settings.

Similar to the association of certain instruments with the identity of a socioprofessional specialist and with public functions, certain singing styles too may be tied to specific social identities and tasks. The most notable example of this is the praise singing style typical of *jeli* women, characterized by the rapid enumeration of fixed formula of praise names and lines.

In the case of instruments for which no hereditary restrictions apply and that are played for general entertainment, there often exists a relationship of competition between musicians of *jeli* or *nyamakala* background on one side and musicians of freeborn or other social descent on the other, over concert invitations, well-paying customers, and audience attention. The rivalry between drummers and singers of *nyamakala* origin (and also among them!) and musicians who are of other social origin dates back to the colonial times, when the loosening of the ties between *jeli* speakers and family historians and their former patron families pushed more *jeli* performers to perform for changing patrons. The competition among these different types of musicians has been reinforced with changes in the market of musical production that started in the 1960s, with an expanding market for entertainment music in town. At that time, instrumentalists (some of whom played electronically fortified instruments) entered into competition with drummers; and female singers gained in prominence in the context of both drumming and song performances. Some of the most famous *jeli* women singers and male instrumentalists of that period benefited considerably from the political and financial support they received in exchange for their praise performances on behalf of the new political leadership. The loss in state support of artistic creativity since the privatization of the sector of musical production following the demise of President Traoré's single-party rule in the early 1990s further forced many musicians in town to look out for new income opportunities. Also, inviting musicians to provide good entertainment during family celebrations has become a question of prestige for many families in town. As a result, gifted musicians, regardless of their social birth, seek to find a niche in the sector of musical production and engage in musical activities, such as speech and song, that was conventionally considered the privileged domain of *jeli* musicians. Whether they are of *jeli* or other social origin, musicians tend to blame the other group of musicians for this situation of heightened competition and to charge one another for stealing customers or dominating a public performance to which both groups have been invited. *Djembe* playing illustrates the effects of these developments. Although a *djembe* may be played by anyone, conventionally *djembe* drummers were often of *jeli* or blacksmith origin. Today, however, with the professionalization of *djembe* entertainment music, in a situation in which providing musical entertainment for family and other public celebrations has become an important source of income, *jeli* drummers increasingly compete with instrumentalists of other social origins over paying clients. The pop star Salif Keita is another notable illustration of the ways in which music making, formerly closely associated with *jeli* and *nyamakala* origin, has been diversified under the effects of urbanization and the commercialization of music. Because Salif Keita comes from a freeborn family; his musical activities were initially strongly resented by his family, who considered them inappropriate for a person of noble descent. Only his success at the national and later international level gradually convinced his family elders that they should give up their strong reservations. Today, Salif Keita is nationally and internationally admired as one of Mali's leading musicians. Yet whenever he appears on stage in Mali to give a public concert, he first follows the conventional prescriptions for proper noble conduct by requesting the permission to speak and sing from those people in the audience who are of *jeli* origin. By this, Salif Keita openly acknowledges that his own social origins do not authorize him to engage in public speech. Another example of musicians who, although not of *nyamakala* origin, have benefited immensely from the professionalization of entertainment music is the women singers from the Wassulu region, most famously represented by international pop icon Oumou Sangaré. In the Wassulu region in Mali's south, women of freeborn descent have conventionally engaged in public song performances. Although their music bears certain features that make it resemble the stylistics of *jeli* praise, the singers commonly justify these similarities by arguing that lauding exemplary figures of the community was a task that freeborn women in the Wassulu region were traditionally allowed—and expected—to do. In this fashion, women singers from the south capitalize on a conventional genre of female song, and on the vivid rhythmic patterns of the Wassulu music, to take over leading positions in the national musical scene and on the world stage.

CATEGORIES OF MUSIC

Malian music can be roughly classified into different musical categories or repertories, according to the occasions on which they are performed and the social identity of the person on whose behalf the music is made. Musical repertories may also be associated with specific categories of musicians. In the case of *jeli* musicians (and only in their case), specific melodic-rhythmic patterns are classified as *juru,* that is, pieces dedicated to commemorate and laud the doings of a grand person, such as a political leader, a warrior, a wealthy patron, or a woman of great standing and respectability. The person to whom the piece is dedicated is referred to as the holder (Bamanakan, *tigi*) of the song.

However, only in some cases is it possible to clearly demarcate one category of music from others. For instance, although many Malians tend to contrast music with a ritual, religious, or political function against music made only for play (*tlòn* in Bamanakan), musical pieces that may be grouped under these two rubrics share a number of formal features. Moreover, the notion of entertainment (*njanaje* in Bamanakan) refers to a range of contexts that are associated with drumming, dancing, and public celebrations. Thus, in practice, the division between music made to entertain people and music with a serious intent is difficult to maintain.

Music and songs performed during agricultural and other work demonstrate this difficulty. These songs are either sung by the workers themselves or they are performed by musicians who have been expressly invited for that purpose. Many of these songs celebrate virtues such as physical strength, endurance, patience, and perseverance. Although meant to encourage people to work harder and faster, the songs clearly constitute a form of entertainment and distraction and simultaneously remind listeners of key values of community life.

Songs also form an important element of panegyric music. Panegyric music denotes a musical repertoire that is dominated by, but not entirely restricted to, the musical activities of musical specialists, such as *jeli* instrumentalists and singers. Panegyric music comprises a range of musical pieces and stylistic elements that aim at highlighting the accomplishments of historical figures and of contemporary people of eminent standing. Important elements of panegyric music are recitations of genealogy and praise songs. These laudatory performances are often considered a service that the praised person and her family should reciprocate through a generous donation. Only some of these musical pieces are based on vocal music. Other panegyric music is played by instruments only, in which case the laudatory message of the piece is entailed in the rhythmic-melodic patterns that refer to specific legendary heroes or past events. Praise songs are not only performed to flatter individual members of the audience. A singer may also praise a legendary figure of the past because of the song's morally edifying effect on audiences. Nor is the performance of these songs necessarily restricted to musical specialists. Among the Tuareg, for instance, there exists a category of songs (called *anzad n-asak*) that is sung by women and men of free birth to the accompaniment of the one-string fiddle *anzad*. Today, men are the preferred performers of *asak*, but it may well be that formerly women held a prominent place in these vocal performances. The texts of these songs belong to the highly prestigious oral poetry, the *tesîwit,* a genre that extols the virtues of heroism and courage on the battlefield and courteous and romantic love at home. These songs may be performed on public festivities and family celebrations and sometimes also on behalf of eminent figures of the community.

MODERN INSTRUMENTATION AND MEDIA TECHNOLOGIES

Traditional music in Mali has never been static and fixed. Because musical performance is subject to frequent improvisation and rearrangement, it is difficult to identify which version of a performance constitutes the authentic original of a song. It is therefore misleading to establish a clear-cut contrast between modern and traditional music. Musical styles in Mali have always been changing, by adapting to new occasions of performance and integrating new stylistic influences and forms of instrumentation. The adoption of new media technologies only forms one element in this process of rearrangement and selective innovation of musical styles.

Some contemporary popular genres of urban music are the product of a thriving urban culture since the 1960s in which people of diverse ethnic background organized themselves into voluntary associations. In these associations, people cultivated their own local performance cultures but also increasingly came to know others and thus to mix them. Also influential for contemporary urban music were the pop music fan clubs created by a young urban elite in the 1960s. Club members defined themselves through their consumption of music and dress styles that corresponded to the latest fads in the European and American metropoles. In this way, young Malians constituted themselves as cosmopolitan connoisseurs of jazz, blues, and prominent musicians such as James Brown.[1] Other urban associations mixed international musical trends and fashion with local musical elements, such as the Gunbe and Sabar associations, both of which are names of specific drums and also stand for particular drum patterns. In the celebrations of these urban associations, drum music played a prominent role.

Djembe drumming is today considered the quintessential music for public celebration in town. But it is important to note that it gained its current significance only in the course of the colonial period. Although practiced since the 1920s, *djembe* performances were increasingly popularized in the 1950s and 1960s. In this process, *djembe* drumming has been firmly established as an urban music tradition, a development that illustrates that any contrast between the allegedly traditional music of rural populations and a modern urban one is misleading.[2] A factor that greatly helped their promulgation in the early postcolonial era was that *djembe* performances were closely associated with the then-emerging transethnic voluntary associations in town. Some of these groups were exclusively designed for young, unmarried people, thereby standing in direct continuity with the rural youth groups that exist among many rural populations of Mali. Today, thanks to the globalization of Malian musical elements, the *djembe* has become the prototypical African drum of world-music production.

Drumming repertoires are highly diverse and thus contrast with the clearly demarcated and relatively standardized musical repertories of *jeli* musicians and oral historians and also with the music of hunters. Drumming has developed various local musical traditions that differ substantially with respect to the musical repertory, the social identity of the performer, and the occasions on which individual pieces are to be played. For instance, among the Soninke people in northwestern and central Mali, only people of *jeli* origin are allowed to play the *tama* drum. Here, the *dunun* drum is played on behalf of people of eminent social standing and associated with important events and legendary figures of the local political past.

Occasions for drumming include celebrations of life-cycle events, such as weddings and circumcision and excision ceremonies that serve to initiate boys and girls into a particular adolescent status. Each of these events is associated with specific drumming patterns. Also frequently played are drumming patterns that were once associated with certain traditional events and contexts, such as the *djembe* rhythms associated with Komo mask performances and other rituals of initiation societies. These drumming patterns have been dissociated from their original context of performance and are conserved in the form of theatrical and other dance performances associated with entertainment and leisure.

Guitar music forms another important element of urban music culture. Electric guitar music, introduced in Francophone West Africa since the early decades of the 20th century, drew initial inspiration from European and Latin American popular music. At that time, it was mostly played and listened to by an emergent French-educated African elite. Already then, guitar music was based on a recombination of these foreign elements with certain local musical and aesthetic conventions. Since the 1960s, guitar music, mostly in its electronically fortified version, was promulgated through the national orchestra and, since the 1980s, by world-famous music stars such as Salif Keita, Boubacar Traoré, Ali Farka Touré, and Habib Koité. Today, the guitar has been so fully Africanized and adapted to local musical taste that is has become an essential element of Malian music.

Religious Music

Music performances, especially drumming and singing, have historically played a prominent role in settings in which traditional religions were practiced. Certain tunes and rhythmic patterns were associated with specific ritual occasions and celebrations of life-cycle events, such as circumcision rituals. Other drum patterns were dedicated to mask performances, whether linked to initiation societies or intended for wider audiences and public entertainment. Finally, as in the case of the *tende* among certain Tuareg groups in northern Mali, certain drumming patterns were—and still are—linked to spirit possession rituals and curing ceremonies. Today, many of these musical airs and drum patterns are still played, but they have often been integrated into a public culture of celebration and urban leisure. Most people who hear these drum and melodic patterns today are no longer aware of their original ritual or religious connotations.

Because Christians constitute only a small minority in Mali, the stylistics of Christian church music, and Christian hymns in particular, have not exerted an important influence on Malian musical conventions.

Contrary to the widespread stereotypes of the music-averse bent of Islam, musical performances have always been important to local Muslim religious practices. Islam has clearly influenced the kinds of musical performances and dances that characterize Mali's different regional cultures today. In the colonial period, as Islam spread into remote corners of Mali's rural areas, certain dances and drumming performances were repressed or marginalized. But Islam also authorized certain musical expressive forms as proper religious behavior, such as songs and dances associated with Muslim festive celebrations.

The question of whether music should be performed and enjoyed at all has remained a thorny and unresolved object of debate among Muslim scholars.

This does not preclude the spiritual, aesthetic, and affective richness of sound practices in Mali, as elsewhere in the Muslim world. Muslims believe that God's ultimate revelation, the Qur'an (literally, recitation), was made accessible to human understanding not through vision, inspiration, or writing but through sound and, more specifically, the sound of the word. God cannot be heard or seen; but His message was made audible by the archangel Gabriel, who told the Prophet Mohammad to recite the Divine revelation and thereby acquaint humankind with God's will. Accordingly, the Muslim art of recitation, conceived as the sonic form of rendering God's recited word, and the attendant science of correct articulation (based on the precise memorization of both word and melodic-rhythmic patterns) underline the uniqueness of the Qur'an. They also establish the fundamental distinctiveness of Qur'anic recitation from other sonorous and musical forms, be they rendered vocally or instrumentally.

One general difficulty with discussing the musical repertories associated with Islam in Mali relates to the fact that the term *music* does not capture the spectrum of practices involved in the making and sensation of sound that are considered religiously significant by many Muslim religious authorities. Nor does the category of sacred music have an equivalent in the Malian context of Muslim religious practice. Muslim authorities tend to consider only certain sound-related practices as conducive to people's experience of God's presence in their lives, and they contrast these sound-related practices which they deem legitimate with music-making proper, which they denounce for its mundane character and the illicit context within which this music is performed. For this reason, sound, as a term that refers to a range of aural perception, is more useful to describe how Muslims in Mali use speech, singing, and hearing as ways to generate spiritual and transcendent experience. Qur'anic recitation is considered an important way by which an observant Muslim may experience God's presence in her life. Recitation, whether done in a simple style or a more elaborate way, is contrasted with music in the proper sense of the term.

Malians' daily lives, be they observant Muslims or adherents of other religious traditions, are shaped by the Muslim call to prayer, *adhan*. Another element of the daily experience for practicing Muslims is the sermons delivered on Fridays, during the congregational worship at the mosque. The murmuring chant of children who labor to memorize the Qur'an also forms part of Malians' everyday sound sensation, which, in combination with other forms of sensual perception, inscribes the sound of divine presence into everyday experience in and outside the sphere of ritual worship.

Malian Muslim practices that are associated with the Islamic mystical traditions reveal a view of the moving capacities of sound and of the spoken word. Specially designed expressive forms (such as poetry), litanies (*dhikr*), and other sonic performances aim to enhance the mystical experience of God's presence and facilitate believers' striving for a state of ecstatic communion with God and his all-encompassing love. Malian Muslims also perform certain devotional expressive forms that combine poetic texts with melodic-rhythmically patterned chants. Among them are praise songs on behalf of the Prophet and his family and also songs that take the form of personal supplication (Bamanakan, *duwa*). Similar to Qur'anic recitation, they are distinguished from other musical genres. Certain chants serve a similar devotional purpose but are explicitly acknowledged to form music in the proper sense of the term. Praise songs may also be directed at particular figures, men and women, who because of their pious conduct and religious erudition are considered to be friends of God (singular *wali*). Whereas the stylistics of Qur'anic recitation follow relatively fixed, universal standards of recitation, the chants and praise songs bear many resemblances to local musical and rhetorical conventions, such as to *jeli* praise performances.

In the area of contemporary Mali, women have historically been centrally involved in the composition and performance of these musical forms of devotion. Women were also instrumental in organizing local Muslim religious festivals, such as the celebration of the Prophet's birthday (*mawlud*) and of the end of Ramadan. The joyous, playful atmosphere that reigns among women during these celebrations, and also the fact that the women accompany their praise on behalf of the Prophet and his family with dancing and drumming, illustrates vividly the difficulty of clearly separating serious ritual music from music for entertainment. After all, the songs performed by Muslim women during their religious gatherings, during but also outside of Muslim religious celebrations, entail at once joy, pleasure, and ritual purpose.

The overwhelming richness of the musical activities and sound experiences that accompanies Muslim religious practice in Mali has been reinforced by new audio and audiovisual recording and broadcast technologies. One effect of these technological innovations is that practices related to the aural perception of divine presence enter into new arenas of daily life, beyond the immediate sphere of ritual action to which these aural forms of spiritual experience used to be restricted. Women may now be able to listen to certain religious forms of musical expression while taking care of their household chores. To a greater extent than before, women may also partake in the production of religious music and speech. These developments illustrate how the production and consumption of music and sacred sound transform over time and create changing possibilities for men and for women to partake in spiritual experience.

THE GLOBALIZATION OF MALIAN MUSIC

Mali's insertion into a global order of musical creativity can be traced back at least as far as the early 20th century, when the guitar was introduced in West Africa and was soon indigenized with respect to playing techniques and to the musical genres performed on the guitar. Over the last 15 years, this development has turned full circle as African music played on the electronic guitar in ways that make it an Africanized European instrument is brought back to Europe and North America, where it takes over a prominent place in the world-music market.

The global spread of certain Malian music genres and instruments goes back at least to the 1960s. At that time, the national orchestras and performance groups traveled in the context of cultural exchange programs to countries allied with Mali's socialist regime, leaving their imprint on local performance conventions over there and returning back home with new musical influences. Since then, certain Malian instruments and performance conventions have become world famous. On the international stage, the *djembe* has emerged as the quintessential African drum since the early 1990s. While music fans outside Africa were acquainted with the drum as early as the 1960s, its rise to fame occurred after the death of former president Sekou Touré when a number of professional drummers from Guinea settled in Europe and North America and started popularizing the *djembe* by offering African dance and drumming courses. Today, there are also other African musical traditions that regularly integrate *djembe* drumming into their traditional performances. A notable example of the spread of the *djembe* to other musical performance contexts within Africa is the Zulu choir music that now makes the *djembe* an integral part of its musical productions.

The rise to world fame by several Tuareg music groups exemplifies the broader process by which different ethnic musical traditions of Mali have come to occupy a prominent place in the sector of world-music production. One of these Tuareg performance groups, Tinariwen, has gained international acclaim since 1998. Its musicians rely heavily on electric guitars to play traditional musical pieces. In 2000, the group released its first album, followed by a tour through Europe and the United States in 2004. Two other internationally known Tuareg music groups are Bombino and Inerane, which are similarly successful in their adaptation of guitar instrumentation to traditional tunes and song lyrics.

In addition to the international reputation earned by the (previously mentioned) male musicians Salif Keita, Ali Farka Touré, Boubacar Traoré, and Habib Koité, a number of female singers, many of them of *jeli* origin, also illustrate the globalization of traditional musical stylistics. Among these internationally acclaimed pop icons are the *jeli* women Ami Koita and Kandia Kouyaté, as well as a number of female stars from the Wassulu region, most illustriously represented by Oumou Sangaré.

THEATER, OLD AND NEW

In Mali, *teatri,* the local term for theater, is one of the most popular genres of entertainment currently played on public occasions and on the mass media. *Teatri* refers to a mixture of music, dance, speech performance, and song. What people today refer to as *teatri* is not a recent invention but goes back to the indigenous forms of drama and comedy that included masks, puppets, and human actors and were traditionally performed by several ethnic groups in Mali. Among the agriculturalist populations, theater performances take place almost exclusively during the dry season, when agricultural work has virtually come to a halt. Theater performances are usually done by the village youth, who are organized into youth associations.

It is difficult to establish a clear-cut typology of the different traditional genres of theater because their names, forms, stylistics, characters, and the stories they recount vary from region to region and according to ethnic affiliation. Traditional forms of theater in Mali were always subject to processes of creative innovation and transformation. Since independence, different regional theatrical forms have been integrated, though to different degrees, into new conventions of theatrical performance that are now presented at the national and regional levels.

Kotetlòn are the theatrical performances—traditionally organized by the Bamana on the occasion of seasonal, family, and individual life-cycle festivities (such as weddings and the celebration of funerals of important people of the village community)—that belong to the best known instances of these traditional forms of theater in Mali. The *kotetlòn* theater comprises parody, farce, and comedy based on the satirical imitation of people, their speech patterns, attire, and body movements. In the village, the *kotetlòn* was conventionally performed only by members of the village male youth association, the *kamalen* (young men's) *ton,* to comment on social and political life. In some areas, the *kotetlòn* performance of young men is framed by other theatrical performances, such as the *koteba,* in which young men and women participate. The *koteba* strongly resembles the *kotetlòn* insofar as it similarly foregrounds parody and farce when commenting on recent events or individual members of the village community. All these forms of theater are meant for the general public, adults and children, and take place in the village public place. In addition, competition among the youth associations of different villages could bring them together occasionally to nominate and celebrate the best theatrical performance association of a region.

While the purpose of the theater performances are general entertainment and relaxation (*nyanaje*), the *kotetlòn* and other theater genres also imply a strong emphasis on rhetorical prowess. In the case of theatrical performances, rhetorical mastery shows first and foremost in the capacity of a speaker to frame his words in a way that is considered comic speech. If the speaker fails to do so, he risks being considered shameless and impolite. Because this kind of mastery of the spoken word is understood to be an important marker of adult status, the *kotetlòn* theater performed by the village youth offers them an important occasion to claim and display social maturity.

Another genre of theater in regions where the Bamana constitute an important part of the population are the dramatic performances of young men (the *koredugaw*) who, during the dry season, travel from one village to another to make some additional income by entertaining the village community with their performances and spectacular costumes at night. The success of their theatrical productions, and that of others such as the genre of marriage parodies, depend on the witty talk and acrobatic dances of the performers.

As this suggests, a characteristic feature of Bamana and other forms of traditional theater is the central importance of skillful, witty, engaging, but also controlled speech. This implies that the characters of the different traditional forms of theater only emerge through their ways of speaking. Their different identities are marked by their lack of politeness, their silliness, goodness, or cleverness, all of them personality features that are evidenced in the characters' speech performances. Audience responses are of central importance to measuring the success of individual characters. It is the audience that, through spontaneous applause, laughter, or disagreement, ultimately decides whether someone's speech is convincing or not. Theater in Mali therefore needs to be understood as an aesthetic performance in which those who watch and consume a performance are also deeply engaged in its production and in determining its success.

Other genres of traditional satirical theater are the *Sogo bò* puppet performances and masquerades of the youth associations among the Bamana and Bozo populations of the Segu region. Most of these theatrical performances are accompanied by songs and drumming. Puppet performances and masquerades may even mix dance, song, and speech and thus present a multisensuous and highly complex aesthetic performance. Masquerades put into play individual masked dancers and large animal constructions (made of huge masks and enacted by dancers who may be hidden from the public eye underneath a cloth or raffia cover). The puppets include several recurring characters representing social stereotypes (as in the case of several Bamana puppets) and water spirits (Bozo puppets). All these puppets are presented in a series of entertaining and laughter-provoking stories that are meant to satirize social life and established hierarchies between elders and the younger members of the village community. But the stories are also meant to offer, although in a lighthearted way, moral lessons of a more general nature. Here again, the role of the audience is paramount. The audience's approval or disapproval structures the turns and twists a puppet performance or masquerade takes and thus ultimately codetermines the story a performance tells and its outcome.

THEATER AND DANCE THEATER (BALLET)

Contemporary dance theater in Mali draws strongly on the various regional and local traditions of theatrical performance. The beginnings of the theater performances that are today displayed in urban and rural settings and that tend to be associated with the domain of state politics go back to the decade preceding Mali's independence. At the time of gaining independence, the governments of the different countries of the former French West African colonial territory created national performance groups that were to play during national holidays, visits of foreign state officials, and other celebrations associated with state politics. The national performance groups created in Mali were the National Orchestra, playing Western-style music with partly Western instruments; the Malian Instrumental Ensemble, composed of *jeli* instrumentalists and vocalists; and the Malian Ballet, an ensemble presenting a mix of dance and theater that relied heavily on local performance traditions and aesthetic standards. In 1969, a national theater company was created, the National Dramatic Group, followed by a national puppet theater company, the Troupe Nationale des Marionnettes, in 1986.

Local drumming conventions, and the musical and oral traditions associated with the *nyamakala* performances of the Bamana and Maninka, offered important sources of inspiration for these artistic groups and the musical, theatrical, and dance forms they created. Over the years, the different national ensembles were instrumental to the creation of standard forms of artistic performance that came to be viewed, by performers and audiences, as instances of typically Malian music and theater. Important for this standardization of national music and theater were the cultural festivals organized at the regional and national levels to stage competition for the prize of the nation's best performance group. These festivals were in part inspired by the cultural competitions, administered by the French colonial administration since the early 1950s, that staged sports competition and also dance and theater performances; the winning teams of the different regions of French West Africa were then to meet for the finals in Dakar.

Another source of inspiration for the dance and theater performances that were to become the bread and butter of the national ballet were laid at the École William Ponty in contemporary Senegal, where the first generation of indigenous clerks for the colonial administration was educated. The first president of independent Mali, Modibo Keita, as well as his wife Mariam Travélé were key figures in the theater performances produced at William Ponty. These productions comprised speech, music, dance, and song. Many pieces treated historical themes and legendary heroes of the past. Because the first generations of graduates enrolled at William Ponty were almost exclusively from the southern peoples of Mali, the theatrical productions they staged drew primarily on the oral traditions of the Bamana and Maninka, such as the epics of the legendary founder of the medieval Mali empire, Sundjata Keita, and of Da Monzon, a political leader associated with the historical kingdom of Segu. These theater plays intended to remind audiences of the illustrious past of the Malian people and—although in a very indirect, subtle fashion—to offer parables with a critical view on French colonial occupation. Other plays sought to teach morals and offer advice by telling stories about contemporary life.

Back in Bamako, many graduates of William Ponty continued with their artistic activities by creating amateur theater groups that staged productions with overt political overtones, militating for an independent nation and for people's greater awareness of their cultural roots and self-esteem. Characteristic of these plays were the integration of song, dance, speech, and drumming. They laid the foundations for what, after independence, was to be produced as national Malian theater by the National Dramatic Group.

All these theater productions contributed to a process by which the national performance ensemble integrated different local cultural practices into national stage productions. By explicitly referring to these cultural and expressive forms as instances of local folklore, the ensemble defined, established, and promulgated a traditional Malian culture among a wider, potentially nationwide public. Yet the major share of the traditional cultural elements used in these theater plays and ballet performances came from the southern triangle of Mali. Very notable Tuareg and Songhai dance genres that are based on self-controlled and sparse body movement (illustrated by the *tagest,* a dance based on the exclusive movement of head, fingers, and shoulders performed by the dancer while remaining seated; and by the *agabas,* a group dance in which men and women may participate) were rarely made part of national ballet and theater performance. This partial representation of Mali's different regional cultural traditions is well documented in a series of now-classical audio-recordings of the Malian national performance groups dating back to the 1960s and 1970s. Of these recordings, more than 80 percent are musical pieces drawn from the Bamanakan- and Maninkakan-speaking societies of southern Mali. These recordings illustrate that the making of a national, Malian culture was based from the outset on a marginalization of northern oral and performance traditions.

The National Ballet gained enormous popularity in the course of the 1960s. Key musical features of its performances were percussion and dance, which complemented the conventional recitations and eulogies of *jeli* singers and instrumentalists (who mainly played the *bala* and *kora*). Gradually a sharper division was established between *ballet,* as a set of performance conventions that comprise a strong element of dance, on one side and *theater,* as a performance genre drawing heavily on speech and song, on the other. Over the years, the outstanding popularity of the National Ballet and of the local folklore it performed reshaped local understandings of what constitutes authentic local tradition. Also important for this process was the creation of a national school for the performing arts, the National Institute for the Arts, in 1964. Some elements of the theatrical and ballet performances that had been designed by the national ensembles, such as certain dance forms integrated into theater pieces, were changed and readapted to performances in rural settings where traditional performance conventions had been more prevalent. The gradual integration of drumming, especially of the *djembe* as the quintessential instrument of entertainment music, into ballet performances at the national level vividly illustrates the process of reconstituting local cultural tradition by the detour of concerted, state-orchestrated celebrations of authentic Malian culture. *Djembe* drum music became popularized through national ballet and national theater stage productions. Thus, whereas in tradition-bound contexts drumming had been associated only with very specific ritual occasions and family celebrations, over the years many spectators, men and women, came to see drumming as an essential element of their authentic traditional entertainment culture and leisure activities.

Since the late 1970s, several private theater companies emerged that sought out private sponsors such as business companies for their theatrical productions. Over the 1980s, with the gradual diminishing of state funding for theater plays, individual actors and companies discovered the sector of development aid as a new source of income, producing plays on command that dealt with HIV/AIDS prevention, environmental protection, governmental health, hygiene and family planning campaigns, and, more recently, the eradication of female circumcision practices. These theater productions differ from the earlier, often politically motivated accounts of honorable figures of Mali's illustrious past. Still, they foreground the long-standing pedagogical impetus of theater productions in Mali that resonate with the aesthetic expectations of spectators. Also, by drawing on a mix of song, dance, drumming, and speech, they do justice to the artistic elements that continue to render theater and dance theater highly popular among local audiences.

NOTES

1. See the autobiographical reminiscences by Manthia Diawara, *In Search of Africa* (Cambridge, MA, and London: Harvard University Press, 1998).

2. See Rainer Polak, *Festmusik als Arbeit, Trommeln als Beruf: Jenbe-Spieler in einer westafrikanischen Großstadt* (Berlin: Reimer, 2004).

Annotated Bibliography

CHAPTER 1: INTRODUCTION

For an overview of the history of Mali and other key information about the country, see the following literature:

Kathleen M. Baker, Andrew Clark, and Pascal James Imperato, "Mali," in *Britannica Online Encyclopedia,* ed. B. O. Encyclopedia (Chicago headquarters), http://www.britannica.com/EBchecked/topic/360071/Mali; CIA Factbook, "Mali," in *The World Factbook* (Washington, DC: CIA Human Resource Management Washington, 2006); John Beierle et al., "Dogon" (electronic resource): FA16, in *eHRAF World Cultures: Africa* (New Haven, CT: Human Relations Area Files), http://ehrafWorldCultures.yale.edu/collection?owc=FA16; R. J. Harrison Church, "Mali, Physical Social Geography," in *Africa South of the Sahara 2003,* ed. Europa Publications, 645 (New York and London: Routledge, 2002); Katharine Murison, "Mali, Recent History," in *Africa South of the Sahara 2003,* ed. Europa Publications (New York and London: Routledge, 2002): 721–28; Charlotte Vaillant, "Mali, Economy," in *Africa South of the Sahara 2003,* ed. Europa Publications (New York and London: Routledge, 2002): 728–32.

For an introduction to the prehistory of the area of today's Mali, see Olivier Dutour, *Hommes fossiles du Sahara: Peuplements Holocènes du Mali Septentrional* (Paris: Editions du Centre National de la Recherche Scientifique, 1989); Roderick Macintosh and Susan Macintosh, *Prehistoric Investigations in the Region of Jenne, Mali* (Cambridge: Cambridge University Press, 1980); Roderick Macintosh and Peter Schmidt, eds., *Plundering Africa's Past* (Bloomington: Indiana University Press, 1996); Roderick Macintosh, *The Peoples of the Middle Niger: The Island of Gold* (Oxford: Blackwell, 1998); Roderick Macintosh, *Ancient Middle Niger: Urbanism and the Self-Organizing Landscape* (Cambridge: Cambridge University Press, 2005); Michel Raimbault and Kléna Sanogo, *Recherches Archéologiques au Mali: Prospections et Inventaire, Fouilles et Études Analytiques en Zone Lacustre* (Paris: Éditions Karthala, 1991).

For a travel account that vividly describes the life situation and political organization in northern Mali prior to French colonial rule, see René Caillié, *Voyage à Tombouctou,* vol. 2. (Paris: François Maspero, 1979); Tayiru Banbera, *A State of Intrigue,* contributed, collected, and trans. David Conrad (Oxford: Oxford University Press, 1990), illuminates the power dynamics of a precolonial kingdom.

For a historical account of the economy in the Niger delta prior to colonial rule, see Richard Roberts, *Warriors, Merchants, and Slaves: The State and the Economy of the Middle Niger Valley, 1700–1914* ([s.l.]: Stanford University Press, 1987). For a historical introduction to the warrior kingdom established by Samori Touré shortly before French colonial occupation of the Malian territory, see Brian Peterson's book on Samori Touré: *Islamization from Below: The Making of Muslim Communities in Rural French Sudan, 1880–1960* (New Haven, CT: Yale University Press, 2011).

For a comprehensive collection of essays on the colonial history of Mali, see Catherine Coquery-Vidrovitch and Odile Georg, eds., *L'afrique Occidentale au Temps des Francais: Colonisateurs et Colonises (c.1860–1960)* (Paris: La Découverte, 1992). Emil Schreyger, *L'office du Niger au Mali 1932–1982: la Problématique d'une Grande Entreprise Agricole dans la Zone du Sahel* (Wiesbaden: Steiner, 1984), grants insight into the workings of the French colonial extractive economy; a complementary perspective on the Office du Niger is provided by Amidu Magasa, *Papa-Commandant a Jété un Grand Filet Devant Nous: L'office du Niger 1902–1962* (Paris: Editions Maspero, 1978). Gregory Mann's book on *tirailleurs sénégalais, Native Sons: West African Veterans and France in the Twentieth Century* (Durham, NC: Duke University Press, 2006), accounts for the social and political transformations effected under French colonial occupation and their repercussions in the early period of postcolonial politics. William Foltz's *From French West Africa to the Mali Federation* (New Haven, CT: Yale University Press, 1965) offers an excellent portrayal of the political dynamics of the struggle for independence and an account of the reasons for the breakup of the Malian Federation.

For a useful bibliographical essay on scholarly research on Mali until the 1970s, see Paule Brasseur, *Bibliographie Generale du Mali, 1961–1970* (Dakar, Senegal: Université de Dakar, 1976).

On the period of US-RDA rule under President Keita, see Nicolas Hopkins, *Popular Government in an African Town: Kita, Mali* (Chicago and London: University of Chicago Press, 1972); Frank Gregory Snyder, *One-Party Government in Mali: Transition Toward Control* (New Haven, CT: Yale University Press, 1965); and the special issue "Modibo Keita's Mali: 1960–1968," *Mande Studies* 5 (2003), ed. Gregory Mann and Baz Lecoq.

A comprehensive account of political and economic developments in Mali after 1991 is offered by the volume *Democracy and Development in Mali,* ed. R. James Bingen, David Robinson, and John M. Staatz (East Lansing: Michigan State University Press, 2000).

Repercussions of administrative reforms since the mid-1990s on local political constellations and dynamics in different regions of the country are addressed in C. Zobel, "Espaces Politiques Locaux, Etat et Représentation: les Communes des Monts Mandingues et de la Haute Vallée du Niger," in *Décentralisation et Pouvoirs en Afrique: en Contrepoint, Modèles Territoriaux Français,* eds. Claude Fay, Y. F. Koné, and C. Quiminal (Paris and Bamako, Mali: IRD and ISH, 2006): 263–78; and Georg Klute and Trutz von Trotha, "Roads to Peace: From Small War to Parasovereign Peace in the North of Mali," in *Healing the Wounds: Essays on the Reconstruction of Societies after War,* ed. Marie-Claire Foblets and Trutz von Trotha (Oxford and Portland, OR: Hart, 2004): 109–43; Baz Lecoq, "Tuareg Rebellions and Competing Nationalisms in Contemporary Mali" (PhD diss., University of Amsterdam, 2002).

Several classical accounts of the different ethnic traditions exist, but many of them tend to reify the divisions between ethnic groups. Prominent examples of such classical accounts are Bokar Ndiaye, *Groupes Ethniques du Mali* (Bamako, Mali: Éditions Populaires, 1970); Bokar Ndiaye, *Structures des Malinkés de Kita* (Bamako, Mali: Éditions Populaires, 1970); and Centre Culturel Abbaye de Daoulas, *Les mondes dogon* (Paris: Hoebeke, 2002).

For studies that portray ethnic identities and interethnic relations in more dynamic ways, see Jean-Loup Amselle, *Mestizo Logics: Anthropology of Identity in Africa and Elsewhere* (Stanford, CA: Stanford University Press, 1998); Mirjam de Bruijn and Han van Dijk, eds., *Peuls et Mandingues: Dialectique des Constructions Identitaires* (Paris: Karthala, 1997); and the special issue "Identity and Belonging in Sahelian Societies," *Cahiers des Sciences Humaines* ORSTOM 31, no. 2 (1995), ed. Claude Fay.

For documentaries and movies that feature key historical events and characteristics of contemporary Malian social life, see *The Bambara Kingdom of Segu,* video recording (Princeton, NJ: Films for the Humanities & Science, Images Sud Nord, 1992); and Susan Vogel, *Living Memory: Six Sketches of Mali Today,* video recording (Brooklyn, NY: First Run/Icarus Films, 2003).

CHAPTER 2: RELIGION AND WORLDVIEW

Much has been written on the religious practices and understandings and related worldviews and mythologies that many Muslims in Mali today consider traditional and un-Islamic. Classic accounts of traditional religion include Germaine Dieterlen, *Essai sur la Religion Bambara,* 2nd ed. (Brussels: Editions de l'Université de Bruxelles, 1988); Germaine Dieterlen, *Dogon: Notion de Personne et Mythe de la Création* (Paris: Harmattan, 1999); Marcel Griaule, *Conversations with Ogotemmêli; an Introduction to Dogon Religious Ideas* (London: International African Institute by Oxford University Press, 1965); Jean-Paul Colleyn, *Les Chemins de Nya: Culte de Possession au Mali* (Paris: Editions de l'Ecole des Hautes Etudes en Sciences Sociales, 1988); and Solange de Ganay, *Le Sanctuaire Kama Blon de Kangaba: Histoire, Mythes, Peintures Pariétales et Cérémonies Septennales* (Paris: Editions Nouvelles du Sud, 1995).

For accounts of the connections between artistic creativity in Mali and broader cultural and religious understandings of the transcendental world, see Sarah C. Brett-Smith, *Making of Bamana Sculpture: Creativity and Gender* (Cambridge and New York: Cambridge University Press, 1994); Patrick R. McNaughton, *The Mande Blacksmiths: Knowledge, Power, and Art in West Africa* (Bloomington: Indiana University Press, 1988); and David Conrad and Barbara Frank, eds., *Status and Identity in West Africa: Nyamakalaw of Mande* (Bloomington: Indiana University Press, 1995). Paul Stoller, Yaya Diallo, and Mitchell Hall offer a related perspective in their book *The Healing Drum: African Wisdom Teachings* (Rochester, VT: Destiny Books, 1989).

An analysis of the sociopolitical implications of non-Islamic religious practices is offered by Clemens Zobel in his "The Spirit of the Kòma: Local Identities, Religious Mentalities, and Sociopolitical Issues in the Manding Mountains, Mali," *Cahiers d'Etudes Africaines* 36, no. 144 (1996): 625–58.

On the ways in which religious beliefs and practices relate to understandings of physical and social integrity and health, see Jean-Paul Colleyn, "Between Deities and Men: A Few Untypical Remarks about the Anthropology of Possession Cults," *Cahiers d'Etudes Africaines* 36, no. 144 (1996): 723–38; Ama Mazama, "Fertility," in *Encyclopedia of African Religion,* ed. M. K. Asante and A. Mazama (Los Angeles: SAGE, 2009), and Molefi Kete Asante, "Shame," in *Encyclopedia of Africa Religion,* ed. M. K. Asante and A. Mazama (Los Angeles: SAGE, 2009); and Jacques Hureiki, *Les Médecines Touarègues Traditionelles: Approche Ethnologique* (Paris: Karthala, 2000).

For ethnographic accounts that document the intermingling of Muslim and local religious beliefs and practices, see Paul Stoller, *Fusion of the Worlds: An Ethnography of Possession among the Songhay of Niger* (Chicago and London: University of Chicago Press, 1989), and Susan Rasmussen, *Spirit*

Possession and Personhood among the Kel Ewey Tuareg (Cambridge: Cambridge University Press, 1995).

On the changing historical relationship between Muslim leaders and the French colonial administration, see Christopher Harrison, *France and Islam in West Africa, 1860–1960* (Cambridge: Cambridge University Press, 1988); and Lansine Kaba, "Islam in West Africa: Radicalism and the New Ethic of Disagreement, 1960–1990," in *The History of Islam in Africa,* ed. N. Levtzion and Randall Powells (Athens: Ohio University Press, 2000): 189–208.

On Muslim religious institutions and practices, see Louis Brenner and Bintou Sanankoua, *L'Enseignement islamique au Mali* (Bamako, Mali: Jamana; London: SOAS [distributor], 1991); Louis Brenner, ed., *Muslim Identities and Social Change in Subsaharan Africa* (Bloomington: Indiana University Press, 1993); Louis Brenner, "Sufism in Africa," in *African Spirituality: Forms, Meanings, and Expressions,* ed. J. Olupona (New York: Crossroad Publishing Company, 2000): 324–49; Louis Brenner, *Controlling Knowledge: Religion, Power, and Schooling in a West African Muslim Society* (Bloomington: Indiana University Press, 2001); R. Niezen, "The 'Community of Helpers of the Sunna': Islamic Reform among the Songhay of Gao (Mali)," in *Africa* 60, no. 3 (1990): 399–424; Benjamin F. Soares, *Islam and the Prayer Economy: History and Authority in a Malian Town* (Ann Arbor: University of Michigan Press, 2005); and Dorothea Schulz, *Muslims and New Media in West Africa: Pathways to God* (Bloomington: Indiana University Press, 2011). On female Muslim authority and religious practice, see Dorothea Schulz, "Remaking Society from Within: Extraversion and the Social Forms of Female Muslim Activism in Urban Mali," in *Development and Politics from Below: Exploring Religious Spaces in the African State,* ed. Barbara Bompani and Maria Frahm-Arp (London: Palgrave Macmillan, 2010): 74–96.

CHAPTER 3: LITERATURE AND MEDIA

Scholarship on early writing systems in northern Mali refutes the misleading yet widespread assumption that African societies were purely oral prior to the arrival of French colonial powers and their Latin writing script. See, for example, John Hunwick and R. S. O'Fahey, *Arabic Literature of Africa* (Leiden and New York: Brill, 1994); P. F. de Moraes Farias, *Arabic Medieval Inscriptions from the Republic of Mali: Epigraphy, Chronicles and Songhay-Tuāreg History* (Oxford and New York: Oxford University Press, 2003); David Robinson, "Fulfulde Literature in Arabic Script," *History in Africa* 9 (1982): 251–61. A useful introduction to the N'ko writing system is offered by Diana White Oyler, "The N'ko Alphabet as a Vehicle of Indigenist Historiography," *History in Africa* 24 (1997): 239–56; D. W. Oyler, "Re-Inventing Oral Tradition:

The Modern Epic of Souleymane Kanté," *Research in African Literatures* 33, no. 1 (2002): 75–93; and Jean-Loup Amselle, "Le N'Ko au Mali," *Cahiers d'Etudes Africaines* 36, no. 144 (1996): 823–26.

On the aesthetic complexity of oral poetry, see Christiane Seydou, "Musique et Literature Orale chez les Peuls du Mali," *L'Homme* 148 (1998): 139–57; Charles Bird (with Mamadou Koita and Bourama Soumaoro), *Kanbili: The Songs of Seydou Camara,* vol. 1 (Bloomington: African Studies Center, Indiana University, 1974); and Karim Traoré, *Le Jeu et le Sérieux: Essai d'Anthropologie Littéraire sur la Poésie Épique des Chasseurs du Mande (Afrique de l'Ouest)* (Cologne: Rüdiger Köppe, 2000). Good illustrations of the richness of proverbial expressions are found in Cécile Leguy, *Le Proverbe chez les Bwa du Mali: Parole Africaine en Situation d'Énonciation* (Paris: Karthala, 2001).

On oral history and on the *jeli* historians and other groups of specialists who are responsible for passing down family and local histories, see Jan Jansen, *The Griot's Craft: An Essay on Oral Tradition and Diplomacy* (Münster, Germany: Lit Publishers; Piscataway, NJ: Transaction Publishers, 2000); Jan Jansen, *Entretiens avec Bala Kanté: une Chronique du Manding du XXème Siècle* (Leiden and Boston: Brill, 2006); Seydou Camara, "La Tradition Orale en Question," *Cahiers d'Etudes Africaines* 36, no. 144 (1996): 763–90; Marloes Janson, *The Best Hand Is the Hand that Always Gives: Griottes and Their Profession in Eastern Gambia* (Leiden: CNRW Research School, 2002); Molly Roth, *Ma parole s'achète: Money, Identity and Meaning in Malian Jeliya* (Münster, Germany: Lit Publishers, 2008); Thomas Hale, *Griots and Griottes: Masters of Words and Music* (Bloomington: Indiana University Press, 1998); and Mamadou Diawara, *La Graine de la Parole* (Stuttgart: Franz Steiner, 1990). For an analysis of the political role of *jeli* performers in postindependent cultural politics, see Dorothea Schulz, *Perpetuating the Politics of Praise: Jeli Singers, Radios, and Political Mediation in Mali* (Cologne: Rüdiger Köppe, 2001).

Of the vast scholarship on the Sundjata epic, the version of the *jeli* historian Fa-Digi Sissoko translated and annotated by John Johnson is particularly accessible: *The Epic of Son-Jara: A West African Tradition* (Bloomington: Indiana University Press, 1992). For other epical accounts of the political past of southern Mali, see the Segu epic (rendered in the Bamana language) presented by Tayiru Banbera, *Segu Maana Bamanankan na: Bamana Language Edition of the Epic of Segu* (Madison: University of Wisconsin-Madison, African Studies Program, 1991).

A useful introduction to the different aspects under which the performance of the Sundjata epic needs to be studied is offered by Ralph A. Austen, ed., *In Search of Sunjata: The Mande Oral Epic as History, Literature and Performance* (Bloomington: Indiana University Press, 1999).

Works that place key examples of the Malian written literature in their historical context are Christopher Wise, ed., *Yambo Ouologuem: Postcolonial Writer, Islamic Militant* (Boulder, CO: Lynne Rienner, 1999); Sebastien Le Potvin, *Lettres Maliennes: Figures et Configurations de l'Activité Litteraire au Mali* (Paris: L'Harmattan, 2005); Ministère de la Culture du Mali, *Tradition et Modernité dans l'Oeuvre Littéraire de Fily Dabo Sissoko* (Bamako, Mali: Jamana, 2001); and Jane Turrittin, "Aoua Keita and the Nascent Women's Movement in the French Soudan," *African Studies Review* 36, no. 1 (1993): 59–89. For writings by female Malian authors, see Aoua Keita's autobiography, *Femmes d'Afrique: La Vie d'Aoua Keita par Elle-Même* (Paris: Presence Africaine, 1975); Aïcha Fofana, *Mariage, on Copie* (Bamako, Mali: Jamana, 1994); and Aïcha Fofana, *La Fourmilière* (Bamako, Mali: Librairie Traoré, 2006).

Other important novels, many of which won international acclaim, are Yambo Ouologuem's, *Bound to Violence,* trans. M. Ralph (New York: Harcourt Brace Jovanovich, 1971); Amadou Hampâté Bâ, *The Fortunes of Wangrin* (Bloomington: Indiana University Press, 1999); Massa Makan Diabaté, *L'Assemblée des Djinns* (Paris: Éditions Présence Africaine, 1985); Massa Makan Diabaté, *Le Boucher de Kouta* (Paris: Editions Hâtier, 1982); Seydou Moussa Diallo, *Devant le Destin et l'Histoire* (Bamako, Mali: Jamana, 2005); Modibo Sounkalo Keita, *L'Archer Bassari* (Paris: Karthala, 1984); and Alpha Mande Diarra, *La niece de l'imam* (Saint-Maur, France: Editions Sépia; Bamako, Mali: Editions Jamana, 1994).

Information on transformations in the media landscape can be found in Dorothea Schulz, "Drama, Desire, and Debate. Mass-Mediated Subjectivities in Urban Mali," *Visual Anthropology* 20, no. 1 (2007): 19–39, and Dorothea Schulz, *Muslims and New Media in West Africa: Pathways to God* (Bloomington: Indiana University Press, 2011). On the printing press, see Panos Institute, *Media, Peace, and Democracy: Information for More Tolerance and Civic Responsibility* (Paris: Panos Institute, 1994). On local radio stations, see Panos Institute, *Radio Pluralism in West Africa: A Survey Conducted by the Panos Institute Paris and l'Union des Journalistes d'Afrique de l'Ouest,* vol. 3 (Paris: Institut Panos and L'Harmattan, 1993); Dorothea Schulz, "In Pursuit of Publicity: Talk Radio and the Imagination of a Moral Public in Mali," *Africa Spectrum* 99, no. 2 (1999): 161–85; and Craig Tower, "Arajo efemu: Local FM Radio and the Socio-technical System of Communications in Koutiala Mali," *Radio Journal: International Studies in Broadcast and Audio Media* 3, no. 1 (2005): 7–20.

World-famous movies by Malian filmmakers include Adama Drabo et al., *Taafe Fanga,* video recording (San Francisco: California Newsreel, 1997); Souleymane Cissé et al., *Yeelen,* video recording (New York: Kino on Video,

2002); Souleymane Cissé, *Baara*, video recording (New York: Kino International, 2002); Souleymane Cissé, *Finye*, video recording (New York: Kino International, 2002).

CHAPTER 4: ART AND ARCHITECTURE

There exists a broad range of literature on the different arts in Mali. Useful literature on prehistoric material culture and art includes Bernard de Grunne, *Ancient Terracottas from West Africa* (Louvain-la-Neuve, Belgium: Institut Supérieur d'Archéologie et d'Histoire de l'Art, Collège Érasme, 1980); Roderick McIntosh, *The Peoples of the Middle Niger: The Island of Gold* (Oxford: Blackwell Publishers, 1998); Rita Bolland, *Tellem Textiles: Archaeological Finds from Burial Caves in Mali's Bandiagara*, trans. Cliff W. Patricia (Amsterdam: Amsterdam Royal Tropical Institute, 1991); Jean Gaussen, *Le Tilemsi Préhistorique et ses Abords: Sahara et Sahel Malien* (Paris: Centre national de la recherche scientifique, 1988); Michel Raimbault and Kléna Sanogo, *Recherches Archéologiques au Mali: Prospections et Inventaire, Fouilles et Études Analytiques en Zone Lacustre* (Paris: Éditions Karthala, 1991); special issue of *African Arts* 28, no. 4 (1995) on the pillage of archaeological sites in Mali; International Council of Museums/UNESCO, *Illicit Traffic of Cultural Property in Africa* (Paris: ICOM, 1995).

On wooden sculpture, see John Goberman and Marc Bauman, *The Art of the Dogon*, video recording (Home Vision, 1988); Dominique Zahan, *Antilopes du Soleil: Arts et Rites Agraires d'Afrique Noire* (Vienna: Edition A. Schendl, 1980); Pascal Imperato, *Legends, Sorcerers, and Enchanted Lizards: Door Locks of the Bamana of Mali* (New York and London: Africana, 2001); Sarah Brett-Smith, *Making of Bamana Sculpture: Creativity and Gender* (Cambridge and New York: Cambridge University Press, 1994); Michel Roussin, *The Dogon* (Paris: Musée Dapper, 1994); Hélène Leloup, Brunhilde Biebuyck, Roger Asselberghs, and Jerry L. Thompson, *Dogon Statuary* (Strasbourg: Amez, 1994); and Kate Ezra, *Art of the Dogon: Selections from the Lester Wunderman Collection* (New York: Metropolitan Museum of Art, 1988); Francine Ndiaye, Geneviève Calame-Griaule, and Bruno Martinelli, *L'Art du Pays Dogon dans les Collections du Musée de l'Homme* (Zurich: Museum Rietberg, 1995); and Coutancier Benoît, *Dogon, Mais Encore—: Objets d'Afrique, Collections d'Europe* (Paris: Somogy, 2002).

On the artists, see Barbara E. Frank, *Mande Potters and Leatherworkers: Art and Heritage in West Africa* (Washington, DC: Smithsonian Institution Press, 1998); and Patrick R. McNaughton, *The Mande Blacksmiths: Knowledge, Power, and Art in West Africa* (Bloomington: Indiana University Press, 1988). On photography, see André Magnin, "Seydou Keita," *African Arts* 28, no. 4 (1995): 91–95; Susan Vogel, *Malick Sidibe: Portrait of the Artist as a Portraitist,* video recording (Brooklyn, NY: First Run/Icarus Films, 2006).

For a useful compilation of Mali's various historical monuments and architectural remains, see Ministère de la Culture du Mali, *Carte Culturelle du Mali: Esquisse d'un Inventaire du Patrimoine Culturel National* (Bamako, Mali: Imprim Color, 2005). On recent public monuments, see Mary Jo Arnoldi, "Symbolically Inscribing the City: Public Monuments in Mali, 1995–2002," *African Arts* 36, no. 2 (2003): 56–65, 95–96.

For general literature on Malian architecture, consult Jean-Paul Bourdier and Trinh T. Minh-ha, *Habiter un Monde, Architectures de l'Afrique de l'Ouest* (Paris: Editions Alternatives, 2005); Arvind Krishan et al., *Climate Responsive Architecture: A Design Handbook for Energy Efficient Buildings* (New Delhi and New York: Tata McGraw-Hill, 2001); Lazlo Mester de Parajd, *Quelle Architecture pour le Bien-être de l'Homme Aujourd'hui au Mali?* (Bamako, Mali: Centre Djoliba, 1994); Michael Paker Pearson and Colin Richards, *Architecture and Order: Approaches to Social Space* (London and New York: Routledge, 1997); and Sergio Domian, *Architecture Soudanaise: Vitalité d'une Tradition Urbaine et Monumentale: Mali, Côte-d'Ivoire, Burkina Faso, Ghana* (Paris: Harmattan, 1989). On Djenné, see Labelle Prussin, *The Architecture of Djenné: African Synthesis and Transformation* (Thesis, Yale University, 1973); Rogier Bedaux, Michiel Alphons, and J. D. van der Waals, *Djenné: une Ville Millénaire au Mali* (Leiden: Rijksmuseum voor Volkenkunde, 1994); Pierre Maas and Geert Mommersteeg, eds., *Djenné: Chef d'Oeuvre Architectural* (Bamako, Mali, and Amsterdam: Institut des Sciences Humaines, Institut Royal des Tropiques, 1992); and Marli Shamir and Albakaye Ousmane Kounta, *Djenné-Ferey: la Terre Habitée* (Brinon-sur-Sauldre, France: Grandvaux, 2007).

On Dogon architecture, see Tito Spini and Sandro Spini, *Togu na: The African Dogon "House of Men, House of Words"* (New York: Rizzoli, 1976); and Wolfgang Lauber, *L'Architecture Dogon: Constructions en Terre au Mali* (Paris: Adam Biro, 1988).

For documentaries on Sudanese architecture, see Susan Vogel, Samuel Sidibé, and Trevor Marchand, *Future of Mud: A Tale of Houses and Lives in Djenne: A Constructed Documentary Video-recording* (Brooklyn, NY: First Run/Icarus Films, 2007); *Art & Architecture of the Arab World,* video recording (Wynnewood, PA: Schlessinger Media, 2005); Ton van der Lee, *Heavenly Mud: Architecture and Magic in Mali,* video recording (New York: Filmakers Library, 2003); Adrian Malone et al., *The Art of Living. Serie: Millennium: Tribal Wisdom and the Modern World Series,* video recording (Chicago: Home Vision Select, New Vision Media Ltd.; distributed by Public Media Inc., 1992).

CHAPTER 5: CUISINE AND DRESS

A variety of publications document the richness of textile production and sartorial choices in Mali. For general literature on dress in Africa, see Joanne Bubolz Eicher, *African Dress: A Select and Annotated Bibliography of Subsaharan Countries* (East Lansing: Michigan State University, 1969); Rene Gardi, *African Crafts and Craftsmen* (New York: Van Nostrand-Reinhold, 1969); Hildi Hendrickson, ed., *Clothing and Difference: Embodied Identities in Colonial and Post-colonial Africa* (Durham, NC: Duke University Press, 1996); Jean Allman, ed., *Fashioning Africa: Power and the Politics of Dress* (Bloomington: Indiana University Press, 2004); Roy Sieber, *African Textiles and Decorative Arts* (New York: Museum of Modern Art, 1972); Barbara Nordquist and Susan Aradeon, *Traditional African Dress and Textiles: An Exhibition of the Susan B. Aradeon Collection of West African Dress at the Museum of African Art* (Washington, DC: Museum of African Art, 1975); Lisa Aronson, "The Language of West African Textiles," *African Arts* 25, no. 3 (1992): 36–100.

Victoria Rovine, "Cotton, Raffia, Beads and Bark: Style and Technique in African Adornments," in *Sense, Style, Presence: African Arts of Personal Adornment,* ed. Susan Cooksey, 12–17 (Gainesville, FL: Samuel P. Harn Museum of Art, 2004).

On dress and textiles associated with particular regions or ethnic groups, see Geneviève Griaule, "Le Vêtement Dogon, Confection et Usage," *Journal de la Société des Africanistes* 21 (1951): 151–61; Rita Bolland, *Tellem Textiles: Archaeological Finds from Burial Caves in Mali's Bandiagara Cliff* (Amsterdam: Royal Tropical Institute, 1991); Pascal Imperato, "Bamana and Maninka Covers and Blankets," *African Arts* 7, no. 3 (1974): 65–67; P. Imperato, "Wool Blankets of the Peul of Mali," *African Arts* 4, no. 3 (1973): 40–47; P. Imperato and Marion Johnson, "Cloths on the Banks of the Niger," *Journal of the Historical Society of Nigeria* 4, no. 4 (1973): 353–63; Patrick McNaughton, "The Shirts that Mande Hunters Wear," *African Arts* 15, no. 3 (1982): 54–58, 91; Susan Rasmussen, "Veiled Self, Transparent Meanings," *Ethnology* 30, no. 2 (1991): 101–16; R. Murpy, "Social Distance and the Veil," *American Anthropologist* 66 (1964): 1257–74.

On the world-famous mudcloth, see Victoria Rovine, *Bogolan: Shaping Culture Through Cloth in Contemporary Mali,* 2nd ed. (Bloomington: Indiana University Press, 2008).

On the variety and complex meanings of dress practices in contemporary urban Mali, see Bernard Gardi, *Le Boubou c'est Chic: Les Boubous du Mali et d'Autres Pays de l'Afrique de l'Ouest* (Basel, Switzerland: Museum der Kulturen Basel and Editions Christoph Merian, 2000); and Dorothea Schulz, "Competing Sartorial Assertions of Femininity and Muslim Identity in Mali," *Fashion Theory* 11, nos. 2/3 (2007): 253–80.

On cuisine and culinary practices, see Gérard Dumestre, "De l'Alimentation au Mali," *Cahiers d'Etudes Africaines* 144, no. 46-4 (1996): 689–702; Susan Rasmussen, "Matters of Taste: Food, Eating, and Reflections on 'the Body Politic' in Tuareg Society," *Journal of Anthropological Research* 52 (1996): 61–83. Changes in food habits among Tuareg pastoralists that result from the periods of prolonged famine are analyzed in J. Swift, "Une Economie Nomade Sahelienne Face à la Catastrophe: Les Touaregs de l'Adrar des Iforas (Mali)," in *Sécheresses et Famines du Sahel,* vol. 2, ed. P. Bonté (Paris: François Maspéro, 1975), 87–101; A. G. Hill, ed., *Population, Health and Nutrition in the Sahel: Issues in the Welfare of Selected West African Communities* (London: Kegan Paul, 1985).

CHAPTER 6: GENDER ROLES, MARRIAGE, AND FAMILY

On gender relations and roles, see the special issue "Gender in the Mande World," *Mande Studies* 4 (2002), ed. Barbara Hoffman. On kinship, family dynamics, and changing marriage strategies, see R. Murphy, "Tuareg Kinship," *American Anthropologist* 69 (1967): 163–70; Maria Grosz-Ngaté, "Monetization of Bridewealth and the Abandonment of 'Kin Roads' to Marriage in Sana, Mali," *American Ethnologist* 15, no. 3 (1988): 501–14; M. Samaké, *La famille Bamanan du Jitumu: Rôle Social, Économique et Politique* (Bamako, Mali: Centre Djoliba, 1987); Susan Rasmussen, "Female Sexuality, Social Reproduction, and the Politics of Medical Intervention in Northern Niger," *Culture, Medicine, and Psychiatry* 19 (1994): 1–30; Saskia Brand, *Mediating Means and Fate: A Socio-Political Analysis of Fertility and Demographic Change in Bamako, Mali* (Leiden: Brill, 2001); Mirjam de Bruijn and Han van Dijk, *Arid Ways: Cultural Understandings of Insecurity in Fulbe Society, Central Mali* (Amsterdam: Thela Publishers, 1995); B. A. Worley, "Bedposts and Broadswords: Twareg Women's Work Parties and the Dialectics of Sexual Conflict," in *Dialectics and Gender: Anthropological Approaches,* ed. R. Randolph et al. (Boulder, CO, and London: Westview Press, 1988).

On the changing economic, political, and legal conditions for the regulation of family life, see Mirjam de Bruijn, "The Hearthhold in Pastoral Fulbe Society, Central Mali: Social Relations, Milk and Drought," *Africa* 67, no. 4 (1997): 625–51; Sally Findley, "Does Drought Increase Migration? A Study of Migration from Rural Mali during the 1983–1985 Drought," *International Migration Review* 28, no. 3 (1994): 539–53; Mariken Vaa, Sally Findley, and Assitan Diallo, "The Gift Economy: A Study of Women Migrants' Survival Strategies in a Low-Income Bamako Neighborhood," *Travail, Capital et Société* 22, no. 2 (1989): 234–60; Dorothea Schulz, "Political Factions, Ideological Fictions: The Controversy over the Reform of Family Law in Democratic Mali," *Islamic Law and Society* 10, no. 1 (2003): 132–64.

On the shifting social hierarchies among different status categories, but also within the family, that resulted from political and economic transformations in the northern regions over the last three decades, see Baz Lecoq, "Bellah Question: Slave Emancipation, Race and Social Categories in the Late Twentieth Century Northern Mali," *Canadian Journal of African Studies* 39, no. 1 (2005): 42–68.

On notions and ideals of female beauty, see the novel by Sylviane Anna Diouf: *Bintou's Braids* (San Francisco: Chronicle Books, 2001); Christopher Roy, *Birds of the Wilderness: The Beauty Competition of the Wodaabe People of Niger,* video recording (United States: University of Iowa, 2001); Dorothea Schulz, "Mesmerizing 'Missis', Nationalist Musings: Beauty Pageants and the Public Debate on 'Malian' Womanhood," *Paideuma* 46 (2001): 111–35.

On women and politics, see Rosa de Jorio, *Female Elites, Women's Formal Associations, and Political Practices in Urban Mali, West Africa* (PhD diss., University of Illinois, 1997).

CHAPTER 7: SOCIAL CUSTOMS AND LIFESTYLE

On the relevance of kinship relations and discourse for the structuring of political relations in the family and in society, see Jan Jansen and Clemens Zobel's, *The Younger Brother in Mande: Kinship and Politics in West Africa* (Leiden: CNWS Research School, 1996).

On life in town, see Monique Bertrand, *La Question Foncière dans les Villes du Mali: Marchés et Patrimonies* (Paris: Karthala, Editions de l'ORSTOM, 1994); Dieudonné Ouédraogo et Victor Piché, *L'Insertion Urbaine à Bamako* (Paris: Karthala, 1995); Dorothea Schulz, "Music Videos and the Effeminate Vices of Urban Culture in Mali," *Africa* 71, no. 3 (2001): 325–71; and Dorothea Schulz, "Renewal and Enlightenment: Muslim Women's Biographic Narratives of Personal Reform in Mali," *Journal of Religion in Africa* 41 (2010): 93–123. A useful introduction to the ways in which practices of withholding information and of creating or keeping secret knowledge play into the social and political dynamics of everyday life is offered by the special issue "Secrets and Lies in the Mande World," *Mande Studies* 2 (2000), ed. Molly Roth and Jan Jansen.

On changing modes of livelihood among different nomadic groups of central and northern Mali, see Mirjam de Bruijn and Han van Dijk, *Arid Ways: Cultural Understandings of Insecurity in Fulbe Society, Central Mali* (Amsterdam: Thela Publishers, 1995); for the Tuareg, see H.T. Norris, "Tuareg Nomadism in the Modern World," *African Affairs* 51, no. 203 (1952): 152–55; Gerd Spittler, *Les Touaregs Face aux Sécheresses et aux Famines: Es Kel Ewey de l'Air (Niger) (1900–1985)* (Paris: Editions Karthala, 1993); and Johannes

Nicolaisen and Ida Nicolaisen, *The Pastoral Tuareg, Ecology, Culture, and Society*, vol. 2 (Copenhagen: Carsberg Foundation, 1997). On the changing modes of livelihood and forms of social organization that resulted from political and economic transformations in the northern regions over the last three decades, see Baz Lecoq, "Unemployed Intellectuals in the Sahara: The Theshumara Nationalist Movements and the Revolutions in Tuareg Society," *Internationaale Instituute voor Sociale Geschiedenis* 49 (2004): 87–109; and Jennifer Seely, "A Political Analysis of Decentralisation: Coopting the Tuareg Threat in Mali," *The Journal of Modern African Studies* 39, no. 3 (2001): 499–524.

On the ways in which people with a serious physical affliction tend to be considered and treated, see Eric Silla's *People Are Not the Same: Leprosy and Identity in Twentieth-century Mali* (Portsmouth, NH: Heinemann; Oxford: J. Currey, Ltd., 1998). For a film documentary on initiatives that seek to move beyond these tendencies to stigmatize those with serious afflictions, see Louise Manon Bourgault and Leila Dullo, *AIDS and the Arts in Africa*, video recording (Marquette, MI, and Glenwood Springs, CO: Department of Communication and Performance Studies, Northern Michigan University, 2001). For a film documentary on changing economies and lifestyles related to development projects and initiatives, see Martin Harbury, *Peanuts*, video recording (Oley, PA: Bullfrog Films, 2002).

CHAPTER 8: MUSIC, DANCE, AND PERFORMING ARTS

For a useful introduction to African music and dance, see Ruth Stone, *The Garland Handbook of African Music* (New York: Routledge, 2008); Eric Charry, *HipHop Africa* (Bloomington: Indiana University Press, forthcoming 2012); Wolfgang Bender, *Sweet Mother: Modern African Music* (Chicago: Chicago University Press, 1991); John Mill Chernoff, *African Rhythm and African Sensibility* (Chicago: Chicago University Press, 1979); Ronnie Graham, *Stern's Guide to Contemporary African Music* (London: Zwan, 1988); John Collins, *African Pop Roots* (London: Foulshams Publications, 1985). For a useful introduction to Tuareg music, instruments, and musicians, see Caroline Card Wendt, "Tuareg Music," in *The Garland Handbook of African Music*, ed. Ruth Stone (New York: Routledge, 2008): 258–79; and Susan Rasmussen, "Moving Beyond Protest in Tuareg *Ichumar* Musical Performance," *Ethnohistory* 53, no. 4 (2006): 633–55.

For a comprehensive account on the different musical traditions and instruments of the Mande-speaking societies of Mali and neighboring countries, see Eric Charry, *Mande Music: Traditional and Modern Music of the Maninka and Mandinka of Western Africa* (Chicago: Chicago University Press, 2000).

On drummers and drumming performance contexts in southern Mali, see Rainer Polak, *Festmusik als Arbeit, Trommeln als Beruf: Jenbe-Spieler in einer westafrikanischen Grossstadt* (Berlin: Reimer, 2004). See also the biography of Salif Keita by Chérif Keita, *Salif Keïta: l'Ambassadeur de la Musique du Mali* (Brinon-sur-Sauldre, France: Grandvaux, 2009).

On the lyrics and popularity of the music performed by *jeli* musicians on behalf of the new political elites of postindependent Mali, see Charles Cutter, "The Politics of Music in Mali," *African Arts* 1, no. 3 (1967): 38–39, 74–77; Dorothea Schulz, *Perpetuating the Politics of Praise: Jeli Singers, Radios, and Political Mediation in Mali* (Cologne: Rüdiger Köppe, 2001); Dorothea Schulz, "The World Is Made by Talk: Female Youth Culture, Pop Music Consumption, and Mass-mediated Forms of Sociality in Urban Mali," *Cahiers d'Etudes Africaines* 168 (2002): 797–829; Adama Dramé, *Jeliya, Être Griot et Musicien Aujourd'hui* (Paris: Editions L'Harmattan, 1992); Chérif Keita, "Jaliya in the Modern World," in *Status and Identity in West Africa: The Nyamakalaw of Mande,* ed. David Conrad and Barbara Frank (Bloomington: Indiana University Press, 1995), 182–96.

On the development of modern theater and its roots in various local dance and performance traditions, see Gaoussou Diawara, Victoria Diawara, and Alou Koné, "Mali," in *World Encyclopedia of Contemporary Theatre,* vol. 3, ed. Don Rubin (1994): 183–90; Sada Sissoko, *Le Kòtèba et l'Evolution du Theatre Moderne au Mali* (Bamako, Mali: Éditions Jamana, 1995); Nicholas Hopkins, "Persuasion and Satire in the Malian Theatre," *Africa* 42, no. 3 (1972): 217–28; James Brink, *Organizing Satirical Comedy in Kote Tlon: Drama as a Communication Strategy among the Bamana of Mali* (Bloomington: Indiana University Press, 1980); James Brink, "Speech, Play and Blasphemy: Managing Power and Shame in Bamana Theater," *Anthropological Linguistics* 24, no. 4 (1982): 423–31; and Famedji-Koto Tchimou, *Langage de la Danse chez les Dogons* (Paris: L'Harmattan, 1995).

On Bamana puppetry theater, see Mary Jo Arnoldi, *Bamana and Bozo Puppetry of the Segou Region Youth Societies: From the Collection of Joan and Charles Bird* (West Lafayette, IN: Department of Creative Arts at Purdue University, 1976); Mary Jo Arnoldi, *Playing with Time: Art and Performance in Central Mali,* Traditional Arts of Africa (Bloomington: Indiana University Press, 1995).

Index

About the Author

DOROTHEA E. SCHULZ is professor of anthropology at the University of Cologne, Germany. Dr. Schulz has worked for more than 20 years in Mali. Her published works include *Perpetuating the Politics of Praise: Jeli Praise Singers, Radios, and Political Mediation in Mali* (Cologne: Rüdiger Köppe, 2001) and *Muslims and New Media in West Africa: Pathways to God* (Bloomington: Indiana University Press, 2011).

Recent Titles in Culture and Customs of Africa

Culture and Customs of South Africa
Funso Afolayan

Culture and Customs of Cameroon
John Mukum Mbaku

Culture and Customs of Morocco
Raphael Chijioke Njoku

Culture and Customs of Botswana
James Denbow and Phenyo C. Thebe

Culture and Customs of Liberia
Ayodeji Oladimeji Olukoju

Culture and Customs of Uganda
Kefa M. Otiso

Culture and Customs of the Central African Republic
Jacqueline Woodfork

Culture and Customs of Zambia
Scott D. Taylor

Culture and Customs of Angola
Adebayo Oyebade

Culture and Customs of Mozambique
George O. Ndege

Culture and Customs of Rwanda
Julius O. Adekunle

Culture and Customs of Senegal
Eric S. Ross

Culture and Customs of Namibia
Anene Ejikeme